ENERGY

Volume I: Demands, Resources, Impact, Technology, and Policy

ENERGY

Volume I
by S. S. Penner and L. Icerman

Demands, Resources, Impact, Technology, and Policy, 1974

Volume II
by S. S. Penner and L. Icerman

Non-nuclear Technologies, 1975

Volume III
by S. S. Penner et al.

Nuclear Energy and Energy Policies, 1976

ENERGY

Volume I
Demands, Resources, Impact, Technology, and Policy

One of a Three-Volume Set of Lecture Notes

S. S. Penner and **L. Icerman**

Energy Center and
Department of Applied Mechanics and Engineering Sciences
University of California, San Diego
La Jolla, California

1974
Addison-Wesley Publishing Company, Inc.
Advanced Book Program
Reading, Massachusetts

London · Amsterdam · Don Mills, Ontario · Sydney · Tokyo

First printing, 1974
Second printing, with corrections, 1976
   (ISBN 0-201-05566-X, ISBN 0-201-05567-8(pbk.))

Library of Congress Cataloging in Publication Data

Penner, S   S
    Energy : demands, resources, impact, technology, and
policy.

    Includes index.
    1. Power resources. 2.   Energy policy.
I. Icerman, L., joint author. II. Title.
HD9502.A2P46   333.7   74-23133

Reproduced by Addison-Wesley Publishing Company, Inc., Advanced Book Program,
Reading, Massachusetts, from camera-ready copy prepared by the authors.

Copyright © 1974 by Addison-Wesley Publishing Company, Inc.
Published simultaneously in Canada.

Manufactured in the United States of America

ABCDEFGHIJ-HA-79876

CONTENTS

GLOSSARY OF SYMBOLS

bbl = barrel

Bev = 10^9 electron volts

Btu = British thermal unit

$^\circ$C = degrees Centigrade

cal = calorie

cm = centimeter

d = day

(e) or subscript e = equivalent energy or electrical energy, depending on the context

$^\circ$F = degrees Fahrenheit

ft = foot

g = gram

gal = gallon

h = hour

hp = horsepower

in. = inch

kcal = kilocalorie = 10^3 calories

kg = kilogram = 10^3 grams

km = kilometer = 10^3 meters

kw = kilowatt = 10^3 watts

lb = pound

m = meter

Mev = 10^6 electron volts

mi = mile

mph = miles per hour

mt = metric ton = 2,200 pounds

Mw = megawatt = 10^6 watts

oz = ounce

p = person

ppm = parts per million

Q = 10^{18} Btu

sec = second

SCF = standard cubic foot

t = ton = 2, 000 pounds

(th) or subscript t = thermal energy

w = watt

y = year

Syllabus for Use of the Volume I on
Energy: Demands, Resources, Impact, Technology, and Policy
in a Lower-Division Course

Chapter 1 - Elaborate on the discussion in Section 1.2 by using standard material from an introductory physics text.

Delete Section 1.7 except for the introductory statements on pages 59 to 61, a discussion of Tables 1.7-2 to 1.7-5, Eq. (1.7-5) and elaboration of Eq. (1.7-7).

Chapter 2 - Delete Section 2.1, except for a discussion of Figs. 2.1-2 and 2.1-3.

Delete all but the first two paragraphs of Section 2.21.

Chapter 3 - Delete Section 3.5.

Chapter 4 - Delete Section 4.6.

Chapter 5 - Delete Section 5.4A.

Chapter 6 - Delete Sections 6.1 and 6.2.

Chapter 7 - Delete Appendix 7-A.

Chapter 8 - No deletions.

Contents of Volume II, 1975

Contents of Volume III, 1976

PREFACE

It is reasonable to expect that people, who are unable to verify demand, resource, or economic estimates on the basis of their own knowledge, should quote the evaluations of experts with care and indicate proper credits for the source in order to avoid making false impressions on unsuspecting readers. This obvious requirement is not always satisfied in energy-related evaluations. We shall try to be careful with statements of doubts and qualifications concerning the available factual data. Nevertheless, the reader would do well to adopt a highly skeptical attitude from the beginning and to insist on using his own best judgment and his own factual verification of important matters. We shall on occasion deliberately quote contradictory or incompatible evaluations in order to emphasize uncertainties in the data base.

Energy technology is related to very many areas of pure and applied physical science. In our discussion of energy demands, resources, economics, impact, policy, and technology, we shall quote applicable physical laws as required while avoiding detailed presentation of classical disciplines of physical science, such as thermodynamics, combustion science, meteorology, chemical-process technology, nuclear physics, etc.

We begin the discussion with an extensive assessment of energy demands and resources. In order to gain perspective on our level of understanding and on doubts concerning the data base, we shall on occasion quote now "invalid" data that are, however, of historical interest. We shall find uncertainties in both methodology and fact. Nevertheless, the careful reader,

who examines all of the information, should be left with insight and apprecia-
tion of energy-demand and resource projections. Next we discuss energy
consumption by sector in order to indicate the dominant consumer applications where energy is used. Energy and economics, not primarily energy
costs but rather the relation between economic well-being and energy utilization, constitute the next major topic that is considered in this text.

With Chapter 5, we begin a first look at energy-related technologies.
We review in some detail estimates of energy-utilization efficiencies and
waste recovery before considering two important and often neglected environmental-impact problems, namely, the potential geophysical implications of
increasing energy applications and societal costs of energy use as exemplified
by an evaluation of the influence of coal use for electricity generation. We
conclude this first volume with an illustration of methodologies involved in
the making of energy policy and resource development.

In succeeding volumes, we shall examine new non-nuclear energy
technologies (e.g., oil recovery from tar sands and oil shale, coal liquefaction
and gasification, the hydrogen economy, solar-energy utilization, geothermal
energy from hot rocks, etc.) and nuclear-energy technologies (fission,
breeder, and fusion reactors) before returning to a more detailed evaluation
of energy policy, including such current topics as nuclear strategies.

We are happy to acknowledge the contributions of our UCSD undergraduates,
who have helped with the development of this material by their participation in
early classes where energy problems were discussed. Greg Trigeiro has
greatly contributed to the preparation of the figures.

The reader should note that reference numbers refer to individual Sections.

S.S. Penner and L. Icerman

ENERGY
Volume I: Demands, Resources, Impact, Technology, and Policy

CHAPTER 1

ENERGY DEMANDS

1.1   Introduction

A discussion of energy demands in early 1974 would appropriately have begun with the "November 1973 U.S. Oil Crisis," which was precipitated by an Arab embargo on the export of Middle Eastern oil to the U.S. as a political weapon. The published figures on the dimensions of the problem, coming from authoritative industrial and governmental commentators, covered a bewildering range of impact estimates.

The 1973 U.S. oil-utilization rate was about 17.7×10^6 bbl/d (bbl = 1 barrel = 42 gallons, d = day) before the oil embargo.[1] Total imports amounted to ~35% or ~6.2×10^6 bbl/d and seemed to be approaching ~39% or ~7.4×10^6 bbl/d for the higher estimated consumption rate of ~19×10^6 bbl/d during the first quarter of 1974. Imports of Arab crude oil amounted to 0.85×10^6 bbl/d during the first seven months of 1973 and were scheduled to grow to ~1.2×10^6 bbl/d by November 1973. Imports of refined crude totaled nearly 3×10^6 bbl/d. By the end of December 1973, the accumulated shortage from foreign imports was expected to grow to ~3×10^6 bbl/d, corresponding to 17% of petroleum needs. The shortage was expected to be

---

[1]National Petroleum Council estimate, as published in Chemical and Engineering News 51, 10, November 26, 1973.

divided into $\sim 1.8 \times 10^6$ bbl/d of crude oil and $\sim 1.2 \times 10^6$ bbl/d of refined

product. Some authorities stated that the shortage should be made up, in

part, by using the Elk Hills, California, U.S. Navy reserve with a capacity

of about 0.359×10^6 bbl/d, conversion of utility and other plants from oil

to gas use to save about 0.150×10^6 bbl/d, conversion of utility and selected

industrial plants from oil to coal use for additional savings of about $0.250 \times$

10^6 bbl/d, running newly-installed nuclear plants at full capacity to generate

the energy-equivalent of 0.50 to 1.00×10^6 bbl/d, and curtailing consumption

through various economy measures. A summary of imported and domestic

oil resources for 1973 is shown in Table 1.1-1, while end uses of oil are

defined in Fig. 1.1-1. The year 1971 production of crude in the major source

countries is listed in Table 1.1-2. Major exporting and importing countries

for 1971 are listed in Table 1.1-3. Representative gasoline costs in dollars

per gallon paid during late 1973 are summarized in Table 1.1-4.

The 1973 U. S. petroleum-refining capacity amounted to $\sim 13 \times 10^6$

bbl/d. The deficit of more than $\sim 4 \times 10^6$ bbl/d of refined petroleum,

which represented 23.5% of U.S. consumption during the first half of the

year, had to be imported.[1] Since the investment cost per bbl/d of re-

fining capacity was $\$2 \times 10^3$ in 1973 dollars, the total required investment

in new refining capacity alone to make the U. S. self-sufficient was estimated

to be $\$8 \times 10^9$. However, the construction time for new refineries is two to

three years without unusual supply problems. During this time, the U. S.

oil needs, according to pre-crisis projections, would again be substantially

Table 1.1-1 Sources of U.S. oil supplies in 1973; reproduced from a release
by the U.S. Bureau of Mines and reprinted with permission from
Chemical and Engineering News 51, 8, December 10, 1973.
Copyright by the American Chemical Society.

	10^6 bbl/d	% of total
total domestic production[a]	10.959	62.85
crude oil	8.801	50.47
natural-gas liquids	1.732	9.93
lease condensate	0.425	2.44
total crude-oil imports	3.171	18.19
Canada	1.033	5.92
Middle East (mostly Saudi Arabia)	0.852	4.89
Nigeria	0.436	2.50
South America	0.416	2.39
Indonesia	0.191	1.10
Iran	0.182	1.04
other countries	0.061	0.35
imports of refined products[b]	2.918	16.73
other domestic sources	0.389	2.23
total	17.437	100.00%

[a] For January through August 1973.

[b] Includes some unfinished oil and plant condensates.

larger. The refining-capacity deficiency was the direct result of a hiatus

in the construction of U.S. refineries, presumably because of import-control

and pricing problems or difficulties in meeting domestic environmental regu-

lations, as well as because of political pressures by oil producers for con-

struction of refineries near producing wells in order to allow accrual of the

benefits of higher finished-product prices to the crude-oil producers. In

fact, the total number of U.S. refineries actually shrank from about 400 in

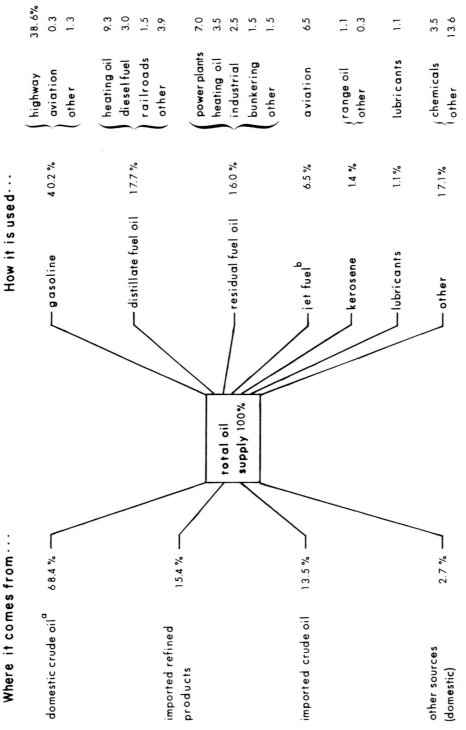

Fig. 1.1-1 Sources and uses of U. S. oil during 1973. Based on a release from the U. S. Bureau of Mines and published in Chemical and Engineering News _51_, 8, December 10, 1973. Copyright by the American Chemical Society.

[a] Includes natural-gas liquids and lease condensate.
[b] Includes naphtha- and kerosine-based jet fuels.

1958 to about 250 larger units in 1973. When a U.S. refinery (a Mobil Oil Co. refinery with a capacity of 0.15×10^6 bbl/d) was completed in January 1973, not a single unit remained under construction. However, by November 1973, there were reports of 40 planned new refineries with a combined output of 4.5×10^6 bbl/d. Later reports suggested that many of these refineries would, in fact, not be built.

Table 1.1-2 The year 1971 production of crude oil in the major producing countries; based on a release from the United Nations.

Country	Total crude production, 10^6 tons/year
U.S.A.	490
U.S.S.R.	377
Iran	227
Saudi Arabia	223
Venezuela	147
Libya	132

The Alaska-pipeline project for delivery of crude oil from the Alaskan North slope to the South for tanker shipments made speedy progress in Congress during the "crisis" period, although it was realized that construction of the pipeline would require from about May 1974 to May 1977, with scheduled 1977 deliveries of 0.6×10^6 bbl/d and ultimate delivery schedules reached in 1979 of 2×10^6 bbl/d. Published estimates for the total Alaskan oil reserves ranged from as low as 9×10^9 bbl to more than 50×10^9 bbl.

Table 1.1-3 Foreign oil-exporting and -importing countries during
1970; based on data of the U.S. Bureau of Mines.

Major exporters, 10^6 bbl				Major importers, 10^6 bbl			
country	crude	refined	total	country	crude	refined	total
Saudi Arabia	1,174	152	1,326	Japan	1,142	250	1,392
Venezuela	889	378	1,267	Germany	780	240	1,020
Iran	1,090	132	1,222	Italy	767	25	792
Libya	1,209	2	1,211	U.K.	767	21	788
Kuwait	944	116	1,060	France	730	44	774

Table 1.1-4 Gasoline costs per gallon in late 1973; compiled from
reports published in various newspapers during
December, 1973.

Country	Approximate $/gallon paid at retail for gasoline
F.R.G.	1.65
Italy	1.20
France	1.10
U.K.	0.95
U.S.A.	0.45

Alternative developments (e.g., drilling in California's Santa Barbara Channel to recover an estimated 200 to 300 $\times 10^6$ bbl) gained support, in spite of opposition from citizens concerned about possible repetition of disastrous earlier oil spillages. Many people took comfort in the knowledge of our large coal reserves and recommended early exploitation of this rich resource. We soon learned that mining of the additional coal represented a major technological effort for which the country was unprepared, the more so because [2] U.S. coal production had declined from 625×10^6 mt (mt = metric ton $\simeq 2,200$ lb) in 1947 to 375×10^6 mt in 1961, with recovery to 535×10^6 mt by 1970. Production in 1985 was projected as 0.9 to 1.4×10^9 mt. Coal exports from the U.S. have amounted traditionally to about 10% of total production. Incremental production of 500×10^6 mt of coal with conversion to synthetic natural gas (syngas) or synthetic oil (syncrude) would add the energy-equivalent of about 2.8×10^6 bbl/d of fuel to the economy and would thus provide substantial relief for U.S. energy needs, which would, however, nearly double by 1985 if normal growth projections were followed. In the light of these numbers, it is not difficult to understand the pessimistic reaction of the business and investment communities as the dimensions of the November 1973 oil and energy crisis became apparent.

Public response to the energy shortage indicated an almost immediate decline in the electricity consumption rate: instead of the yearly growth rate of about 7% registered during the first 9 months of 1973, electricity use actually declined by the equivalent of 1.5% during the last quarter of 1973. At the same time, increased imports and decreased oil consumption led to an increase in the stockpiles of crude and refined-products reserves (see Fig. 1.1-2).[3] A U.S. Bureau of Mines program was initiated to increase oil flow from wells by

---

[2]U.S. Energy Outlook: Coal Availability, National Petroleum Council, Washington, D.C., 1973.

[3]American Petroleum Institute, January 1974, as quoted in Science 183, 183 (1974).

explosive fracturing and micellar or polymer flooding; the breaking of rock

formations should be particularly conducive to improve yields in regions of

low permeability. [4]

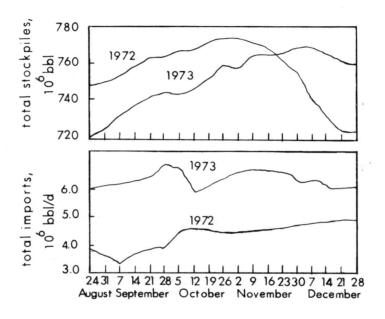

Fig. 1.1-2   The lower set of curves depicts U.S. imports of
              crude oil and refined products. The values are
              averages for the 4 weeks ending on the day listed.
              The upper curves show total inventories held by
              major suppliers. Reproduced from Ref. [3]. Copy-
              right 1974 by the American Association for the
              Advancement of Science.

By mid-1974, a substantial return to "normalcy" had occurred. Im-

ports were approaching 40% of U.S. petroleum consumption, the foreign-

_____

[4]Chemical and Engineering News <u>52</u>, 18, February 18, 1974.

trade bill was running at a rate of over $\$20 \times 10^9$ per year, and the U.S. had become even more dependent on foreign supplies than it had been before the "crisis" of 1973-74. The needed dedication to implement Project Independence was absent.

The preceding superficial remarks answer none of the following important questions:

a. What are the quantitative dimensions of present and future energy demands?

b. Which technological developments promise significant relief and on what time scale?

c. What is an optimized strategy for reduction of energy use while new energy sources are being developed?

d. What are the economic implications of reduction in energy use? Must a deficit of 3.0×10^6 bbl/d necessarily imply a loss in GNP (GNP = gross national product) of about $\$90 \times 10^9$ as one oil-company executive claimed and as may be inferred from a superficial interpretation of some of the data presented in Chapter 4?

e. What is a reasonable priority list for large-scale industrial implementation, prototype or pilot-plant testing, and support of basic research?

It is our purpose in the following pages to present factual information that bears on the intelligent resolution of these critical questions for the U.S., for selected foreign countries, and for the entire world.

1.2   The Meaning of Energy

We know how to measure energy changes and how to use energy very effectively. But we do not really understand what energy is. Perhaps no other concept has been as vital to the development of physical science as the idea of energy conservation.[1] This concept underlies Newton's formulation of classical mechanics, as well as the great nineteenth and twentieth century syntheses of scientific thought: thermodynamics (the first law is "the" principle of energy conservation, which is required in the formulation of quantitative thermo-chemistry as we apply it in defining the limits of energy utilization associated with fossil-fuel combustion, engines, electrochemical devices such as batteries, etc.), electromagnetic theory, the theory of relativity (with its basic theorem that the energy - equivalent of the rest mass m is mc^2 if c is the velocity of light, a physical law that has opened our vista to the realization of the enormous energy-utilization potential associated with nuclear transformations), quantum mechanics (where the restriction of atomic energy levels to discrete values, in the form of Planck's constant times a characteristic frequency, provided a precise methodology for understanding atoms, molecules, and subatomic particles), and cosmology.

---

[1] For an illuminating discussion of this notion and of its implications, see R. P. Feynman, R. B. Leighton and M. Sands, The Feynman Lectures on Physics, Volume I, Chapter 4, Addison-Wesley Publishing Co., Inc., Reading, Mass. 1963.

Freeman Dyson[2] has examined the problem of energy in the universe and has emphasized the preponderance of gravitational energy on a cosmological scale. Noting that the second law of thermodynamics gives us a quantitative measure of disorder through the entropy, he classifies the forms of energy according to their entropy per unit energy with a low value denoting a high degree of order which permits extensive energy abstraction while a high value for the entropy per unit energy indicates a state of disorder with a relatively low potential for useful energy conversion. Rather than elaborating on this topic, we refer to Table 1.2-1 for examples of achievable energy-conversion efficiencies.

In a practical sense, we may define energy units according to the applicable laws of physics. Thus the erg (= 1 g-cm^2/sec^2), the centimeter-gram-second (c.g.s.) unit of energy, is the work done by a force of 1 dyne (= 1 g-cm/sec^2) during a displacement of 1 cm; the newton (= 1 kg-m/sec^2) is the unit of force when the kilogram-meter-second (kg. m. s.) system is used in place of the c.g.s. system, with 1 newton = 10^5 dyne; a newton-m is 10^7 erg and is called a joule.

The 15° calorie is defined as the quantity of heat or energy required to raise the temperature of 1g of liquid water from 14.5 to 15.5°C; the 60° Btu is defined as the energy required to raise the temperature of one pound mass of water from 59.5 to 60.5°F. The 15° calorie and the 60° Btu are usually

---

[2]F. J. Dyson, "Energy in the Universe, "Scientific American **224**, 51-59 (1971).

Table 1.2-1 Energy forms and their practically achievable
utilization efficiencies.

Energy forms	Applications	Practically achievable efficiency, percent	Fundamental limitation in utilization efficiency
energy released by relocation of material bodies	flywheels to produce translational motion	~100	energy conservation (first law of thermodynamics)
energy released by nuclear reactions	nuclear reactors to generate electricity	35 to 45	Carnot efficiency for the thermal cycles used
energy released by chemical reactions	fossil-fuel power plants to generate electricity	35 to 45	Carnot efficiency for thermal cycles used
	fuel cells to generate electricity	80 to 120 for the definition of efficiency used	energy conservation
solar radiation	photosynthesis	~1	energy conservation
	solar space and water heaters	5 to 20	Carnot efficiency for the thermal cycles used
	wind energy to generate electricity	10 to 60 (?)	energy conservation
	hydroelectric power conversion	60 to 80	energy conservation
	photovoltaic cells	1 to 20	energy conservation
fusion energy	the goal is electricity generation	probably 35 to 45	Carnot efficiency for the thermal cycles used

replaced by the International Table calorie (I. T. cal) or simply cal and I. T.
Btu or simply Btu, according to which the mechanical equivalent of heat is defined as $3,600/860 = 4.18605$ I. T. joule/cal; similarly, there are 778.28 ft-
lb per Btu. The precise determination of the mechanical equivalent of heat
was one of the great challenges during the early development of thermodynamics.

In the practical applications with which we shall be concerned, it is generally
sufficient to use one or, at most, two significant figures for resource and
consumption estimates. Nevertheless, we shall often use three or more significant
figures. We summarize in Table 1.2-2 some useful data on units, conversion
factors, and energy consumption. The data summarized in this one table yield,
with proper interpretation, practically a complete evaluation of the energy
problems facing the world.

A. Energy Consumption

A convenient energy unit for the description of global energy consumption is
the $Q = 10^{18}$ Btu. The 1970 world energy consumption by 4×10^9 people was
0.24 Q/y while the year 2000 projection (which is uncertain by a factor of 2 or
more) is 2.1 Q/y for 7×10^9 people. The corresponding U.S. figures are
0.07 Q/y for 2×10^8 people in 1970 and 0.16 Q/y for 3×10^8 people in the year 2000.
Noting from the top of Table 1.2-2 that 0.949×10^{-3} Btu = 2.78×10^{-7} kwh, we
see that 0.07 Q/y = $(0.07 \times 10^{18}$ Btu/y) $\times (2.78 \times 10^{-7}$ kwh/0.949×10^{-3} Btu) $\times$
$(1 \text{ y}/8.76 \times 10^3 \text{ h}) = 2.34 \times 10^9$ kw or kw(th), where the supplementary symbol
(th) stands for thermal in order to emphasize the fact that we are using thermal
energy rather than electrical energy units even though we are employing the kw

Table 1.2-2 Units, conversion factors, energy consumption.*

1 joule $= 10^7$ erg $(= 10^7$ dyne-cm$) = 6.24 \times 10^{12}$ Mev $= 6.24 \times 10^9$ Bev $=$ 1.0 newton-m $= 0.736$ ft-lb $= 0.24$ cal $= 0.949 \times 10^{-3}$ Btu $= 2.78 \times 10^{-4}$ wh $= 3.73 \times 10^{-7}$ hph $= 2.78 \times 10^{-7}$ kwh $= 2.38 \times 10^{-10}$ ton of TNT equivalent $= 1.22 \times 10^{-13}$ of the fusion energy from the deuterium in 1 m^3 of seawater $= 1.11 \times 10^{-14}$ g of matter equivalent $= 1.22 \times 10^{-14}$ of the fission energy of 1 kg of U-235 equivalent $= 6.7 \times 10^{-23}$ of the average daily input of solar energy at the outside of the atmosphere of the earth $= 5.8 \times 10^{-32}$ of daily energy output from the sun.

1 metric ton of coal $\simeq 27.8 \times 10^6$ Btu (1 metric ton = 1 mt $\simeq 2,200$ lb)
1 bbl of petroleum $\simeq (5.60$ to$) 5.82$ (or more) $\times 10^6$ Btu (1 bbl ≈ 42 gallons)
1 SCF of natural gas $\simeq 10^3$ Btu
1 cord of wood $\simeq 1.95 \times 10^7$ Btu (1 cord = 128 ft^3)

9,500 Btu (th)/kwh$_e$ at 36% conversion efficiency.

1 Q $= 10^{18}$ Btu $= 1.05 \times 10^{21}$ joule $= 2.93 \times 10^{14}$ kwh(th) $= 1.22 \times 10^{10}$ Mwd(th)
$= 3.35 \times 10^7$ Mwy(th) $= 1.7 \times 10^{11}$ bbl of petroleum equivalent;
1 y $= 8.76 \times 10^3$ h

Coal conversion to oil: $\geqslant 2$ bbl/mt ($\geqslant 42\%$ energy-conversion efficiency)

Energy consumption estimates:**

USA (1970)	-- 0.07 Q/y	[2×10^8 people, 11.7 kw(th)/p].
(2000)	-- 0.16 Q/y	[3×10^8 people, 17.8 kw(th)/p].
(2020)	-- 0.3 Q/y	[4×10^8 people, 25 kw(th)/p].
WORLD (1970)	--- 0.24 Q/y	[4×10^9 people, 2 kw(th)/p].
(2000)	-- 2.1 Q/y	[7×10^9 people, 10 kw(th)/p].
(2050)	-- 6 Q/y	[10×10^9 people, 20 kw(th)/p].

Note: See footnotes to this table on the following page.

Footnotes to Table 1.2-2

* Table 1.2-2 abbreviations used: bbl = barrel; Btu = British thermal unit;
  cal = calorie; d = day; g = gram; h = hour; hp = horsepower; kg = kilogram;
  kw = kilowatt = 10^3 watt; m = meter; Mw = megawatt = 10^6 watt = 10^3 kw;
  p = person; SCF = standard cubic foot, corresponding to the gas volume
  at a pressure of 14.73 psi (=1 atmosphere) and a temperature of 60°F;
  w = watt; y = year; the symbol (e) or the subscript e identify electrical
  energy; the symbol (th) or the subscript t identify thermal energy. The
  subscript e is also used occasionally in place of the phrase "equivalent
  energy"; the particular meaning attached to e should generally be clear from
  the context.

**Representative estimates from various sources; forecasts to the year 2000
  and beyond are uncertain by factors of 2 or more.

---

or kwh. Because of energy loss in conversion, only about 30 to 40% of the

thermal energy liberated by combustion processes in a utility boiler is currently

available as electrical energy or as kwh(e) or kwh_e. If we divide the average total

power used continuously in the U.S. during 1970, namely, 2.34×10^9 kw(th), by

the population of 2×10^8 people, we see that the equivalent per capita continuous

power consumption was 11.7 kw(th)/p in the U.S.

A similar calculation, starting with 0.24 Q/y and 4×10^9 people for the

world in 1970, shows that the average continuous per capita power consumption

for the entire world population was 2 kw(th)/p or about one-sixth of the U.S.

consumption. Another way of looking at the same data is to note that, with 5%

of the world population in 1970, we accounted for more than 29% of the world's

energy consumption.

The growth rate in world and U.S. energy consumption between 1970 and 2000 is seen to be projected at factors of 8.75 and 2.3, respectively, reflecting the fact that the rest of the world has much catching up to do in order to arrive at an energy-use rate approaching ours.

B.   Coal Conversion

One mt of coal is seen to have the thermal energy-equivalent of ($27.8 \times 10^6/5.82 \times 10^6$) bbl = 4.8 bbl of petroleum for complete combustion to H_2O, CO_2, SO_2, etc.   However, the best available conversion procedures for making syncrude (= synthetic crude oil) from coal have an overall efficiency of only about 42%.   Hence, we shall generally have to be satisfied with a coal-to-syncrude fuel-conversion process that yields 2 bbl of syncrude per mt of coal.

With 100% energy-conversion efficiency of coal to syngas (= synthetic gas, mostly methane), we should be able to make 2.78×10^4 SCF/mt where SCF stands for a standard cubic foot or for standard cubic feet (i.e., a gas volume under standard conditions of 1 atmosphere pressure and 60^oF temperature). In practice, we shall again have to be satisfied with substantially less (perhaps 50% less) than 2.78×10^4 SCF of syngas per mt of coal.

C.   Fission Energy

The fission energy released by 1 kg of U^{235} is seen to be equivalent to (0.949×10^{-3} Btu/1.22×10^{-14}) $\times$ (1 bbl of petroleum/5.82×10^6 Btu) = 1.34×10^4 bbl of petroleum when completely burned.   Some authors will give somewhat different estimates because they use a different value for the energy released from 1 bbl of petroleum, reflecting the variability occurring in natural crude

oil. Thus, in place of 1.34×10^4 bbl, the estimate might be as low as $1.32 \times$

10^4 bbl or as high as 1.40×10^4 bbl equivalent to the fission energy released from

1 kg of U^{235}.

A typical low-grade U_3O_8 rock deposit, which is mined at a cost of \$10/lb

of U_3O_8, might be 5m thick with a density of $2.5 g/cm^3$. Hence one m^3 of rock

would weigh $(10^2 cm)^3 \times (2.5 g/cm^3)/(453 g/lb) \times (2,200 \ lb/mt) = 2.5$ mt. This

rock contains about 60g of U per mt (6×10^{-3} weight percent) corresponding to

150g of U per m^3 or 750g of U per m^2 of surface for the 5m thick deposit. Thus

12.5 mt of deposit dug out below $1m^2$ surface area have a uranium content of

0.750 kg of U or (see Section 1.4) of 0.0053kg of U^{235} which, when used as a

fission fuel, would release the same thermal energy as 71 bbl of petroleum.

At late 1973 prices, the cost for the oil would be about \$710 (to perhaps as much

as \$1,420 by year-end for uncommitted foreign crude) compared with a fissionable

uranium fuel cost at \$10/lb of U_3O_8 with 6×10^{-3} weight percent of uranium in

the rock or ($10/lb of U_3O_8) $\times$ ($12.5 \times 2.2 \times 10^3$ lb of rock/m^2 of surface) $\times$

(6×10^{-5} lb of U/lb of rock) $\times [(16 \times 8 + 238.07 \times 3)/238.07 \times 3$ in lb of $U_3O_8/$

lb of U] $\simeq \$19.50/m^2$. The raw-material cost for the fission fuel is thus seen

to be lower by about a factor of forty than the cost for the bbl-energy-equivalent of

oil. Of course, there is more involved in making fission fuel for a nuclear reactor

than digging raw uranium ore out of the ground.

D. Fusion Energy

Reference to Table 1.2-2 shows that the energy released by fusion of the

deuterium present in 1 m^3 of sea water is equivalent to

$$\frac{0.949 \times 10^{-3} \text{ Btu}}{1.22 \times 10^{-13} \text{fusion energy in } 1m^3} \times \frac{1 \text{ bbl of petroleum equivalent}}{5.82 \times 10^6 \text{ Btu}}$$
of seawater

$$= 1.34 \times 10^3 \text{ bbl of petroleum equivalent to the fusion energy}$$
in 1 m^3 of seawater.

The conversion factor of 1.22×10^{-13} per joule refers to deuterium fusion

with the release of 4.96 Mev (Mev = millions of electron volts, the value of

mc^2 for an electron is about 0.5 Mev) per deuterium atom fused.

The 1973 U.S. oil consumption amounted to nearly 17.7×10^6 bbl/d. This

energy could, with 100% conversion efficiency, be supplied by deuterium fusion

using 1.32×10^4 m^3/d of sea water as raw material. With this unachievable,

ideal conversion efficiency, 1 km^3 of sea water would last $10^9/1.32 \times 10^4 =$

7.6×10^4 days $\simeq 210$ years at the 1973 oil-utilization rate.

   E.   The Solar-Energy Input to the Earth

The total solar-energy input received per day by the earth is equivalent

to
$$\frac{0.949 \times 10^{-3} \text{ Btu}}{6.7 \times 10^{-23} \text{ solar energy}} \times \frac{1 \text{ bbl of petroleum equivalent}}{5.82 \times 10^6 \text{ Btu}}$$
input in one day

$$= 2.43 \times 10^{12} \text{ bbl of petroleum equivalent to the solar energy}$$
input in one day,

which is about equal to the estimated upper limit of the total recoverable oil

reserves (2.1×10^{12} bbl) stored on the entire earth. The upper limit for the

estimated total coal recoverable on earth has been given as 7.6×10^{12} mt

$= 3.63 \times 10^{13}$ bbl of petroleum equivalent. If this coal were used with 100%

efficiency to replace the sun as input source of radiation on the earth, it would last less than about 15 days.

Of course, the surface of the earth receives only a tiny fraction of the daily energy output of the sun. The total solar-energy output amounts to 2.8×10^{21} bbl of petroleum equivalent.

F. Per Capita Oil Consumption in the U.S. During 1970

The total energy used in the U.S. during 1970 was 0.07 Q/y = 7×10^{16} Btu/y $\simeq 33 \times 10^{6}$ bbl of petroleum equivalent per day. Thus the average continuous U.S. power consumption of 11.7 kw(th)/p, which corresponds to an annual energy use of 4.27×10^{3} kw-d/py, was equivalent to a per capita oil consumption of 0.165 bbl/ d-p. Since one bbl has 42 gallons, the per capita energy consumption corresponded to about 7 gallons of oil equivalent per day for every man, woman, and child in the U.S. during 1970. Of course, we all used more in 1973. The 7 gallons of oil equivalent per person per day used in 1970 were roughly equally divided between electricity production, transportation, manufacturing, and commercial-combined-with-residential use.

1.3   Qualitative Description of Fossil Fuels

Since we shall be referring repeatedly to the fossil fuels by their common appellations, it is desirable to present a brief qualitative description of these important compounds, from which we derive thermal energy by combustion.

Natural gas is mostly methane, CH_4, after treatment. We show in Table

1.3-1 representative compositions of natural gas at various stages of refinement.

Table 1.3-1 Representative composition of natural gases recovered during the nineteen forties at Santa Fe Springs, Calif.

Type of sample	% by volume of						
	CO_2	Air	CH_4	C_2H_6	C_3H_8	C_4H_{10}	C_nH_{2n+2} $(n \geq 5)$
wet gas	0.7	1.4	64.3	10.8	10.4	6.7	5.1
average gas	0.3	—	80.7-85.3	7.0 to 8.4	3.3-5.0	2.4-3.2	1.5-2.4
average gas after treatment	0.5	—	88.4	6.8	2.9	1.2	0.2

Natural-gas liquids (NGL) or casing-head gasolines are hydrocarbons extracted during the production of natural gas, with the general chemical formula C_nH_{2n+2} ($n \geq 5$). The NGL amounted to 17.5% of total liquid HC (= hydrocarbon) production in 1967. Liquefied petroleum gases (LPG) are mixtures of propane (C_3H_8) and butane (C_4H_{10}). Typical compositions of unstabilized and stabilized natural gasolines are listed in Table 1.3-2.

Table 1.3-2 Composition of typical natural gasolines.

Natural gasoline	% by weight of					
	CH_4	C_2H_6	C_3H_8	iso-C_4H_{10}	n-C_4H_{10}	C_nH_{2n+2} ($n \geq 5$)
unstabilized	0.3	0.6	8.3	6.3	31.9	52.6
stabilized	---	---	---	1.6	45.1	53.3

Liquid crude oil is obtained from underground reservoirs by means of oil wells. It ranges from natural gasolines to very heavy viscous oils with colors from green-red to black. The green-red crude may have a gravity corresponding to 14° A.P.I. (A.P.I. = American Petroleum Institute) and a specific gravity of $0.97 g/cm^3$, while the lighter black oil might be classified as 54° A.P.I. with a density of 0.76 g/cm^3. The A.P.I. gravity scale is defined as follows: A.P.I. gravity in degrees = $(141.5/\rho)$ - 131.5, where ρ = specific gravity of a particular oil in g/cm^3 at $60^{\circ}F$.

Gasoline made from paraffin-base petroleums contains hydrocarbons from C_5H_{12} (pentane) to $C_{12}H_{26}$ (dodecane); it boils (is distilled into the component hydrocarbons) between 35 and $220^{\circ}C$.

The word petroleum is formed from the Greek words petra (rock) and oleum (oil). Petroleum is formed by the decay and partial (incomplete) oxidation of vegetable and animal debris buried in sedimentary rocks during geologic times. The oil and gas displace the water which is normally found in sedimentary rocks. They usually occur in relatively constant proportions.

Oil may be recovered from tar sands, which contain highly viscous organic hydrocarbon liquids (bitumens) in sand (silicate) grains with a variable amount of silt and clay.

Oil shale, from which shale oil may be recovered, contains the waxy solid hydrocarbon kerogen, which is tightly packed in clay, mud, and silt.

Coal was formed from organic matter 40 to 250 million years ago, with high-grade coal corresponding to the older deposits. Anthracite or hard coal is generally located in the deeper beds; it burns with a smokeless flame and sells at the highest prices paid for coal. Bituminous coal or soft coal, which makes up about 50% of the world's coal reserves, has been used extensively for electric-power production (about 43% of the bituminous coal used was employed for this purpose in the U.S. during 1970), for coke and steel making (about 19% of the total used), for other industrial applications (about 21%), for export (about 10%), and for home heating (about 7%). <u>Subbituminous coal</u> or <u>still softer coal</u> contains about 25 weight percent of water. <u>Brown coal</u> or <u>lignite</u> contains about 50% by weight of water. <u>Peat,</u> which is the first product formed during the decay of plants, contains up to 90% of water. All coals contain some hydrogen, sulfur, hydrocarbons, nitrogen compounds, etc. Representative analyses of coal samples are shown in Table 1.3.-3.

Table 1.3-3   Analyses of typical U.S. coal samples; based on U.S. Bureau of Mines data.

Type of coal	Origin	Proximate analysis (weight %)				Heating value, Btu/lb
		moisture	volatile matter	fixed carbon	ash	
anthracite	Pennsylvania	4.4	4.8	81.8	9.0	13,130
bituminous						
low-volatility	Maryland	2.3	19.6	65.8	12.3	13,200
medium-volatility	Alabama	3.1	23.4	63.6	9.9	13,530
high-volatility	Ohio	5.9	43.8	46.5	3.8	13,150
subbituminous	Washington	13.9	34.2	41.0	10.9	10,330
	Colorado	25.8	31.1	38.4	4.7	8,580
lignite	North Dakota	36.8	27.8	30.2	5.2	6,960

1.4   Qualitative Description of Nuclear Fuels

A proper understanding of the utilization of fission and fusion reactors requires some knowledge of nuclear physics. The applicable aspects of this subject will be discussed when we consider prototypes of commercial nuclear reactors. Here we content ourselves with a brief commentary on the raw materials required in fission and fusion nuclear reactors.

A. Resources for Fission Reactors

Fission-nuclear reactors are classified as burners if they consume the

naturally-occurring fissile isotope $^{235}_{92}$U. Here, the left superscript denotes the

approximate atomic mass (which is equal to the sum of the number of protons

and neutrons), while the left subscript identifies the atomic number (which

equals the number of protons). The isotope $^{235}_{92}$U is the only naturally-occurring

isotope which undergoes nuclear fission as the result of absorption of slow

(thermal) neutrons. Naturally-occurring uranium ores contain 6×10^{-5} of the total

uranium in the form of $^{234}_{92}$U, 7.11×10^{-3} of the total as $^{235}_{92}$U, and the

balance (0.99283 of the total) as $^{238}_{92}$U. A typical low-grade uranium ore is

the Chattanooga Shale of Devonian age (formed 330,000,000 to 290,000,000

years ago), which is found in Illinois, Indiana, Kentucky, Ohio, and Tennessee.[1]

The Gassaway Member of this shale deposit is about 15 feet in thickness and

covers an area of hundreds of square miles. This ore contains 6×10^{-5} parts

by weight of uranium, which is distributed among the various isotopic constituents

in the proportions specified above.

Fission-nuclear reactors are converters or breeders if they convert such

nuclear fuels as $^{238}_{92}$U and $^{232}_{90}$Th into fissile compounds as the result of

neutron absorption. These neutrons are initially supplied by the fission of $^{235}_{92}$U.

Thorium is a widely-distributed element. For example, the Conway Granite

deposits in New Hampshire extend over an area of more than 300 square miles

[1]V. E. Swanson, "Oil Yield and Uranium Content of Beach Shales" in Uranium
and Carbonacous Rocks, U.S. Geological Survey Paper 356, Washington, D.C.,
1960.

and are probably a mile or more in depth.[2] This granite has an essentially

constant Th-content of 56 g per ton of rock.

For efficient planning of nuclear-fuel reserves, it is necessary to maintain

a supply of ore covering the period from the present to eight years later, in

order to assure ample supplies for fuel-rod preparation.[3]

The availability of uranium for nuclear fuels is measured in terms of the

supply of U_3O_8 and depends on the price which the consumer is willing to pay

per pound of U_3O_8. A recent estimate [4] of availability of U_3O_8 as a function

of price is given in Table 1.4-1. Hubbert[3] was somewhat more pessimistic

about the availability of U_3O_8 and wrote (in 1969) of reasonably assured U.S.

supplies of 310,000 t and estimated additional reserves of 350,000 t at a cost

of not more than \$10/lb of U_3O_8 (t = ton = 2,000 lb).

B. Resources for Fusion Reactors

At the present time, the most likely candidates for controlled thermo-

nuclear fusion reactions are deuterium ($_1^2$D), for the deuterium-deuterium fusion

process, and lithium ($_3^6$Li), for the lithium-deuterium fusion process.

---

[2] J. A. S. Adams, M. C. Kline, K. A. Richardson, and J. J. W. Rogers, "The Conway Granite of New Hampshire as a Major Low-Grade Thorium Source," Proc. Nat. Acad. Sci. 48, 1898-1905 (1962).

[3] M. King Hubbert, Chapter 8 on "Energy Resources" in Resources and Man, quote of R. L. Faulkner, p. 223, W. H. Freeman and Co., San Francisco, California, 1969.

[4] Potential Nuclear Power Growth Patterns, U.S. Atomic Energy Commission, WASH 1098, Washington, D.C., 1970. Reported by M. Benedict in "Electric Power from Nuclear Fission," Bulletin of the Atomic Scientists 27, 8-16, September 1971.

Table 1.4.1   Availability of U.S. uranium resources as a function
of price (the 1972 price was \$8/lb); reprinted by per-
mission of Science and Public Affairs from Ref. [4].
Copyright 1971 by the Educational Foundation for
Nuclear Science.

Price, \$/lb of U_3O_8	Cumulative supply at this or lower price, t(=tons) of U_3O_8
8	594,000
10	940,000
15	1,450,000
30	2,240,000
50	10,000,000
100	25,000,000

The abundance of ^2_1D atoms in water relative to that of ^1_1H atoms is 1 to 6,500. Thus, 1 m^3 of liquid water contains about 1.029×10^{25} atoms of ^2_1D with a total mass of 34.4 grams.

Lithium occurs in sea water with a mass ratio of about 1 part in 10^7, while its abundance in the rocks of the earth crust is 20 to 32 per 10^6 by mass. Only 7.42% of all lithium occurs as the isotope ^6_3Li. Minable lithium deposits in the U.S. amount to 5 to 10×10^6 t of Li_2O (see Hubbert, Ref. [3], p. 231).

1.5 Past and Future Estimates of Energy Demands for Selected Regions of the World

While it is reasonable to speak of pre-1972 energy demands, it is questionable that the post-1973 energy-demand projections will turn out to be accurate. One of the reasons for this view is the following consideration: in the pre-1972 period, energy was supplied in response to demand at very low

prices. The determinant consideration was what the consumers wanted.

In the post-1973 period, at least for some time to come, actual demand will

be affected by costs and may have to be adjusted according to availability of

supplies. Nevertheless, we shall pretend in this section that supplies in

the future will be determined by demand, as in the past. In this manner,

we shall be able to derive some estimated supply-goal functions for future

years.

A. Estimated Demand Functions for Selected Regions of the World*

The estimated future-demand function is a "reasonable" extrapolation

of the past use rate. This type of information is often obtained by simply

postulating desirable, needed, or allowable future growth rates, determined

by considerations other than energy-availability such as population growth,

per capita income, maximum environmental loading in view of constraints

relating to allowable air and water pollution, etc. Thus, projections of

future demand or growth estimates are generally little more than educated

extrapolations of available statistical data. A representative set of projections

---

* For a very extensive compilation of data referring to the period 1925 to 1970, see J. Darmstadter (with P. D. Teitelbaum and J. G. Polach), Energy in the World Economy, A Statistical Review of Trends in Output, Trade and Consumption Since 1925, 876 pages, published for Resources for the Future, Inc., by the Johns Hopkins Press, Baltimore, Maryland, 1971. An example of a regional demand projection for electricity use is given in Section 1.7; this type of analysis constitutes the basic information that is required for making rational demand-growth estimates.

made in 1972 for the entire "Free" World (i.e., the world exclusive of the Communist countries), the U.S., Western Europe, and Japan, is reproduced in Figs. 1.5-1 to 1.5-4 from a report issued by the Stanford Research Institute.[1] The total energy demands are listed in Figs. 1.5-1 to 1.5-4 in terms of millions of barrels per day of petroleum equivalent to the energy derived from all sources, including petroleum, coal, natural gas, hydroelectric-power generation, and nuclear-power generation. Since these projections antedate the rapid price escalations of 1973 and 1974, they represent intelligent 1972 projections of demands rather than realistic 1974 estimates of demands.

Reference to Figs. 1.5-1 to 1.5-4 leads to the following conclusions:

1. Nuclear-energy generation was a minor contributor to the total demand as late as 1970.

2. Since 1955, the energy-use rates of petroleum and natural gas have increased rapidly in comparison with energy growth rates supplied by either coal burning or hydroelectric-power generation.

3. Future projections for all countries show nuclear-power generation as the most rapidly-growing component, even though its application will be initially restricted to electricity production.

4. The recent relative growth rate of natural-gas use in Western Europe is greater than in other parts of the non-Communist world, reflecting,

---

[1]S. H. Clark, *World Energy*, Stanford Research Institute, Menlo Park, California, 1972.

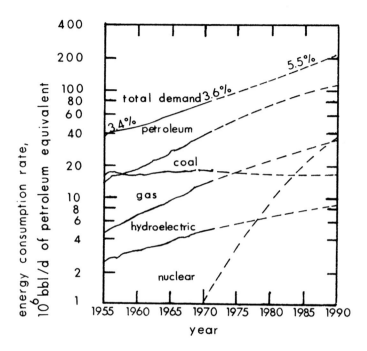

Fig. 1.5-1   A 1972 evaluation of recent and extrapolated annual
              consumption of primary energy resources in the
              "Free" World; reproduced with some modifications
              from Ref. [1]. Percentages on the total demand
              curve indicate approximate applicable growth rates
              for the time periods where the percentages are
              shown.

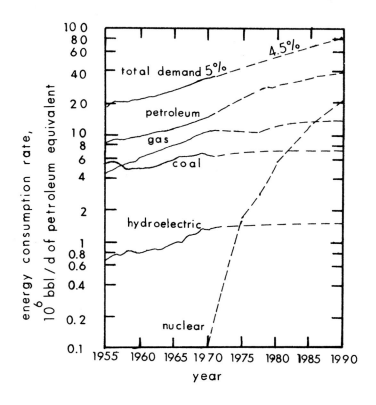

Fig. 1.5-2   A 1972 evaluation of recent and extrapolated annual
             consumption of primary energy resources in the
             United States; reproduced with some modifications
             from Ref. [1].   Percentages on the total demand
             curve indicate approximate applicable growth rates
             for the time periods where the percentages are
             shown.

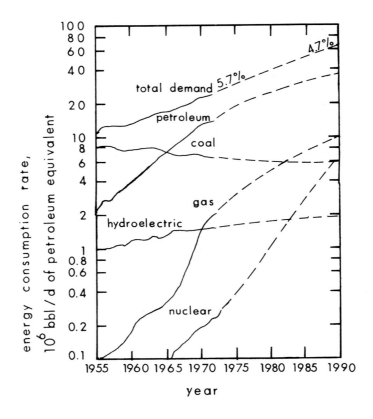

Fig. 1.5-3   A 1972 evaluation of recent and extrapolated annual
             consumption of primary energy resources in Western
             Europe; reproduced with some modifications from
             Ref. [1].   Percentages on the total demand curve
             indicate approximate annual growth rates for the
             time periods where the percentages are shown.

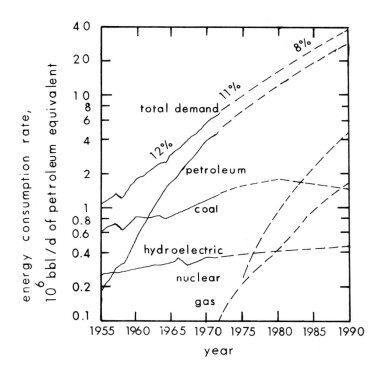

Fig. 1.5-4   A 1972 evaluation of recent and extrapolated annual
consumption of primary energy resources in Japan;
reproduced with some modifications from Ref. [1].
Percentages on the total demand curve indicate approximate annual growth rates for the time periods
where the percentages are shown.

in part, significant discoveries of new supplies in the North Sea.

5.   The Japanese reliance on petroleum imports has been growing at a disproportionately large rate and is projected to continue doing so for some years to come.   Since Japan has no native crude-oil supplies, its dependence on foreign sources is correspondingly heavy.

6.   The U.S. demand function (see Fig. 1.5-2) in the past was a disproportionately large fraction of that of the entire world.   Other countries have now begun to compensate for this "energy gap".   Accordingly, their projected future growth rates (see the percentages shown on the total demand curves in Figs. 1.5-1, 1.5-3, and 1.5-4) are larger than the projected future growth rates for the U.S.   For example, Japan appeared to be heading for an 11% annual growth rate during the early seventies, as compared with 5.7% in Western Europe and 5.0% in the U.S.

B.   A More Detailed Examination of Past and Future U.S. Energy-
Demand Functions

A detailed record of energy utilization in the U.S. is shown in Fig. 1.5-5 for the period 1850 to 1970.   Study of this figure shows that the introduction of new technology has been followed by relatively slow growth before the new technology became an important contributor to the total energy demand.   Coal supplied about one-tenth of the total energy in 1850 when wood burning accounted for 90% of energy generation.   Ten years later, the much more convenient and concentrated energy source coal still contributed only about one-fifth as much energy as wood burning.   By 1870, twenty years

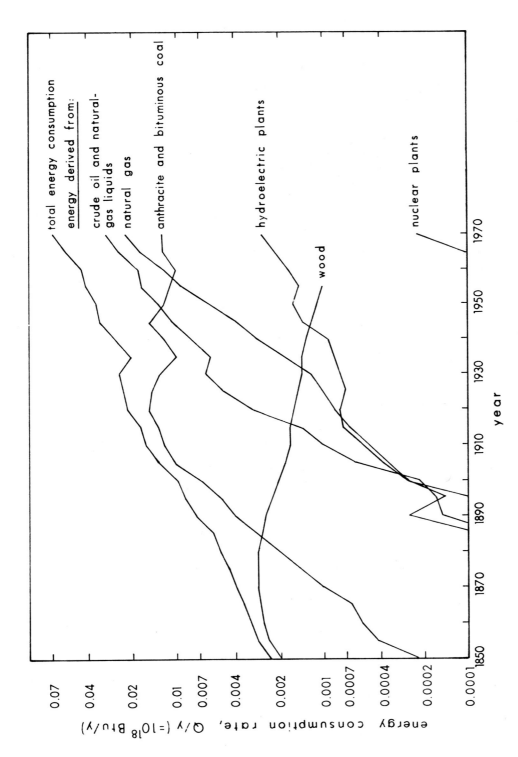

Fig. 1.5-5   Annual energy consumption by source of the United States for the period 1850 to 1970; based on data of the U.S. Department of Commerce. Hydroelectric and nuclear energy are converted to thermal energy at the average efficiency of fossil-fuel plants operating during the specified year. The data are plotted for five-year intervals.

later, coal use had produced about 28% of all energy in the U.S. Coal

burning became more important than wood burning in 1884, about 34 years

after it had been used to supply 10% of the total energy generated. We note

similar growth for the use rates of crude oil and natural-gas liquids (see

Fig. 1.5-5). As of 1970, wood burning was still nearly four times more

important as an energy source than nuclear-power generation. Extrapolation

of the recent use of wood and nuclear-energy sources suggests that these

components of the energy industry will become equally important during 1975.

According to Fig. 1.5-5, the total U.S. energy consumption in 1970

had grown to nearly 7×10^{16} Btu/y or 1.2×10^{10} bbl/y of petroleum equivalent.

This last value is seen to be consistent* with the entry in Table 1.5-2 of about

3.3×10^7 bbl/d equivalent for the U.S. 1970 total energy demand.

A 1972 evaluation of past demand and projected future energy supplies

(in 10^6 bbl/d equivalent) to 1985 for the U.S. is reproduced in Table 1.5-1.

Approximately the same values as those listed in Table 1.5-1 are obtained

for the years 1850, 1900, and 1970 from Fig. 1.5-5 by dividing values in

Btu by $(5.6 \times 10^6$ Btu/bbl) $\times$ (365 d/y). The total year 1900 petroleum

consumption of 120,000 bbl/d corresponds to the output of what would be

considered 20 to 30 moderately rich wells, or of one or two very rich wells

by 1974 standards. The 1985 projection of 33.3×10^6 bbl/d for U.S. oil

---

*   As has already been emphasized, some discrepancies are attributable to
    variations in the Btu-equivalent assignment for a barrel of petroleum.

demand is too high and not in agreement with late 1972 projections by the

National Petroleum Council, which we shall discuss presently.

Table 1.5-1   U.S. energy supply in 10^6 bbl/d equivalent; reproduced from
S. Field, <u>SNG and the 1985 U.S. Energy Picture</u>, Stanford
Research Institute (S. R. I.), Menlo Park, California, 1972.

	1850	1900	1970	1985
gas		0.12	11.00	14.1
coal	0.140	3.28	6.50	7.2
oil		0.12	14.70	33.3
hydroelectric		0.12	1.25	1.4
nuclear			0.10	10.0
wood	1.030	0.95	0.38	0.3
total	1.170	4.59	33.93	66.3
total (excluding wood)			33.55	66.0
approximate population (millions)	23	75	205	240
per capita energy[a] consumption $(bbl/y-p)_e$	19	22	60	100

[a]The subscript e identifies either "electrical energy" or "equivalent
thermal energy". Here it stands for "equivalent thermal energy".

A notable feature of the data in Table 1.5-1 is represented by the entries in

the bottom row, which show that the yearly personal oil-consumption equiva-

lent grew from 19 bbl in 1850 to 22 in 1900 and 60 in 1970. The extrapolated

value of 100 by the year 1985 may well turn out to be too high. An alternative

1972 projection from another S. R. I. report is reproduced in Table 1.5-2 and

shows greater details for the period 1970 to 1978, with values generally

similar to those in Table 1.5-1 for 1970.

Table 1.5-2 Projected U.S. energy demands to the year 1978 in 10^6 bbl/d equivalent; reproduced from S. H. Clark, World Energy, Stanford Research Institute (S.R.I.), Menlo Park, California, 1972.

	1970	1971	1972	1973	1974	1975	1976	1977	1978
coal	6.1	5.9	6.0	6.0	6.0	6.0	6.0	6.0	6.0
oil	14.7	15.1	16.2	17.9	19.5	21.1	22.9	24.3	25.6
gas	10.4	10.7	10.7	10.4	10.1	9.8	9.5	9.5	9.5
hydroelectric	1.3	1.3	1.3	1.3	1.3	1.3	1.3	1.3	1.3
nuclear	0.1	0.2	0.3	0.7	1.2	1.7	2.0	2.4	3.0
total	32.6	33.2	34.5	36.3	38.1	39.9	41.7	43.5	45.4

It is interesting to note that the 1973 oil-consumption projection of 17.9×10^6 bbl/d was not reached because of the Middle Eastern oil embargo for shipments to the U.S. (compare Section 1.1).

Longer-term projections are shown for natural gas (NG) and crude oil plus natural-gas liquids (NGL) in Figs. 1.5-6 and 1.5-7, respectively. The data shown in Figs. 1.5-6 and 1.5-7 are parametric extrapolations with the percentages of annual growth rates representing the variable parameter. At annual growth rates of 6% for NG and for crude oil plus NGL to the year 2020, we shall dispose by ourselves in the U.S. of all of the reserves known in 1972 in the entire world; Hubbert's (1970) estimates of U.S. recoverable resources of NG show that equivalent reserves would disappear before 1990 if we depended on our own resources and allowed consumption to grow at the rate of 6% per year (see Fig. 1.5-6).

Another 1972 estimate of a U.S. resource-exhaustion schedule for various scenarios is summarized in Table 1.5-3. These data show that energy use rates are so high that the differences between low and high

reserve estimates typically correspond to differences of only a few years

in time before resource exhaustion.

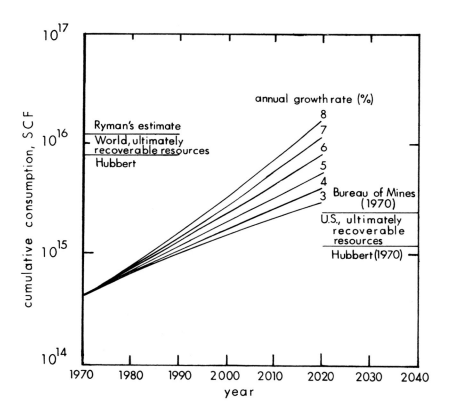

Fig. 1.5-6   Cumulative requirements for domestic natural gas
              as a function of consumption growth rates after 1970;
              reproduced from the Cornell Workshop on Energy
              and the Environment, U.S. Government Printing
              Office, Washington, D.C., 1972.

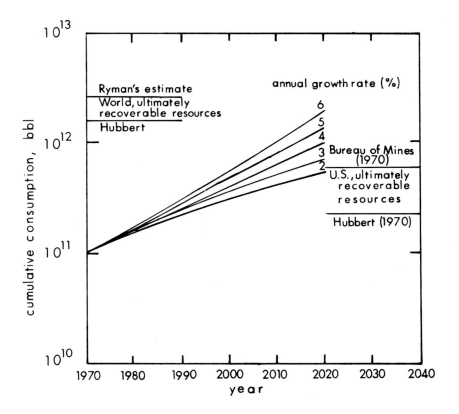

Fig. 1.5-7   Cumulative U.S. requirements for petroleum
(crude and NGL) as a function of consumption
growth rates after 1970; reproduced from the
Cornell Workshop on Energy and the Environment, U.S. Government Printing Office,
Washington, D.C., 1972.

A different method of projection for the years to 1990 is shown in Fig.

1.5-8 in terms of a block diagram showing relative contributions from dif-

ferent energy sources in percentages. According to this particular pro-

jection, we have passed or are currently passing, the time period when NG

makes its largest relative percentage contribution (33%) to the total energy

supply. The relative growth projected for coal in Fig. 1.5-8 is probably too slow, while the maintenance of petroleum as an energy source for 44% of our

needs to 1985 may be optimistic because of logistic or economic problems.

Table 1.5-3   U.S. resource depletion for various energy policies; reproduced from the Cornell Workshop of Energy and the Environment, U.S. Government Printing Office, Washington, D.C.,
1972.

Fuel and case description	Year in which all ultimately recoverable resources are depleted for a			
	low resource estimate		high resource estimate	
	EGM*	RGM**	EGM*	RGM**
natural gas:				
no imports, no synfuel	1989	1991	2000	2007
no imports, synfuel	1990	1992	2008	2016
imports, no synfuel	1993	1997	2010	2025
imports, synfuel	1996	2000	2037	(1)
petroleum:				
no imports, no synfuel	1988	1988	2011	2014
no imports, synfuel	1989	1989	2027	2030
imports, no synfuel	2001	2003	2031	2038
imports, synfuel	2006	2008	(1)	(1)
coal:				
no synfuel	(1)	(1)	(1)	(1)
synfuel	2032	(1)	2044	(1)

*EGM = extrapolated-growth model

**RGM = reduced-growth model.

(1)Beyond the year 2050.

A 1971 National Petroleum Council (NPC) projection is reproduced in

Fig. 1.5-9. This block diagram shows the estimated distribution of oil

and gas resources derived from domestic and foreign supplies. It was

labeled an "initial appraisal," which could be modified advantageously

(i.e., requiring fewer imports) by proper exercise of energy policy to

promote domestic oil production.

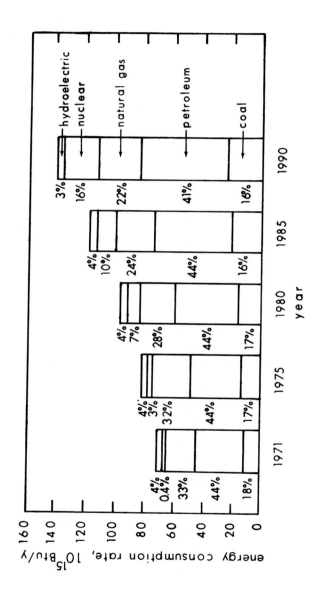

Fig. 1.5-8   The year 1971 energy consumption and estimated future energy
consumption in the United States by source; reproduced from
The Potential for Energy Conservation, U.S. Government
Printing Office, Washington, D.C., 1972.

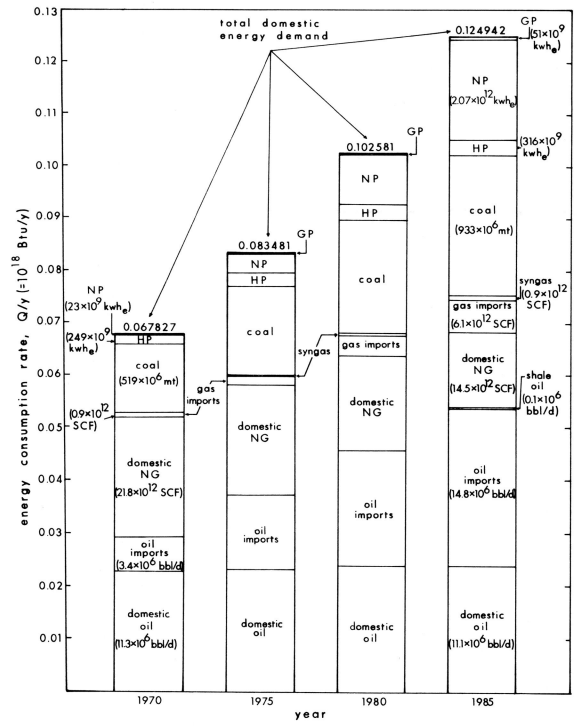

Fig. 1.5-9 A 1971 U.S. energy projection to 1985; reproduced from U.S. Energy Outlook, National Petroleum Council, Washington, D.C., 1971. HP--hydroelectric-power generation; NP-- nuclear-power generation; GP--geothermal-power generation.

The effects of domestic exploration policy are highlighted by the NPC data shown in Fig. 1.5-10 for 1985, where applicable values are identified for high domestic supply (case I), two cases of intermediate domestic supply (cases II and III), and continuation of present (1972) trends (case IV). The serious economic implications of the continuation of present (1972) trends were discussed at length in the NPC report but became hopelessly exaggerated within 12 months of publication because of a totally unforeseen acceleration in foreign fossil-fuel price increases. The coal, nuclear, hydroelectric, and geothermal contributions in Fig. 1.5-10 were assumed to remain largely invariant for the different domestic fossil-fuel supply programs. The high demand, intermediate demand, and low demand limits are defined by the data summarized in Table 1.5-4.

Table 1.5-4 Projections of U.S. energy demand for the high, intermediate and low demand limits of Fig. 1.5-10; reproduced from U.S. Energy Outlook, National Petroleum Council, Washington, D.C., 1972.

Case	Average annual growth rate, % gain		
	1970-1980	1981-1985	1971-1985
high	4.5	4.3	4.4
intermediate (initial appraisal)	4.2	4.0	4.2
low	3.5	3.3	3.4

Some perspective may be gained on the implications of projected U.S. oil and natural-gas demands by comparing extrapolated regional demand and supply data, as is done in Tables 1.5-5 and 1.5-6. These tables show the

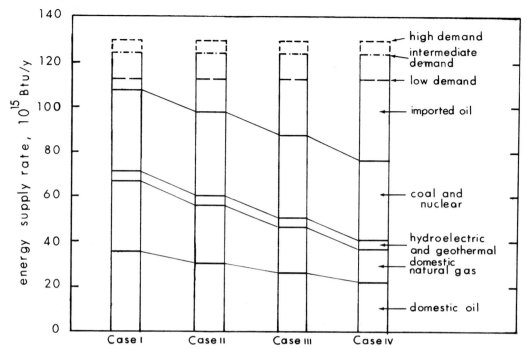

Fig. 1.5-10 The anticipated (in 1972) effect of domestic exploration
policy on the year 1985 distribution of foreign and domestic gas and oil supplies (Case I: high domestic supply;
Cases II and III: intermediate domestic supply; Case IV:
continuation of 1972 trends); reproduced from U.S. Energy
Outlook, National Petroleum Council, Washington D.C.,
1972.

implied stress on oil-producing regions if the U.S. demands, as well as those

of other low producers (Western Europe, Japan), are not modified extensively.

Repeated reference has been made to disproportionately high energy con-

sumption in the U.S. This fact is further clarified by comparing the 1970 de-

mands of U.S. residents with those of residents in other countries, as is done

in Fig. 1.5-11. While Swedes used more oil per capita, their total per capita

energy consumption was only 82.5% of that of U.S. residents, although their

average outside temperatures are significantly lower than ours. All countries,

Table 1.5-5   A 1972 evaluation of regional demands and supplies of petroleum (in 10^6 bbl/d) to the year 1990; reproduced from S. H. Clark, *World Energy*, Stanford Research Institute, Menlo Park, California, 1972.

	1971	1972	1973	1974	1975	1976	1977	1978	1980	1990
demand										
United States	15.1	16.2	17.9	19.5	21.1	22.9	24.3	25.6	27.0	35.0
Canada	1.6	1.7	1.7	1.8	1.9	2.0	2.1	2.2	2.4	4.1
Western Europe	13.2	13.7	15.0	16.5	18.5	19.8	21.0	22.2	24.7	36.0
Japan	4.5	4.9	5.5	6.2	7.1	7.9	8.8	9.8	12.4	27.0
other	6.9	7.4	7.9	8.5	9.0	9.5	10.0	10.6	11.8	15.5
total	41.3	43.9	48.0	52.5	57.6	62.1	66.2	70.4	78.3	117.6
supply										
United States	11.6	11.2	11.2	11.0	10.5	10.0	10.3	10.3	11.5	14.5
Canada	1.6	1.8	2.0	2.2	2.4	2.5	2.5	2.6	2.8	4.0
Venezuela	3.8	3.2	3.0	3.0	3.0	3.0	3.0	3.0	3.0	3.0
other Latin American countries	1.5	1.5	1.6	1.7	1.8	1.9	2.0	2.5	2.5	3.5
Western Europe	0.4	0.5	0.7	1.0	1.5	2.0	2.8	3.5	5.0	10.0
Africa	5.8	5.7	6.5	7.0	8.0	8.5	9.0	9.5	11.0	17.0
Middle East	15.0	18.2	20.8	24.1	27.5	30.9	32.9	35.2	37.7	57.6
Indonesia	0.9	1.1	1.4	1.6	1.9	2.1	2.3	2.5	3.0	5.0
other Pacific Basin countries	0.7	0.7	0.8	0.9	1.0	1.2	1.4	1.6	1.8	3.0
total	41.3	43.9	48.0	52.5	57.6	62.1	66.2	70.4	78.3	117.6

Table 1.5-6 Crude-oil and natural-gas production and reserves in 1971; reprinted with permission from Chemical and Engineering News **51**, 62, April 16, 1973. Copyright by the American Chemical Society.

	Oil			Natural gas		
	production	reserves	years supply	production	reserves	years supply
	(in 10^6 mt)			(in 10^9 m^3)		
North America	619.1	7,484.0	12.1	753.8	9,465.0	12.7
Canada	66.3	1,368.0	20.6	70.8	1,570.0	20.6
U.S.	552.8	6,116.0	11.1	683.0	7,895.0	11.6
Western Europe	18.7	1,998.0	106.8	101.7	4,530.0	44.5
Austria	2.5	27.0	10.8	1.9	16.0	8.4
France	1.9	13.0	6.8	8.1	190.0	23.4
West Germany	7.4	82.0	11.1	13.8	390.0	28.3
Italy	1.3	33.0	25.4	13.0	170.0	13.1
Netherlands	1.7	37.0	21.8	46.2	2,350.0	50.9
Turkey	3.4	80.0	23.5	na	5.0	
U.K.	0.1	690.0		18.7	1,100.0	58.8
other	0.4	1,036.0		0.0	309.0	
Eastern Europe	390.4	10,535.0	27.0	250.4	15,793.0	63.1
Hungary	2.0	130.0	65.0	3.7	85.0	23.0
Romania	13.5	116.0	8.6	26.7	277.0	10.4
U.S.S.R.	369.5	10,200.0	27.6	212.0	15,000.0	70.8
other	5.4	89.0	16.3	8.0	431.0	82.0
Middle East	795.7	48,883.0	61.4	101.7	10,854.0	106.7
Bahrain	3.7	86.0	23.2	0.5	690.0	
Iran	224.2	7,531.0	33.6	37.0	5,700.0	
Iraq	84.0	4,840.0	57.6	6.0	600.0	
Kuwait	160.7	10,770.0	67.0	18.6	1,661.0	
Oman	14.2	700.0	42.3	2.2	57.0	
Qatar	20.4	780.0	38.2	2.5	230.0	
Saudi Arabia	237.3	21,460.0	90.4	27.7	1,600.0	
United Arab Emirates	51.2	2,716.0	53.0	7.2	316.0	
Rest of Asia	88.2	4,374.1	49.6	19.4	1,454.0	74.9
China	25.0	2,700.0	108.0	4.2	100.0	23.8
India	7.4	128.0	17.3	1.4	42.0	30.0
Indonesia	44.3	1,400.0	31.6	3.4	130.0	38.2

Table 1.5-6, continued.

	Oil			Natural gas		
	production	reserves	years supply	production	reserves	years supply
	(in 10^6 mt)			(in 10^9 m^3)		
Rest of Asia (cont'd)						
Israel	6.0	1.0		0.1	2.0	20.0
Malaysia	3.3	120.0	36.4	0.0	210.0	
Pakistan	0.5	5.0	10.0	3.4	550.0	
other	1.7	20.1	30.0	6.9	420.0	71.6
Latin America	265.1	4,408.1	16.6	92.8	2,053.0	22.1
Argentina	21.7	358.0	16.5	8.1	215.0	26.5
Bolivia	1.7	25.0	14.7	2.3	140.0	60.9
Brazil	8.7	137.0	15.7	1.2	140.0	
Columbia	11.1	236.0	21.3	2.4	70.0	29.2
Mexico	25.0	630.0	25.2	18.2	326.0	25.2
Trinidad	7.0	215.0	30.7	3.0	140.0	46.7
Venezuela	185.0	1,984.0	10.7	47.6	720.0	15.1
other	4.9	65.1	25.5	10.0	302.0	44.6
Australasia	14.9	407.0	27.3	2.5	870.0	348.0
Australia	14.8	379.0	25.6	2.2	700.0	
other	0.1	28.0		0.3	170.0	
Africa	275.2	7,884.3	28.6	33.4	5,426.9	162.5
Algeria	36.3	1,590.0	43.8	3.0	3,000.0	
Egypt	15.5	570.0	36.8	1.1	210.0	
Libya	132.3	3,300.0	24.9	15.8	830.0	
Nigeria	75.4	1,579.0	20.9	12.4	1,120.0	
other	15.7	845.3	65.0	1.1	266.9	
World total	2,467.3	85,973.5	34.8	1,355.7	50,455.9	37.2

except for Canada and Sweden, had per capita energy-use rates less than one-half of ours during 1970.

We conclude this section with a summary of bituminous coal production during the years 1969, 1970, and 1971 in various countries (see Table 1.5-7). It is interesting to note that U.S. coal production did not change greatly during the specified three-year period.

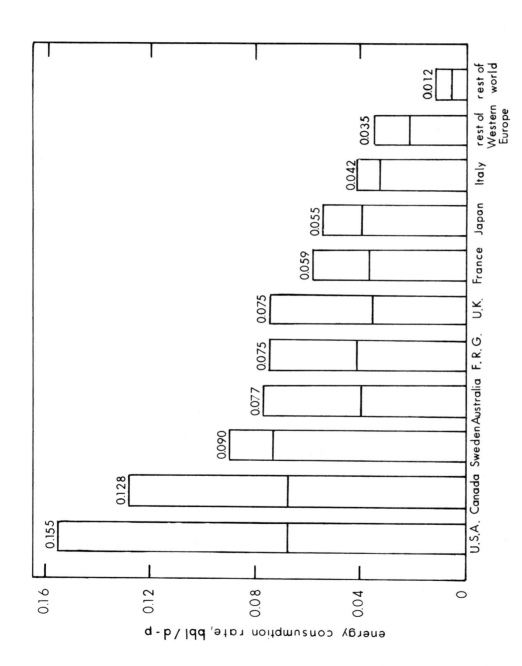

Fig. 1.5-11 The 1970 contribution of oil consumption to total energy use in barrels per day per person; reproduced from Energy Users Guide, The Bureau of National Affairs, Inc., Washington, D.C., 1973. The lower section of the bars corresponds to energy derived from oil, while the upper section represents energy derived from other sources.

The story of natural-gas demands is considered in some detail in the following Section 1.6.

Table 1.5-7 Bituminous coal production in units of 10^6 metric tons, during the recent past; reprinted with permission from Chemical and Engineering News $\underline{51}$, $\underline{63}$, April 16, 1973, and based on a United Nations release. Copyright 1973 by the American Chemical Society.

Country	1969	1970	1971
U.S.	512	541	495
U.S.S.R.	425	432	480
U.K.	153	144	147
Poland	135	140	145
West Germany	112	111	111
India	75	74	70
South Africa	53	55	59
Australia	43	45	49
Japan	45	40	33
France	41	37	33
Czechoslovakia	27	28	29
Canada	8	12	15
South Korea	10	12	13
Belgium	13	11	11

C. Comments on Procedures for Rational Projection of the Energy-Demand Function in the U.S. and Elsewhere

Decisions relating to transportation, land use (and, hence, industrial and commercial development), and electricity production in the U.S. are made on a regional basis with the determinant unit (e.g., a county) consisting typically of a metropolitan complex and adjoining rural areas. The total U.S. demand function is the sum of the regional demand functions and corresponds to actual energy use if the hypothesis that demand determines supply holds, which we are assuming to be the case for the sake of argument in the present discussion.

Regional-demand projections, in turn, depend on such factors as population-growth projections, increased industrial and commercial development as determined by land-use allocations, transportation-system development, per capita income and standard of living, efficiency of energy conversion in devices such as cars, airplanes, refrigerators, etc. There is no satisfactory methodology at hand for making reliable projections even on a regional basis. As an illustration of some of the required complex considerations, we shall discuss in Section 1.7 the relatively simple problem of electricity-demand projection for a region (the San Diego region has been chosen in the example).

1.6   Natural-Gas Demands in the United States

In many respects, natural gas is an ideal fuel for industrial and consumer applications. It is transportable through pipelines at relatively low cost and is a preferred fuel, compared with coal and oil, because of relatively low pollutant output. We have exploited this valuable resource so rapidly that its peak growth rate for application probably has already been passed. Furthermore, price constraints have impeded production so severely that it may disappear as a major component of the energy-resource picture even more rapidly than needs to be the case in view of remaining reserves.

A. Past Uses and Supplies and Estimated Future Availability

The 1970 distribution of natural-gas demand by application sector is summarized in Table 1.6-1 and by region in Table 1.6-2. In order to accomplish the regional utilization specified in Table 1.6-2, the gas production and gas-flow transfers shown in Fig. 1.6-1 had to be accomplished. Future projections of gas supplies for the U.S. are listed in Table 1.6-3.

Table 1.6-1 Approximate 1970 natural-gas allocation by application sector; reproduced from S. Field, SNG and the 1985 U.S. Energy Picture, Stanford Research Institute, Menlo Park, California, 1972.

Sector for use	Demand, 10^{12} SCF	Percentage of total natural-gas demand
residential and commercial	7.5	32.7%
industrial	10.1	44.5
electric-power generation	4.1	18.2
transportation	0.5	2.3
manufacture of chemicals	0.5	2.3
total	22.7	100.0%

Table 1.6-2 Approximate 1970 natural-gas utilization by region; reproduced from S. Field, SNG and the 1985 U.S. Energy Picture, Stanford Research Institute, Menlo Park, California, 1972.

Region	Demand, 10^{12} SCF	Percentage of total natural-gas demand
West South Central	7.81	34.4%
East North Central	4.05	17.9
Pacific	2.54	11.2
West North Central	2.06	9.1
Middle Atlantic	1.91	8.4
South Atlantic	1.58	7.0
Mountain	1.28	5.6
East South Central	1.20	5.3
New England	0.25	1.1
total	22.68	100.0%

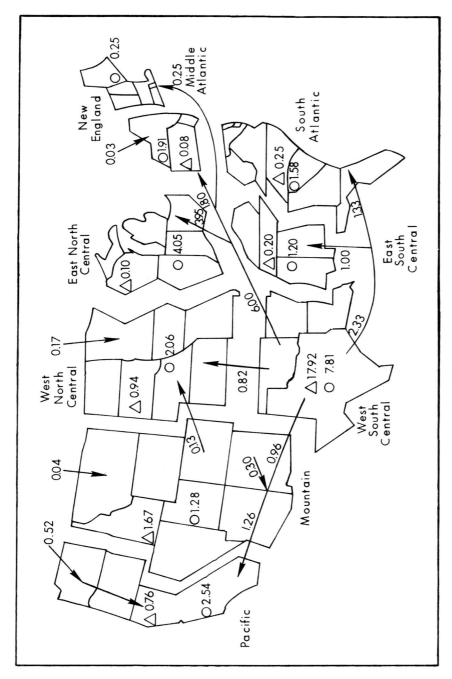

Fig. 1.6-1 Approximate productions and transfers of natural gas in the U.S. in 1970; reproduced from S. Field, SNG and the 1985 U.S. Energy Picture, Stanford Research Institute, Menlo Park, California, 1972. The numbers adjacent to circles correspond to regional total demand, while the figures preceded by triangles represent regional indigenous production. The arrows indicate inter-regional shipments and all data are in units of 10^{12} SCF.

It is interesting to note (see Table 1.6-1) that industrial use amounted to 44.5% of the total in 1970, residential and commercial application was 32.7%, while only 18.2% of the consumed natural gas was employed for electric-power production. This low utilization rate by the utility industry reflects, at least in part, supply problems which were apparent for NG as early as 1970.

The regional distribution of natural-gas utilization (see Table 1.6-2) also reflects availability of this resource and is not simply related to population or industrial activity. The preferred availability of NG in the West South Central region is responsible for the relatively heavier use of NG, as compared with that in the East North Central Region. Reference to Fig. 1.6-1 shows that Texas was the principal exporter of NG and that the Pacific Region, including California, was a heavy importer (1.78×10^{12} SCF out of 2.54×10^{12} SCF were imported).

The values summarized in Table 1.6-3 have been used in Fig. 1.6-2, which shows a 1972 estimate of anticipated U.S. natural-gas supply problems to the year 1990. We note a projected lower-48 state potential reserve considerably less than the 1970 use rate and a substantial and growing dissatisfied demand (see Fig. 1.6-2), which was estimated (in 1972) to reach about 14×10^{12} SCF/y by the year 1990. It remains to be seen if the production of syngas, as well as the exploration rates in the lower 48 states and in Alaska, cannot be significantly accelerated by allowing prices to rise as required by prevailing market conditions.

Table 1.6-3   The 1970 U.S. gas supplies and estimated future supplies in 10^{12} SCF; reproduced from S. Field, <u>SNG and the 1985 U.S. Energy Picture</u>, Stanford Research Institute, Menlo Park, California, 1972.

	Year				
	1970	1975	1980	1985	1990
proven reserves in the lower 48 states:					
interstate	10.5	9.0	4.6	2.4	1.0
intrastate	11.4	11.0	6.9	3.6	1.5
subtotal	21.9	20.0	11.5	6.0	2.5
potential reserves in the lower 48 states		4.0	8.5	13.0	16.5
subtotal for the lower 48 states	21.9	24.0	20.0	19.0	19.0
Alaskan supplies			1.2	2.0	2.3
Canadian supplies	0.8	1.1	1.5	2.5	2.5
LNG imports		0.6	1.5	2.4	3.2
SNG from oil		0.3	1.3	1.3	1.0
SNG from coal			0.4	2.0	4.0
total gas supplies	22.7	26.0	25.7	29.2	32.0
residential and commercial demand	7.5	8.8	10.8	13.7	15.9
gas available for industrial use and electric-power generation	15.2	17.2	14.9	15.5	16.1

B.   The Effect of Pricing on Natural-Gas Availability

Natural gas has been recovered in such a manner as to keep supply and demand in balance.   No effort has been described to develop an optimal utilization and corresponding production schedule for the country as a whole.

Figure 1.6-3 shows the time history of natural-gas production from the beginning of 1970 to the end of 1973.   Relative peak growth in production occurred during the second quarter of 1970 when NG was used at a rate about 8% higher than during the corresponding time period of the preceding year. Production continued to exceed that of the preceding year until the beginning of 1972, when it began to decline.   By the fourth quarter of 1973, NG production was projected (in 1972) to lie 5% below that accomplished during the fourth quarter of 1972.

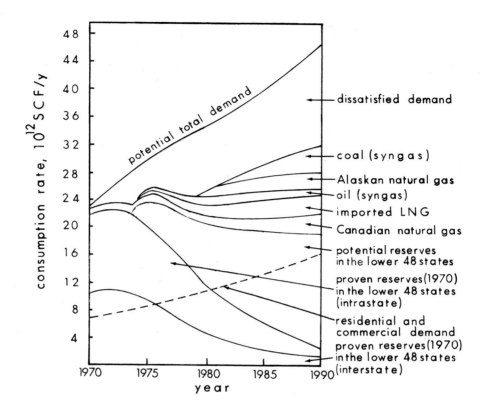

Fig. 1.6-2   A 1972 estimate of U.S. gas demands and supplies to
             the year 1990; reproduced from S. Field, <u>SNG and the
             1985 U.S. Energy Picture</u>, Stanford Research Institute
             Menlo Park, California.

The rate of gas production has been estimated[1] as a function of the field

price, which is given in cents per 10^6 Btu $\simeq$ cents per 10^3 SCF.   Figure 1.6-4

[1]S. H. Clark, <u>World Energy</u>, Stanford Research Institute, Menlo Park,
California, 1972.

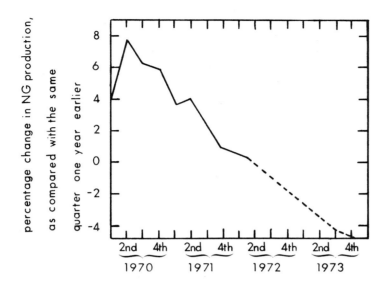

Fig. 1.6-3   NG production as a function of time, expressed
as the percentage change from the quarter of the
prior year; reproduced from Ref. [1].

shows a projection[1] of how production might be stimulated by selective price

increases. In this connection, it is interesting to note that the energy cost for

one gallon of petroleum at \$1.00/gallon is \$7.20 per 10^6 Btu. Thus, even at

\$1.00/10^6 Btu, the cost of NG is, relatively speaking, low.

Supply estimates as a function of time and both field and city-gate prices

for NG are projected[1] in Fig. 1.6-5 to the year 2000. According to these

data, simply maintaining the 1970 supply of about 23×10^{12} SCF will require

about a six-fold increase in field prices by the year 1990. Reference

to Fig. 1.6-5 also shows that city-gate prices exceeded field prices by 20¢/

10^6 Btu in 1970 and are projected to exceed field prices by 30 to 40¢/10^6 Btu

by the early nineties.

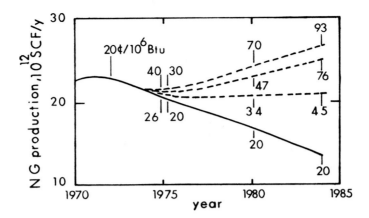

Fig. 1.6-4   A 1972 estimate of NG production as a function of
field price in cents/10^6 Btu ($\simeq$¢/10^3 SCF); reproduced from Ref. [1]. At 20¢/10^6 Btu, production
was (in 1972) expected to decline to about one-half
of the 1970 production by the year 1985.

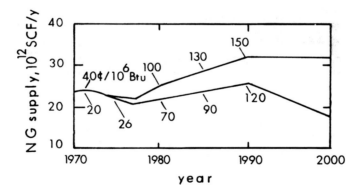

Fig. 1.6-5   A 1972 estimate of NG supplies for the U.S. from
all sources (upper envelope) and from the lower 48
states and Canada (lower envelope) projected to the
end of the century, together with estimated field and
city-gate prices in cents/10^6 Btu; reproduced from
Ref. [1]. The numbers on the upper envelope correspond to average city-gate prices, while the numbers on the lower envelope represent average field
prices.

Projected delivered natural-gas price trends by application are shown in Fig. 1.6-6. The disproportionately higher prices charged for residential use, as compared with large-scale use, do not reflect accurately the higher costs associated with distribution to low-volume users. The estimated cost increases for NG use are large for all consumer segments. The question of demand-price elasticity, i.e., of the relation between consumer use and prices, is difficult to answer precisely. It evidently depends on availability of other energy sources, on the energy-intensivity of the application (which is generally low in industrial use), on limits set by environmental control standards, etc.

As prices rise, productivity is stimulated, while demand tends to be curtailed. A 1972 estimate for the rise in supply with increasing prices and the decrease in demand with increasing prices by 1980 is reproduced in Fig. 1.6-7. The intersection of these two curves for 1980 represents the projected stable supply-and-demand point for this calendar year, i.e., at a price of about 55 cents/10^3 SCF higher than in 1971, about 25×10^{12} SCF of NG become available and are consumed. Operation under these stable conditions may not be attainable and may not be a desirable national objective. It is conceivable that the interests of the country will be best served by a long-term gas-conservation program designed to assure availability of limited supplies of NG for chemical synthesis, at least to the middle of the twenty-first century.

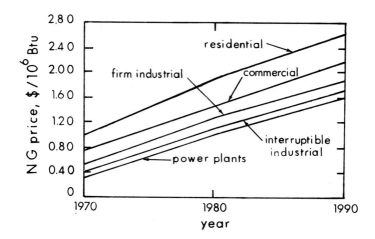

Fig. 1.6-6   Projected price trends to the year 1990 for NG use
by different consumers; reproduced from Ref. [1].

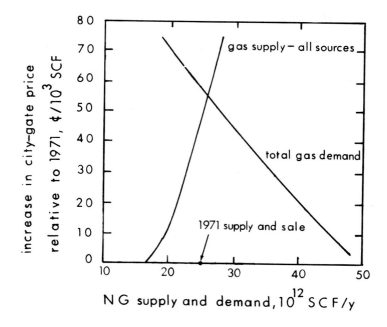

Fig. 1.6-7   Estimated 1980 U.S. gas supply and demand curves;
reproduced from Ref. [1].

1.7   An Electricity Demand Projection to the Year 2000 for the San Diego Region*

World energy consumption is the sum of the energies used by the countries composing the world.   The U.S. consumption of energy is obtained by addition of the energies utilized in the individual states.   Energy consumption in a state is the sum of the energies used by the regions of which the state is composed.   Energy planning (insofar as electricity production, land use, local transportation networks, etc. are concerned) is effectively performed at the regional level.   For this reason, it is important to understand how regional demand projections are made.   The following discussion will be confined to electricity growth projections for a region, in particular, for the San Diego region in California.

Growth of residential electricity demand in the San Diego region between 1950 and 1970 will be shown to be primarily associated with increasing saturation levels of appliance usage.   Only a relatively minor contribution to the demand function is attributable to increased consumption per appliance unit and is probably the result of development of a more elaborate or extensive performance function.   Using past saturation growth figures and an estimate of somewhat less than 1% per year for the increase in consumption per appliance, we

---

*This discussion follows closely an analysis by G. Dimonte, "A Growth Projection for Electricity Demand in San Diego County to the End of the Century," Report EC-R.1, Univ. of Calif., San Diego, La Jolla, Calif., August 1973. Dimonte's analysis was a student summer project performed under the supervision of S. S. Penner and M. Rotenberg.

arrive at a year 2000 electrical-energy consumption level of about 12, 000 kwh_e per average household, as compared with a 1970 level of about 4, 900 kwh_e. Technological innovation, such as electrical-car development with home re- charge capability, will increase average household electricity consumption significantly.

The electrical-energy consumption in the commercial and industrial sector in kwh_e/year is estimated on the assumption that consumption is a linear function of commercial and industrial floor area. The 1972 estimate for the electricity loading function per ft^2 was 27. 6 kwh_e/(ft^2-year). Pro- jection of this function to later times is based on the assumption that growth occurs along logistics curves to limiting values appropriate for all-electric structures.

Projections of total regional electrical-energy consumption to the year 2000 are made by combining the private and commercial (including industrial) growth rates and multiplying the final value by 1. 04 in order to account for unallowed growth in agriculture, street and highway lighting, and other sales. The final limiting values for household electricity consumption and commer- cial electrical loading are assumed to be reached by the year 2035 along logistics curves. Both "high" and "low" projections are made. We estimate that actual electrical-energy consumption in the San Diego region by the year 2000 will be 24% to 31% of the value obtained by straightforward extrapolation of past and current energy-use rates.

An inadequate though conventional time-series regression analysis for household electricity demand in San Diego County shows the expected positive correlation with the size of the household. Positive exponents appear also in the terms measuring time and average real yearly household income. Weak negative exponents were obtained for the prices of electricity and gas. Local temperature variations appear to be unimportant. Some of these results are immediately plausible, others can be accounted for by the fact that the regression analysis is not physically significant because we did not introduce explicitly the dependence of household electricity demand on appliance-saturation level.

A. Introduction

Electrical-energy demand in San Diego (S. D.) County was 5.98×10^9 kwh_e in 1970 and has been growing at the average rate[1] of 9.5%/y since 1950 (see Fig. 1.7-1). California demand[2] was 124×10^9 kwh_e while it was $1,540 \times 10^9$ kwh_e nationally.[3] Both have been growing at an average rate of 7%/y since 1960. The population of S. D. County was 1.36 million in 1970. Thus, the 6.3% of California residents who lived in the County consumed 4.8% of the California electrical-energy production.

---

[1] These data were collected from annual reports of the San Diego Gas and Electric Company (SDG&E).

[2] Annual Report, 1971-72, p. 56, Public Utilities Commission, State of California, Sacramento, Calif., 1972.

[3] Statistical Abstract of the United States, U.S. Bureau of the Census, U.S. Government Printing Office, Washington, D.C., p. 507, 1972.

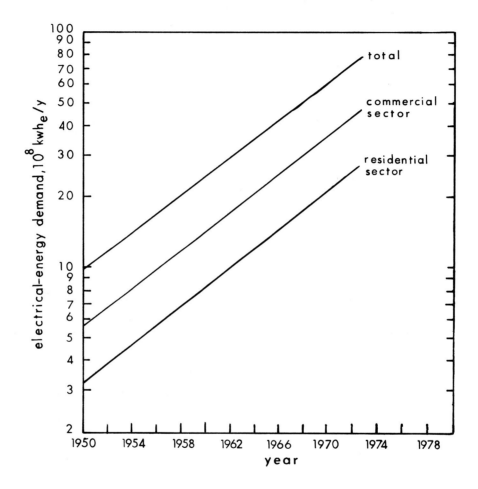

Fig. 1.7-1 Electrical-energy demand in San Diego County. The
average growth rate in the total electrical-energy
demand was 9.5%/y from 1950 to 1972. The sources
for the data are SDG&E annual reports. This figure
has been reproduced with modifications from Dimonte's
analysis.

If the past growth rate is sustained to the year 2002, S. D. will consume as much electricity as the entire State did in 1970. Let us suppose, for illustrative purposes, that this energy is provided by 2,000 Mw_e plants located at coastal sites, with a 65% capacity factor. Then we would require eleven such plants in the San Diego region separated by an average distance of 7.2 miles, which is evidently unacceptable. A better solution is desert siting of air- or water-cooled nuclear stations.

The desirability of energy expansion is controversial because it may prove to be an excessive burden to the environment although many economic and other social benefits are derived from additional electric services.

Future energy-use rates are sometimes estimated by a simple extrapolation of past trends. While this procedure is reasonable (and often the most useful) for short-term projections, one must consider the effects of approaching saturation when making long-term projections. In the following discussion, we shall study electricity consumption in S. D. County and determine reasonable growth rates in order to project energy needs to the end of the century.

It is desirable to divide demand into principal user categories, namely, residential and commercial (combined with industrial use). This analysis in the residential sector will consist of a description of the increase in demand since 1950, using saturation data for major electrical appliances and reasonable estimates of the average energy consumption by appliances. It is then possible to draw some conclusions about future demand growth rates in the residential sector. Regression techniques, as employed in independent studies conducted by Wilson,[4] Kline,[5] and Anderson,[6] will be applied to the S. D. region; the results are reported in Appendix A1.7.

The analysis in the commercial and industrial sectors parallels the study conducted by Lees[7] for the South Coast Air Basin (SCAB), in which he found that floor space was the important scaling variable. However, the model for San Diego County was changed because industry does not play as important a role as it does in SCAB. E. J. List[8] has reported that industrial electricity demand was 3.6% of the total for San Diego County in 1969.

B.   Residential Sector

B1   Residential Demand

Residential electricity demand was 2.1×10^9 kwh$_e$ (35% of the total) in 1970 and has been growing at an average rate of 9.7%/year since 1950 (see Fig. 1.7-1). Figure 1.7-2 shows the time history of growth for population

[4] J. W. Wilson, "Residential Demand for Electricity," The Quarterly Review of Economics and Business 11, 7-19 (1971).

[5] P. Kline, "An Econometric Model for Residential Electricity Demand, "The 1970 National Power Survey, Part IV, Appendix B-1, Federal Power Commission, U.S. Government Printing Office, Washington, D. C., 1971.

[6] Kent P. Anderson, "Residential Demand for Electricity: Econometric Estimates for California and the United States," Rand Corporation Report R-905-NSF, Santa Monica, California, January 1972.

[7] L. Lees, "Implications of the Growth in Demand for Commercial and Industrial Electrical Energy in the South Coast Air Basin," Environmental Quality Laboratory Report #2, California Institute of Technology, Pasadena, California, November 1971.

[8] E. J. List, "Energy Use in California: Implications for the Environment," Environmental Quality Laboratory Report #3, California Institute of Technology, Pasadena, California, December 1971.

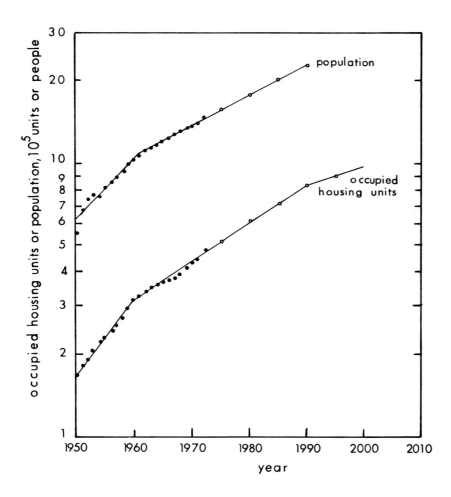

Fig. 1.7-2   Dimonte's (•) estimates and San Diego County Comprehensive Planning Organization (o) projections of population and occupied housing units for S. D. County. The
growth rate for occupied housing units is 3.2%/y from
1960 to 1990 and 1.5%/y from 1990 to 2000.

and occupied housing units in S. D. County. According to these estimates,[*] the average household consumption of electricity was 1,610 kwh_e in 1950 and rose to 4,953 kwh_e in 1970.

Appliances consume electricity but the extent to which they are owned and used is determined by people who are trying to maximize their utility function, subject to defined household constraints. Thus, in order to understand the trend in residential demand properly, one should study the evolution of the parameters defined by the relation

$$DH = \sum_i \beta_i g_i, \qquad (1.7\text{-}1)$$

where DH is the average annual household electricity consumption, g_i is the current use (or saturation) level for the ith appliance, and β_i is the average annual household consumption of electricity when the ith appliance is used. A list of terms is given in Table 1.7-1. The sum in Eq. (1.7-1) should include all appliances but, as will be shown in Section 1.7B2, it is sufficient to consider contributions only from major appliances.

The problem of understanding how a number of independent variables affect β_i and g_i is a formidable one because the final judgment may well be subjective; in particular, analytical procedures, such as simple regression analysis, may not apply (see Appendix A1.7 for details concerning regression analysis). Possible exceptions are applicances which use a large

---

*Values were calculated by dividing residential electric sales volume, given in SDG&E annual reports, by U.S. Census figures of occupied housing units for S. D. County.

Table 1.7-1 Definition of terms.

Symbol	Definition	Units
DH	average annual household electricity demand	kwh_e/housing unit-y
ρ_i	average annual consumption of electricity for appliance i	kwh_e/y
g_i	saturation (fraction of homes owning appliance i per year)	per y
$(kwh_e)_c$	annual electricity consumption by the commercial and industrial sectors	kwh_e/y
S	commercial and industrial floor area	ft^2
λ	electrical loading per ft^2 of commercial and industrial floor area	$kwh_e/(ft^2$-y)
N	number of occupied housing units in S. D. County	
RYH	average real yearly household income	$(1967)
SOH	number of occupants per housing unit	p
RPE	real price of electricity per kwh_e for customers using at least 500 kwh_e/month	¢/kwh_e(1967)
RPG	average real price of gas	¢/10^3SCF (1967)
t	time in years	1950 $\equiv$ 1
T_A	average August temperature	^{o}F
T_J	average January temperature	^{o}F
$\langle T_A \rangle, \langle T_J \rangle$	average values of T_A and T_J, respectively, for the period 1950-72	^{o}F

amount of electricity in such a way that a cost analysis is appropriate (e. g. ,

space heating). In general, the cost of electricity in S. D. County has been

less than 1% of the total family income during the last 22 years and it is,

therefore, a priori unlikely that past demand has been sensitive to modest

price increases. Furthermore, the process of accumulation of appliances

takes years and should not be attributed to family income for a specific year.

Even without detailed understanding of individual factors relating to ap-

pliance purchase, it is still possible to gain some information about future

demand by looking at recent trends of f_i and g_i. This problem will now be

examined.

B2 Results of a Saturation Study for 1950, 1960, and 1970

Tables 1. 7-2, 1. 7-3 and 1. 7-4 display the calculations of DH using data

for β_i and g_i for 1950, 1960 and 1970, respectively. Saturation values for

the major appliances were taken from census data, except where indicated.

For those appliances for which regional census data were not available, national

estimates appearing in Merchandising Week[9] were used.

The values of f_i for 1970 were obtained with the help of tables,[10]

which provided estimates for a family of four in a 1, 500 ft^2 house. However,

the numbers taken from these tables were scaled down slightly because the

average housing unit in S. D. County consisted of 4. 7 rooms and was inhabited

---

[9] Merchandising Week, Billboard Publications, New York, N. Y., volume 104,
    February 28, 1972.

[10] The tables for "Estimated Annual kwh_e Consumption of Electric Appliances"
    were provided by the Edison Electric Institute (1969) and SDG&E.

Table 1.7-2 Major appliance use in composite S. D. households
for the year 1950; reproduced with modifications from
Dimonte, loc. cit.

Electric appliance	Estimated annual consumption, kwh$_e$	S. D. County[a] saturation, %	Annual use in a composite household, kwh$_e$
central heating	6,100	0.3%	18
water heater	2,900	(not available)	--
air conditioning			
room	1,000	(0.8)[b]	8
central	2,600	(not available)	--
range	850	9.6	82
freezer	850	7.2	61
dryer	900	(1.4)	13
refrigerator	525	85	445
T.V.	280	10.3	29
dishwasher	270	(2)	5
washing machine	80	(75.2)	60
radio	80	96	77
		subtotal:	798
lighting (4.3 rooms)	200/room	99	850
total	16,285[c]		1,648
actual			1,610

a. U. S. Census of Housing: General Characteristics, Alabama-Georgia, 1950, Volume 1, Part 2, U. S. Bureau of the Census, U. S. Government Printing Office, Washington, D. C., 1953.

b. Figures in parentheses are national values for 1950 published in Ref. [9].

c. Total for a home with all major appliances.

Table 1.7-3 Major appliance use in composite S. D. households for the year
1960; reproduced with modifications from Dimonte, loc. cit.

Electric appliance	Estimated annual consumption, kwh_e	S. D. County[a] saturation, %	Annual use in a composite household, kwh_e
central heating	6,700	5.3	355
water heater	3,200	7.2	230
air conditioning			
room	1,100	3.2	35
central	2,900	0.9	26
range	950	17.5	166
freezer	950	18.5	176
dryer	900	6.5	58
refrigerator	700	98	685
T. V.	300	90	270
dishwasher	300	(7.1)[b]	21
washing machine	85	69	59
radio	90	100	90
			subtotal: 2,171
lighting (4.5 rooms)	225/ room	100	1,010
total	18,085[c]		3,181
actual			2,920

a. U.S. Census of Housing: State and Small Areas, 1960, HC(1) No. 6, U.S.
Bureau of the Census, U.S. Government Printing Office, Washington, D.C.,
1963.

b. Figures in parentheses are national values for 1960 published in Ref. [9].

c. Total for a home with all major appliances.

Table 1.7-4 Major appliance use in composite S. D. households for the year
1970; reproduced from Dimonte, loc. cit.

Electric appliance	Estimated annual consumption, kwh$_e$	S. D. County[a] saturation, %	Annual use in a composite household, kwh$_e$
central heating	7,500	10.2	765
water heater	3,600	10.3	361
air conditioning			
room	1,200	9.6	115
central	3,200	3.8	122
range	1,050	28	294
freezer	1,050	22.5	236
dryer	1,000	20.6	206
refrigerator	900	100	900
T. V.	430	95.3	410
dishwasher	330	23	76
washing machine	90	63	57
radio	100	100	100
		subtotal:	3,642
lighting (4.7 rooms)	250/ room	100	1,175
total	20,425[b]		4,817
actual			4,953

a. U.S. Census of Housing: Detailed Housing Characteristics, California,
1970, HC(1)-B6, U.S. Bureau of the Census, U.S. Government Printing
Office, Washington, D.C., 1972.

b. Total for a home with all major appliances.

by 2.9 people in 1970. The figure of 7,500 kwh_e annually for space heating in S.D. County is an average over many households with different types of built-in electrical heating units.

All values for f_i in 1960, except two, were obtained by subtracting 10% from the 1970 estimates. The first exception involves the use of television; here, an allowance had to be made for the more widespread ownership of color T.V. in 1970 than in 1960 and 1950. The second exception refers to refrigerators. In this case, consumption was calculated on the assumption that the average refrigerator had a capacity of 9 cu. ft. in 1950, 12 cu. ft. in 1960, and 14 cu. ft. (refrigerator-freezer) for 1970.

The calculated values of DH agree within about 10% with the actual values, which were computed by dividing the total electrical sales to residential customers by SDG&E by the census figures for the total number of occupied housing units. This result indicates that the three-fold increase in household electricity consumption from 1950 to 1970 in S.D. County can be attributed primarily to increases in the saturation levels of the major electrical appliances and the specified minor increases in electricity consumed by each unit. The major contributions to the rise came from increased saturation of (a) electric units to control the environment (space heating, cooling, and refrigeration), (b) television, and (c) electric ranges and clothes dryers.

It will now be assumed that the saturation, g_i, of all major appliances will continue to grow at the same rates as it has since 1950. At the same time, we assume that the average consumption rate per appliance will grow at a rate of slightly less than 1%/year. With these assumptions, we conclude that the average household will consume 12, 020 kwh$_e$ in the year 2000, as indicated in Table 1.7-5.

There is the possibility that new technology will provide us with important new applications for electricity utilization in the home. However, during the past 25 years, only the introduction of television has made a significant contribution to the increase in demand. It is also conceivable that technological advances such as improved design efficiency will reduce the electrical energy needed for existing appliances. Methods for more efficient utilization of electricity in the home have been discussed by Doctor et al. [11]

A major potential user of electricity is the all-electric car with power cells that can be energized in residential outlets. Design values for a prototype, battery-operated vehicle indicate that the energy consumption for 10, 000 miles of driving would be 2, 800 kwh$_e$. [12] Thus, the technological revolution associated with this possible development will increase our year 2000 estimates appreciably.

Table 1.7-5 displays a model calculation for average household electricity consumption in the year 2000. As indicated above, an extrapolation

[11] R. D. Doctor, K. P. Anderson, M. B. Berman, S. H. Dole, M. J. Hammer, P. T. McClure, and C. B. Smith, California's Electricity Quandry: III. Slowing the Growth Rate, Rand Corporation Report R-1116-NSF/CSA, Santa Monica, California, 1972.

[12] G. Caprioglio and A. Weinberg, Fabrication and Initial Testing of an Experimental Zinc-Oxygen Battery for Electric Vehicles, Gulf General Atomic Company, GA-10559, San Diego, California, 1971.

Table 1.7-5   Estimated major appliance use in composite S. D. households for
the year 2000; reproduced with minor modifications from Dimonte,
loc. cit.

Electric appliance	Estimated annual consumption, kwh_e	S. D. County saturation, %	Annual use in a composite household, kwh_e
central heating	9,500	25	2,375
water heater	4,500	25	1,125
air conditioning			
room	1,400	25	350
central	4,200	20	840
range	1,300	60	780
freezer	1,300	40	520
dryer	1,300	60	780
refrigerator	1,500	100	1,500
T. V.	600	100	600
dishwasher	420	50	210
washing machine	100	70	70
radio	120	100	120
			subtotal: 9,270
lighting (5.0 rooms)	350/ room	100	1,750
other			1,000
total (without electric transportation)	27,590		12,020
electric transportation	2,800/car	100	4,200
total	31,790[a]		16,220[a]

a.   Calculations have been made[12] for 1.5 vehicles per home with prototype
electricity use. The prototype vehicle weights 2,200 lb and has a 250 lb
payload. It is used 80% (of mileage) in urban traffic and 20% at cruising
speed.

b.   Total for a home with all major appliances.

of past trends has been used to arrive at the year 2000 demand of 12, 020 kwh$_e$

to 16, 220 kwh$_e$, depending on whether or not 1.5 electrified cars for trans-

portation are included.

B3 Least-Squares Fit of the Residential Demand to a Logistics Curve

Figure 1.7-3 shows that the average household demand for electricity

grew at the average rate of 5.5%/y from 1950 to 1972.   The procedure

used to estimate data points for DH is described in Appendix A1.7.   In order

to approximate these points with a smooth function, which does not increase

indefinitely, we use the logistics curve given by

$$DH(t) = \frac{D_0 D_\infty}{D_0 + (D_\infty - D_0)\exp(-rt)} . \qquad (1.7\text{-}2)$$

This function exhibits the following limiting behavior:

$$DH(t) = \begin{cases} D_0\exp(rt) \text{ for } rt \ll \ln[(D_\infty/D_0) + 1], \\ D_\infty \text{ as } t \to \infty . \end{cases} \qquad (1.7\text{-}3)$$

Rearranging Eq. (1.7-2) and taking natural logarithms, we find that

$$\ln\left\{\left(\frac{D_\infty}{DH(t)} - 1\right)\left(\frac{D_0}{D_\infty - D_0}\right)\right\} = -rt , \qquad (1.7\text{-}4)$$

which is amenable to simple regression analysis for the determination of r

for a specified value of D_∞.

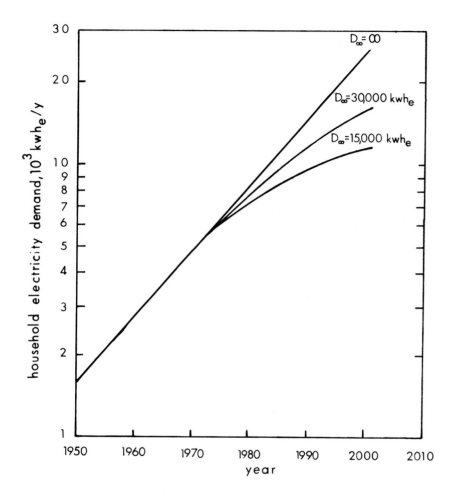

Fig. 1.7-3   Household electricity demand in S. D. County.   The
             average growth rate was 5.5%/y for the 1950-72 period.
             Projections follow logistics curves with D_∞ as the max-
             imum demand.   This figure has been reproduced with
             modifications from Dimonte's analysis.

Good least-squares fits were found for many values of D_∞ (see Fig. 1.7-3) but only those two which predict 12,020 kwh_e and 16,220 kwh_e for the year 2000 will be used in Section 1.7D in making total, year 2000, consumption estimates.

C. Commercial Sector

C1 Commercial-Sector Electricity Demand

Commercial electricity demand in S.D. County was 3.68×10^9 kwh_e (61% of total demand) in 1972 and has been growing at the average rate of 9.4%/y since 1950 (compare Fig. 1.7-1). Lees[7] has shown that, for the South Coast Air Basin, "the strongest factors driving up the demand for commercial electrical energy are the growth in commercial floor area and the increased electrical loading per square foot of floor area." In this spirit, we postulate the following functional relationship for S.D. County:

$$(kwh_e)_c = \lambda S, \qquad\qquad (1.7-5)$$

where $(kwh_e)_c$ is the annual consumption of electricity by the commercial sector in kilowatt-hours, S is the commercial floor area in ft^2, and λ is the average electrical loading in $kwh_e/(ft^2 - y)$.

The objective of this study is to seek a time profile of $\lambda = \lambda(t)$ for S.D. County by dividing actual values of $(kwh_e)_c$ by estimates of commercial floor space. The period of study is limited, by the availability of reliable data, to the interval 1964-72.

The model for the commercial sector includes the industrial sector because it consists of only about 15% of the total floor space and uses a relatively small amount of electrical energy in S.D. County.

C2 Commercial Floor Space

Data for commercial floor area for S. D. County are very sparse but may nevertheless be estimated. The major groups which compose the commercial and industrial sector are taken to be retail stores, business, personal and professional services; schools; churches; city and county governments; transportation and industrial activities.

Annual statistical data on dollar valuation of new non-residential buildings in the county are available in the Construction Review[13] from 1964 to 1972. National averages of cost/ft^2 for newly-constructed commercial and industrial buildings can be obtained on a yearly basis in the Statistical Abstract.[14] If we assume that the national averages are valid for San Diego, we can find the annual incremental change in commercial floor space by dividing dollar valuation by cost/ft^2.

The total floor area was estimated in the following way. San Diego[15] conducted an inventory of non-residential land for 1965, which provides a listing of floor area by standard industrial classification for the city. The aggregate for the major groups listed above was 70. 6 million ft^2 in 1965 (15% of the total was industrial floor space). Dollar valuation of non-residential

[13] Construction Review, U.S. Department of Commerce, U.S. Government Printing Office, Washington, D. C., 1964-73.

[14] Statistical Abstract of the United States, U.S. Bureau of the Census, U.S. Government Printing Office, Washington, D. C., p. 678, 1972.

[15] City of San Diego, Nonresidential Land Use Inventory, pp. 30-32, San Diego, California, 1966.

building permits indicates that an average of nearly 60% of the construction

in S. D. County from 1955 to 1971 was located in the city. If we assume that

60% of the floor area in the County is in the city, we find it to be $118 \times 10^6 ft^2$

in 1965. This procedure is compatible with the fact that an average

of 62% of the County population[*] resided in the city during the period 1910-1970.

The time history of commercial floor space from 1964-1972 is displayed

in Fig. 1.7-4 and shows that it has been growing at the rate of 4.2%/y. It

is interesting to note that the number of occupied housing units exhibited an

average growth rate of approximately 4.1%/y for the same period.

If we divide commercial electric sales volume provided by SDG&E by

the estimates of floor area, we can generate data points for the commercial

electrical loading, $\lambda(t)$, as shown in Fig. 1.7-5. This scheme indicates an

average loading of 27.6 $kwh_e/(ft^2 -y)$ for 1972.[**]

C3 Projections of Commercial Electrical Loading Along Logistics Curves

The causes for the increase in electrical loading per ft^2 are difficult to

define because there is great diversity of businesses and structures in the

commercial sector. A proper treatment of the problem would include dividing

the sector into major groups which have similar energy requirements, but

this procedure is beyond the scope of the present analysis. Instead, we can

_____

[*] This estimate was obtained from official U.S. Census figures.

[**] By comparison, electrical loading for the University of California, San Diego,
without use of electric space heating or electric cooling, was 24.66 $kwh_e/$
(ft^2-y) for the fiscal year 1971-72.

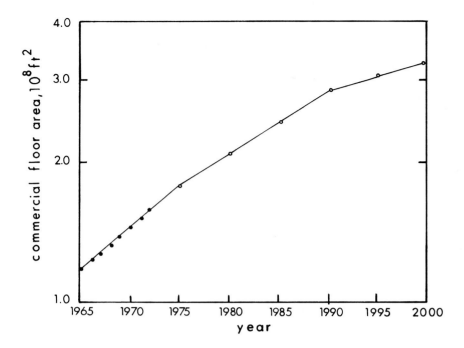

Fig. 1.7-4   Estimates (•) and projections (o) of commercial floor
              area in S. D. County. The growth rate for the commer-
              cial floor area is taken to be 3.2%/y from 1972 to 1990
              and 1.5%/y from 1990 to 2000. This figure has been
              reproduced from Dimonte's analysis.

use the data generated in the previous discussion to perform least-squares

fits to logistics curves for projection purposes.

In two studies for the electrical loading in all-electric buildings, the

authors[7,16] report values of 35.8 $kwh_e/(ft^2-y)$ and 44.6 $kwh_e/(ft^2-y)$.

---

[16] R. G. Stein, "Architecture and Energy," unpublished paper presented at
     the Philadelphia Meeting of the American Association for the Advance-
     ment of Science, December 1971.

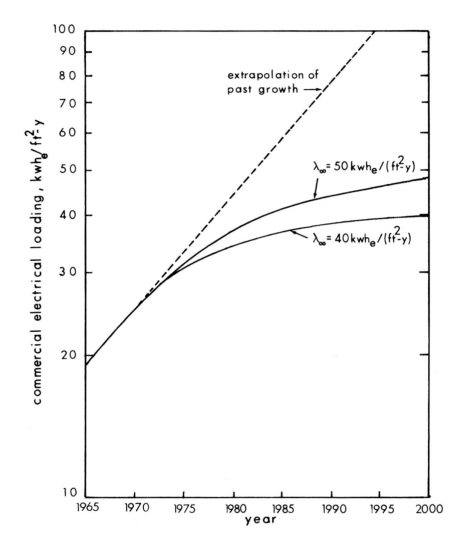

Fig. 1.7-5   Commercial electrical loading for S. D. County. Projections follow logistics curves that have been fitted to
estimated data points from 1964 to 1972 and to estimated
equilibrium values. This figure has been reproduced
with modifications from Dimonte's analysis.

Accordingly, two least-squares fits to logistics curves were made as follows:

$$\lambda(t) = \frac{\lambda_0 \lambda_\infty}{[\lambda_0 + (\lambda_\infty - \lambda_0)\exp(-rt)]} \tag{1.7-6}$$

with $\lambda_\infty = 40 \ kwh_e/(ft^2-y)$ and $50 \ kwh_e/(ft^2-y)$. The motivation for this procedure is the idea that average loading could not exceed that of the all-electric structure. The results are displayed in Fig. 1.7-5.

D. Projections of Total Electricity Consumption to the Year 2000

In order to make projections that are more meaningful than extrapolations, one must construct plausible models and use these as guides. Here, total demand will be approximated by

$$E_T = 1.04 \times \{DH \times N + \lambda \times S\}, \tag{1.7-7}$$

where the factor 1.04 is included in order to account for additional total consumption associated with unallowed-for growth in agriculture, street and highway lighting, and miscellaneous other sales. During the last 22 years, the electrical sales to the residential, commercial, and industrial sectors have amounted to an average of roughly 96% of the total annual electrical sales, as indicated in SDG&E annual reports. In order to make a more accurate estimate of total electrical sales, we must also multiply the combined sales to the residential, commercial, and industrial sectors by the factor of 1.04.

A Comprehensive Planning Organization (CPO) for S. D. County projection for occupied housing units (N) was used and S was calculated by employing the same growth rates as the CPO in calculating N (see Section 1.7C3).

Projections of DH and λ have been taken from fits to logistics curves, as

explained in Sections 1.7B3 and 1.7C3.

The high projection includes electrified transportation and assumes that

household electricity consumption will reach a maximum of 30,000 kwh_e/(H.U.-y)

by 2035 and that commercial electrical loading will increase to 50 kwh_e/(ft^2-y).

The low projection assumes that DH will stabilize at 15,000 kwh_e/(H.U.-y) by

2010 and that λ will reach an equilibrium of 40 kwh_e/(ft^2-y). The results are

displayed in Fig. 1.7-6 and Table 1.7-6.

Our best projections lead to the conclusions that total electricity demand

will be 24% to 31% of the estimate derived from extrapolation (see Fig. 1.7-6) to

the year 2000. The principal reasons for the decreased growth rate are (a) an

expected decline in the growth rate for population to 1.5% per year in the

period 1990-2000 in S.D. County and (b) electricity consumption per housing

unit or ft^2 of commercial floor area is not expected to grow at the current

rates to the end of the century.

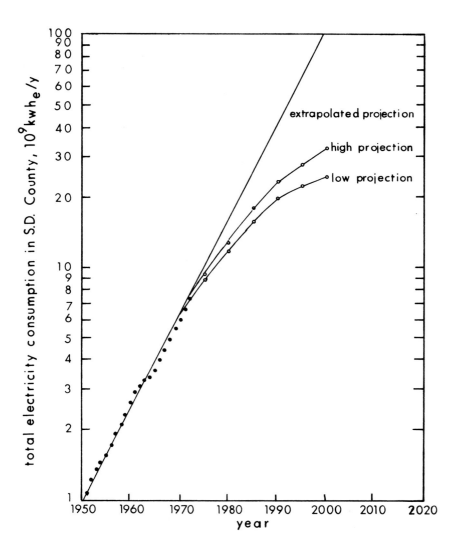

Fig. 1.7-6   Total actual (•) and projected (○) electricity consumption
in S. D. County; reproduced from Dimonte, loc. cit.

Table 1.7-6 Projection of total electricity consumption in S.D.
County; reproduced from Dimonte, loc. cit.

Year	Low projection, 10^9 kwh$_e$	Rate of growth, %/y*	High projection, 10^9 kwh$_e$	Rate of growth, %/y
1975	8.8	6.4	9.1	8.0
1980	11.9	6.0	12.9	6.7
1985	15.6	5.3	17.8	6.1
1990	19.6	4.5	23.3	5.8
1995	22.2	2.5	27.8	3.4
2000	25.0	2.5	32.7	3.4

*The decrease in the rate of growth is due, in part, to an expected
decline in the population growth rate in S.D. County.

A1.7 Appendix - Dimonte's Time-Series Analysis for the Residential-Demand Function from 1950 to 1972 in S.D. County*

Linear regression analysis[17] is a standard econometric tool which has been used to ascertain elasticities and significance levels for various independent variables which influence average household electricity demand. We have applied this time-series analysis to S.D. County for the period 1950 to 1972. The explanatory variables have been taken to be average real yearly household income (RYH), size of household (SOH), real prices of gas (RPG) and of electricity (RPE), and summer (T_A) and winter (T_J) temperature characterizations.

It should be noted that, contrary to the conclusions reached in Section 1.7B, we have not introduced the appliance saturation levels as explanatory variables. We, therefore, do not expect to obtain physically-meaningful results, even though an excellent empirical fit can be made to the available data.

The following functional form is assumed:

$$DH = C_0(RYH)^{\alpha_1}(SOH)^{\alpha_2}(RPE)^{\alpha_3}(RPG)^{\alpha_4}\exp(\alpha_5 t)$$

$$\times [1 + \alpha_6(T_A - \langle T_A \rangle)] \times [1 + \alpha_7(T_J - \langle T_J \rangle)]. \qquad (A1.7\text{-}1)$$

---

*This Appendix may be deleted by readers who are not especially interested in applications of regression analysis. The regression methodology turned out to be a less satisfactory tool for demand projections than the simple analysis presented in the main part of Section 1.7.

[17]J. Johnston, Econometric Methods, McGraw-Hill, New York, N.Y., 1960.

Linear regression techniques are used after taking the natural logarithms of both sides of Eq. (A1.7-1). Thus,

$$\ln DH = \alpha_0 + \alpha_1 \ln(RYH) + \alpha_2 \ln(SOH) + \alpha_3 \ln(RPE) + \alpha_4 \ln(RPG)$$

$$+ \alpha_5 t + \alpha_6 \Delta T_A + \alpha_7 \Delta T_J, \qquad\qquad (A1.7-2)$$

where we define $\alpha_0 \equiv \ln C_0$, $\Delta T_A \equiv T_A - \langle T_A \rangle$, $\Delta T_J \equiv T_J - \langle T_J \rangle$, and assume that $\alpha_6 \Delta T_A$ and $\alpha_7 \Delta T_J$ are much smaller than unity.

The explicit time dependence is included for two reasons. First, its inclusion is a means for describing the availability of new or improved appliances over the years. Second, it is expected that a family will accumulate more electrical appliances with time and thereby increase electricity demand, although there are no changes in the other variables. This accumulation is expected because most appliances do not need to be replaced every year, thus allowing the savings to be used for acquisition of other appliances although the family income has remained constant. This procedure will not be useful if the other independent variables exhibit a high degree of colinearity with time.

Each year from 1950 to 1972 provides one data point for the regression with $t = 1$ for 1950. Generation of the data base will now be discussed.

Electric sales volumes and revenues, as well as gas sales volumes and revenues, were obtained from SDG&E annual reports for the period from 1950 to 1972. Prices charged to residential users of 500 kwh_e/month were calculated from rate schedule D-1, which was provided by SDG&E back to 1946.

In order to estimate* the total number of occupied housing units (H. U.) in S. D. County, the procedure described in the following sentences was used. The Building Inspection Departments (BID) for the cities and the unincorporated area of S. D. County provide data on the number of housing units authorized for building during each year. If the 1960 census figure for total H. U. is used as the base point, it is possible to obtain a time history from 1950 to 1972 using BID statistics and assuming zero demolition rate from 1950 to 1960 and a 0. 5%/y rate from 1960 to 1972. This method recovers the 1950 and 1970 census points and agrees well with the S. D. County Planning Department estimates for the years from 1965 to 1972. An average occupancy rate of 95% is assumed.

The average size of the households is found by dividing the population numbers by the estimates of H. U.

Personal income estimates made by the Economic Research Department of Copley Press International were used for the years 1950 to 1954, while figures appearing in the California Statistical Abstract were used for subsequent years. All current dollars (e. g., income, prices) were transformed to real 1967 dollars by dividing by the Consumer Price Index for the L. A. - Long Beach area, as given by the U. S. Department of Labor, Bureau of Labor Statistics.

---

*The S. D. County Planning Department has been making estimates of housing units since 1965. The number of customers served by SDG&E is not a correct number for housing units because some multiple-unit structures are served by master meters.

Indices of summer and winter climate are the average August and January temperatures for each year and were obtained from Climatological Data, California (1950 to 1972), which is published by the U.S. Weather Bureau.

Table A1.7-1 contains a summary of the results of the time-series analysis. Household demand seems to be "explained" very well by the chosen set of variables, as is indicated by the F-test (significance is better than the 0.001 level). The most important variables are time, price of electricity, and price of gas. The corresponding significance levels are better than the 0.01 level for the first two and the 0.05 level for the latter.

The elasticity of the real price of electricity is -0.32, which is larger than the results -1.33 and -0.91 quoted by Wilson[4] and Anderson,[18] respectively, in their national cross-sectional studies.

The very small coefficient for ℓnRYH is the result of the fact that the real household income varied by only 15% during the period of interest. Since DH changed by a factor of 3 in this interval, one can see that RYH would not be a very good explanatory variable.

A seemingly anomalous result is the negative value for the elasticity of the price of gas. This observation is, however, without significance and is explained statistically by the fact that electricity consumption has been increasing while the average real price of gas has decreased. It is interesting

---

[18] K. P. Anderson, The Demand for Electricity in California - Dimensions of Future Growth, Rand Corporation Working Note #WN-7550-NSF, Santa Monica, California, 1971.

to note that the average real price of electricity decreased by 50% while the
price of gas decreased by 27% from 1950 to 1972 in S.D. County. Here, the
average price of electricity and gas is calculated by dividing total sales
revenue by total sales volume appearing in SDG&E annual reports; these
current prices are then transformed into real price by dividing by the Consumer Price Index.

Table Al. 7-1   Results of a time-series regression analysis for
household electricity demand in S.D. County (1950-
1972). The adjusted R^2 is 0.997. The F-test significance is better than the 0.001 level. This table
has been reproduced from Dimonte's analysis.

Variable[a]	Coefficient	Standard error	Significance level
constant	7.3	0.39	b
time (t)	0.045	0.0022	b
average real yearly household income (RYH)	0.058	0.10	0.61
size of household (SOH)	0.21	0.15	0.18
real price of electricity (RPE)	-0.32	0.1	b
real price of gas (RPG)	-0.28	0.13	0.05
average January temperature (T_J)	-0.003	0.0024	0.26
average August temperature (T_A)	0.003	0.0039	0.47

a.   All variables were transformed into logarithms except t, T_A, and T_J.

b.   The significance is better than the 0.01 level. There are 14 degrees
of freedom.

In conclusion, we note that regression analysis cannot determine cause and effect and the results must, therefore, be viewed as inadequate. Thus, the excellent significance level achieved in the empirical fit cannot hide the fact that the functional form of the expression used for DH in Eq. (A1.7-1) does not contain explicitly the increased appliance saturation with time, which we have shown in Section 1.7B to be the dominant factor in determining the residential electricity demand function.

1.8 Epilogue

After studying the material presented in the preceding sections, the reader is clearly justified in saying "this was all somewhat informative, but what are the real demand projections?" The answer to the implied criticism in the query must be that we cannot offer definitive demand functions, that energy-demand functions are evolutionary variables which must be reexamined and changed when important determining factors are changed, and that the determining factors are made up of an ill-defined interplay of physical, economic, social, and political forces. In times of shortages, the demand function shrinks because concerned citizens conserve. When a utility offers reduced rates for large-volume users, electricity use may grow because it may become more economical to use more electricity. A governmental imposition of a 55 miles-per-hour speed limit will reduce gasoline consumption because the lower speed limit corresponds to more miles per gallon and because the implied longer travel times may curtail

long-distance travel by automobile. A large export tax for foreign bauxite
may make aluminum less competitive with plastics or steel for some applications and may thereby modify energy demands in manufacture. Aerody-
namic streamlining of trucks may save two or three percent of the total
energy allocated for the transportation sector. Rationing to limit foreign
imports may drastically curtail the energy-demand function. The invention
of a personal, airborne hovercraft may imply a drastic rise in energy consumption.

Energy demands are time-dependent functions that reflect the status
of our technology, our economic well being, our social system, our
leisure-time habits, and existing political realities. They will change with
time. An excellent illustration of demand-supply elasticity is provided by the
data shown for Japan in Fig. 1.8-1: Japan's "Project Sunshine," which is
similar in intent to the U.S. Project Independence, has led to a substantially
lower demand projection in 1974 than was contemplated in 1970 (see Fig. 1.8-1).
The estimated[1] year 2000 demand has been lowered by nearly 40% (corresponding to annual growth of 7% between 1970 and 1980, 5.5% during the next
decade, and 4% from 1990 to 2000). At the same time, accelerated development of plants using coal, hydroelectric and geothermal resources, and nuclear
energy has been proposed in order to limit required oil imports. Japan has
significant supplies of underground heat (including many active volcanoes),

---

[1]"Japan Takes Fresh Look at Long-Range Energy Problems," Chemical and
Engineering News, 52, 12-13, August 12, 1974.

which have not been adequately exploited.   By the year 2000, as much as

50×10^3 Mw$_e$ of geothermal power may be developed, as compared with 35 Mw$_e$

by the end of 1973.

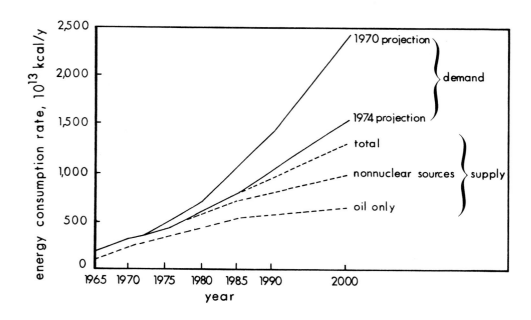

Fig. 1.8-1 Drastic downward revisions in energy-demand projections for
Japan followed the 1973-74 oil embargoes and price rises; reprinted with permission from Ref. [1]. Copyright by the American Chemical Society.

CHAPTER 2

ENERGY RESOURCES

Many of the recently published estimates of energy resources in the
United States and in the world are based on the collation performed by
M. King Hubbert. Some of the following reserve estimates are also abstracted from this authoritative work. Before presenting a summary of resource
estimates, it will be convenient to comment on time histories of cumulative
reserves, production, and remaining reserves in a manner that presents
some extension of related ideas published by Hubbert.

2.1   Time Histories of Cumulative Reserves, Production, and Remaining
       Reserves for any Resource

Let [1]

Q_d = cumulative total discovered reserves,

Q_p = cumulative production,

Q_r = remaining proved reserves, which have not yet been
employed for production;

then

$$Q_d = Q_p + Q_r \qquad\qquad (2.1\text{-}1)$$

---

[1] M. King Hubbert, Chapter 8 on "Energy Resources" in Resources and Man,
A Study and Recommendations by the Committee on Resources and Man of the
Division of Earth Sciences, National Academy of Sciences-National Research
Council, W. H. Freeman and Co., San Francisco, Calif., 1969.

and the rates of change with time of cumulative discovered reserves, cumulative production, and remaining proved reserves are related as follows:

$$dQ_d/dt = dQ_p/dt + dQ_r/dt. \tag{2.1-2}$$

When a resource is first discovered or evaluated for exploitation, its cumulative total value Q_d will rise from zero, exponentially at first as intensive exploration occurs, and finally taper off as exploration becomes largely completed (see Fig. 2.1-1). The value of Q_d as a function of time follows a logistics curve. The initial exponential growth rate appears to be driven by consumers and their friends who demand more and more of the resource for consumption and force a rising consumption rate at a value proportional to the instantaneously applicable consumption rate, which is itself a linear function of total discovered reserves. Thus the initial growth of Q_d follows Malthus' equation, which is well known from population-growth studies:

$$dQ_d/dt = k_1 Q_d \tag{2.1-3}$$

or

$$Q_d = Q_{d,0} (\exp k_1 t) \text{ for small } t, \tag{2.1-4}$$

where k_1 is a constant. Since every available resource is in finite supply, the exponential growth of Q_d with time is soon truncated. Let $Q_{d,\infty}$ represent the constant total value of discoverable reserves for any resource. Then $Q_{d,\infty} - Q_d$ represents the amount of total resource that remains to be discovered at any time t for use by consumers. The Malthus growth equation must be

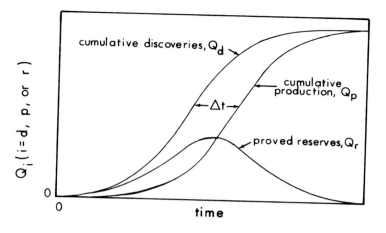

Fig. 2.1-1 Averaged time histories of cumulative discoveries, cumulative
production, and proved reserves for any resource; reproduced
from M. King Hubbert, "Energy Resources, A Report to the
Committee on Natural Resources," National Academy of Sciences-
National Research Council, Publication 1000-D, Fig. 22, p. 55,
Washington, D. C., 1962.

replaced by the <u>Verhulst equation</u> for early and later times, i.e.,

$$dQ_d/dt = k_2 Q_d (Q_{d,\infty} - Q_d),$$

(2.1-5)

where k_2 is a constant such that $k_2 Q_{d,\infty} = k_1$ if Eq. (2.1-2) applies for early

times. The rate of growth of total discovered resource is proportional not

only to the instantaneous value of the discovered resource (which determines

the number of consumers and hence their demand) but also to the amount of

remaining undiscovered resource $Q_{d,\infty} - Q_d$. In order to integrate Eq.

(2.1-5), it is convenient to divide by $Q_{d,\infty}$ and to replace $k_2 Q_{d,\infty}$ by a new

"rate constant" k with the dimensions of reciprocal time. In this manner,

Eq. (2.1-5) is transformed to

$$(1/Q_{d, \infty})(dQ_d/dt) = k(Q_d/Q_{d, \infty})[1 - (Q_d/Q_{d, \infty})]. \qquad (2.1-6)$$

If we now replace $Q_d(t)/Q_{d, \infty}$ by the fraction $f(t)$ of total discovered resource, we see that Eq. (2.1-6) is of the form

$$df/dt = kf(1 - f)$$

or

$$df/f(1 - f) = (df/f) + [df/(1 - f)] = kdt, \qquad (2.1-7)$$

which we may integrate term by term from $f(t)$ at $t = t_1$ [when the known resource has the value $f(t_1)$] to the value $f(t)$ at time t. Thus, we obtain

$$\ell n[f(t)/f(t_1)] - \ell n\{[1 - f(t)]/[1 - f(t_1)]\} = k(t - t_1)$$

or

$$\frac{f(t)}{f(t_1)} \frac{[1 - f(t_1)]}{[1 - f(t)]} = \exp k(t - t_1). \qquad (2.1-8)$$

Equation (2.1-8) may be solved for $f(t)$ with the result

$$f(t) = f(t_1)/\{f(t_1) + [1 - f(t_1)]\exp{-k(t - t_1)}\}$$

or, returning to the cumulative total discovered and discoverable reserves as variables,

$$\frac{Q_d(t)}{Q_{d, \infty}} = \frac{Q_d(t_1)/Q_{d, \infty}}{Q_d(t_1)/Q_{d, \infty} + \{1 - [Q_d(t_1)/Q_{d, \infty}]\}\exp{-k(t - t_1)}}.$$

$$(2.1-9)$$

Equation (2.1-9) is an expression for the logistics curve showing early exponential growth and tapering off to saturation as $Q_d(t)$ approaches $Q_{d,\infty}$ asymptotically.

Discovery of a usable resource is <u>followed</u> by cumulative production and utilization, i.e., the time dependence of Q_p will parallel that of Q_d with a time lag Δt (see Fig. 2.1-1). The growth rate of Q_p will rise exponentially with time initially and then approach $Q_{d,\infty}$ asymptotically as resource exhaustion is accomplished.

The remaining proved reserves Q_r may now be simply estimated by computing the difference between Q_d and Q_p according to Eq. (2.1-1). Because of the time delay Δt, Q_r will increase at first, pass through a maximum, and then decay to zero (see Fig. 2.1-1) as cumulative production (Q_p) approaches the total discoverable reserves ($Q_{d,\infty}$).

The preceding remarks describe the approximate average behavior of resource discovery and exploitation, provided the initial estimate of $Q_{d,\infty}$ remains substantially constant. When an important new resource discovery is made, the $Q_d(t)$ and $Q_p(t)$ curves tend to jump from a given logistics curve to a new logistics curve for a substantially larger value of $Q_{d,\infty}$. Nevertheless, after reasonably complete resource estimation has been accomplished, the idealized curves of Fig. 2.1-1 tend to describe cumulative discovered quantities, cumulative production, and remaining reserves reasonably well.

The time rates of change of Q_d, Q_p, and Q_r are shown in Fig. 2.1-2.

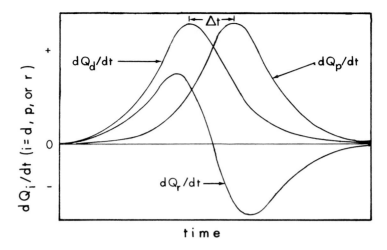

Fig. 2.1-2 The time derivatives dQ_i/dt (i = d, p, or r) as functions of time; reproduced from M. King Hubbert, "Energy Resources, A Report to the Committee on Natural Resources," National Academy of Sciences-National Research Council, Publication 1000-D, Fig. 24, p. 56, Washington, D.C., 1962.

The time interval Δt between peak cumulative discovery rates (dQ_d/dt) and maximum cumulative consumption rates (dQ_p/dt) corresponds to the value of Δt at the maximum slopes shown in Fig. 2.1-1. Particularly interesting is the time dependence of the rate of change of remaining reserves with time, (dQ_r/dt), which generally shows a maximum preceding the maximum of dQ_d/dt, passes through zero when $dQ_d/dt = dQ_p/dt$, reaches a minimum later than dQ_p/dt reaches a maximum, and vanishes at very early and at late times when the resource has either not been discovered or else has been exhausted.

The data in Fig. 2.1-3 have been reproduced from Hubbert[1] and refer to oil discoveries in the United States, exclusive of Alaska. The plots shown in Fig. 2.1-3 are reminiscent of the idealized curves shown in Figs. 2.1-1 and 2.1-2. Because of oil discoveries made since publication of Hubbert's 1969 paper,[1] revisions must be made for later time periods.

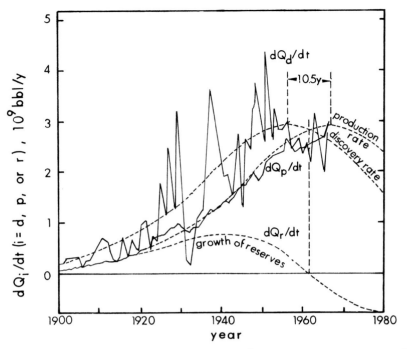

Fig. 2.1-3 Rates of proved discovery (dQ_d/dt), production (dQ_p/dt) and increase of reserves (dQ_r/dt) of crude oil in the United States,
exclusive of Alaska, as functions of time. The dashed curves
are analytical derivatives while the solid lines are actual yearly
data. Reproduced from M. K. Hubbert, "Degree of Advancement of Petroleum Exploration in the United States, "Bulletin
of the American Association of Petroleum Geologists 51, 2207-
2227 (1967).

2.2   Hubbert's 1969 and Later Estimates of Available Oil Reserves in the United States

Published resource estimates have an aura of authority which they do not

deserve. The published estimates look more reliable than they are because

(a) authors of resource estimates tend to give more significant figures than are

justified and (b) authors who do not make their own resource estimates copy

from others who do, without necessarily repeating all of the applicable assump-

tions, constraints, and limitations involved in the original estimates. In this manner, many people may repeat an erroneous value to several significant figures, thereby giving the impression that a highly uncertain number is really well known. We refer to Hubbert's discussion of representative oil estimates, noting only that the "best" estimate of 155 to 175×10^9 bbl for the mainland U.S. cumulative oil discoveries, $Q_{d, \infty}$, has been exceeded by some knowledgeable authors by as much as a factor of four. The functional forms of the idealized curves shown in Figs. 2.1-1 and 2.1-2 may be useful for extrapolating past known production or discovery data to ultimate total production and discovery data.

Such measures as the time history of the rate of discovery of bbl of oil per foot of exploratory drilling have also been used in making resource estimates (see Fig. 2.2-1). It is interesting to observe from Fig. 2.2-1 that the rate of oil discovery in bbl/ft drilled remained nearly constant from 1951 (when 6×10^8 ft of cumulative drilling were completed) until 1967 (when 15×10^8 ft of cumulative drilling were completed).

Hubbert's[1] 1969 estimate of U.S crude-oil production as a function of past and future years refers to $Q_{d, \infty} = 1.65 \times 10^{11}$ bbl. Two other estimates, for substantially larger values of $Q_{d, \infty}$ than were used by Hubbert, are shown in Figs. 2.2-2 and 2.2-3. An estimate of U.S. crude-oil resources, compiled in mid-1973 by the U.S. Geological Survey,[2] is shown in Table 2.2-1. It

[1]Ref. [1] in Section 2.1.

[2]U.S. Geological Survey estimates prepared for the World Energy Conference, Detroit, Michigan, 1974; compiled by R. F. Meyer, Deputy Chief, Office of Energy Resources, U.S. Geological Survey, Reston, Virginia.

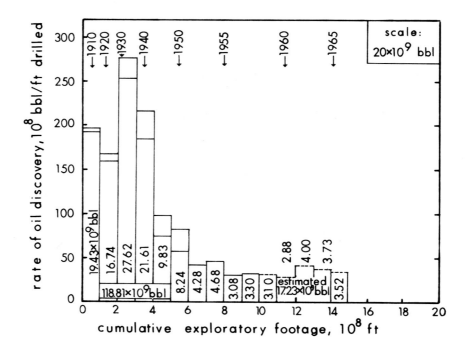

Fig. 2.2-1 Crude-oil discoveries per foot of exploratory drilling as a func-
            tion of cumulative exploratory footage drilled in the United States,
            exclusive of Alaska, 1860-1967. The higher tops in the bar-
            graphs account for total-well exhaustion. Reproduced from
            M. K. Hubbert, "Degree of Advancement of Petroleum Explor-
            ation in the United States, "Bulletin of the American Association
            of Petroleum Geologists 51, 2207-2227 (1967).

Table 2.2-1 Crude-oil resources in the United States and adjacent
             continental shelves; based on data of the U.S.
             Geological Survey. [2]

Previously known reserves		Additional resources, 10^9 bbl	Total resources, 10^9 bbl
Original oil in place, 10^9 bbl	Proven recoverable remaining reserves, 10^9 bbl		
434	42	343	777

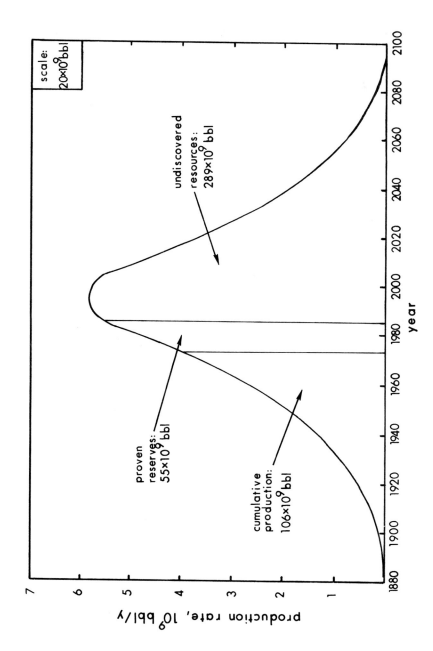

Fig. 2.2-2 Complete cycle of crude-oil production in the United States and adjacent continental shelves, exclusive of Alaska; this curve refers to $Q_{d\infty}$ = 450 × 10^9 bbl and a 1985 U.S. production rate equal to 16 × 10^6 bbl/d (corresponding to about 50% of projected requirements).

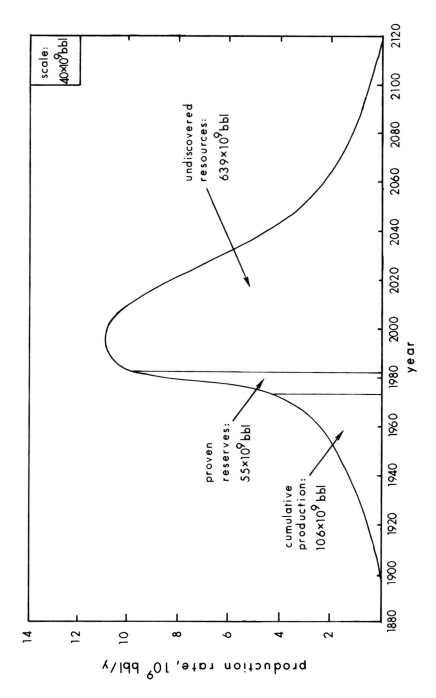

Fig. 2.2-3 Complete cycle of crude-oil production in the United States and adjacent continental shelves, exclusive of Alaska; this curve refers to $Q_{d_\infty} = 800 \times 10^9$ bbl (corresponding to a late 1972 estimate by the National Petroleum Council) and a 1985 production rate of 30×10^6 bbl/d (corresponding to the total projected requirements for 1985).

should be noted that these data have not been generally accepted (see Section 2.7 for details) buy may also turn out to be too low if, for example, exploratory drilling off the Atlantic coast were to be unexpectedly productive.

2.3   Hubbert's 1969 and Later Estimates of Natural-Gas Reserves in the United States

In the U.S., a reasonable estimate could be made in the past for the total natural-gas resource on the assumption that between 6.0 and 7.5 $\times 10^3$ SCF are generally produced per bbl of oil. The relative natural-gas production rate appears, however, to have declined in recent years. Hubbert's[1] 1969 summary curve refers to $Q_{d, \infty}$ = 1.29 $\times 10^{15}$ SCF. An estimate based on 1972 resource determinations by the National Petroleum Council is shown in Fig. 2.3-1. The mid-1973 U.S. Geological Survey[2] estimate of U.S. natural-gas resources is given in Table 2.3-1. Disagreements concerning these estimates are briefly considered in Section 2.7.

Table 2.3-1   Natural-gas resources in the United States and adjacent continental shelves; based on data from the U.S. Geological Survey.[2]

Known reserves		Additional resources, 10^{12} SCF	Total resources, 10^{12} SCF
Original gas in place, 10^{12} SCF	Proven recoverable reserves, 10^{12} SCF		
845	267	1,146	1,991

[1] Ref. [1] in Section 2.1.
[2] Ref. [2] in Section 2.2.

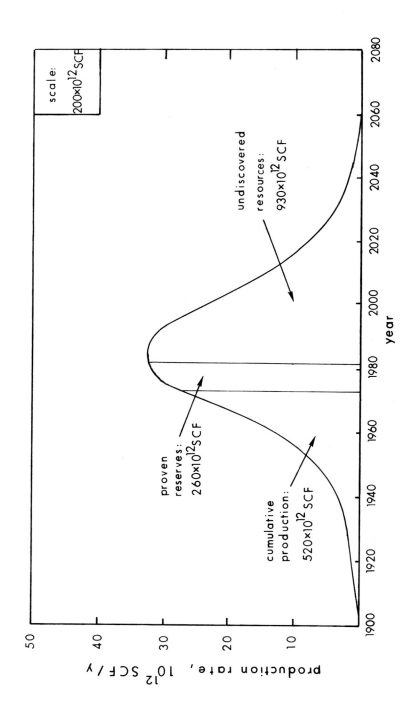

Fig. 2.3-1 Complete cycle of natural-gas production in the United States and adjacent continental shelves, exclusive of Alaska; the curve refers to $Q_{d_\infty} = 1,710 \times 10^{12}$ SCF (corresponding to a late 1972 estimate by the National Petroleum Council).

2.4   Hubbert's 1969 and Later Estimates of Natural-Gas Liquids in the United States

The ratio NG/NGL $\approx$ 2.60 to 3.32 $\times 10^4$ SCF/bbl, with smaller numbers corresponding to later times, is used to calculate the natural-gas liquids resource estimates. Hubbert's[1] 1969 estimate refers to $Q_{d,\infty} = 36 \times 10^9$ bbl. A cycle-of-production curve for $Q_{d,\infty} = 60 \times 10^9$ bbl is shown in Fig. 2.4-1. An estimate by the U.S. Geological Survey[2] for the U.S. resources of natural-gas liquids is shown in Table 2.4-1.

Table 2.4-1 Natural-gas liquids resources in the United States and adjacent continental shelves; based on the data of the U.S. Geological Survey.[2]

Known reserves		Additional resources,	Total resources,
Original natural-gas liquids in place, 10^9 bbl	Proven recoverable reserves, 10^9 bbl	10^9 bbl	10^9 bbl
21.5	6.8	29.2	50.7

2.5   Hubbert's 1969 and Later Estimates of Total Petroleum Liquids in the United States

The total petroleum liquids correspond to the sum of the values for crude oil and NGL. Hubbert's[1] 1969 estimate refers to $Q_{d,\infty} = 201 \times 10^9$ bbl. Two other estimates, for larger total reserves, are shown in Figs. 2.5-1 and 2.5-2. An estimate of U.S. total petroleum liquids, compiled by the U.S. Geological Sur-

---

[1]Ref. [1] in Section 2.1.

[2]Ref. [2] in Section 2.2.

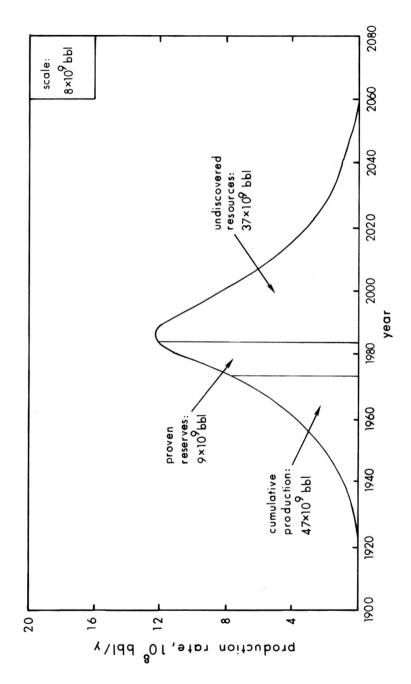

Fig. 2.4-1   Complete cycle of production of natural-gas liquids in the United States and adjacent continental shelves, exclusive of Alaska; the curve has been prepared on the assumption that 1 bbl of natural-gas liquids is produced for every 25,000 SCF of natural gas.

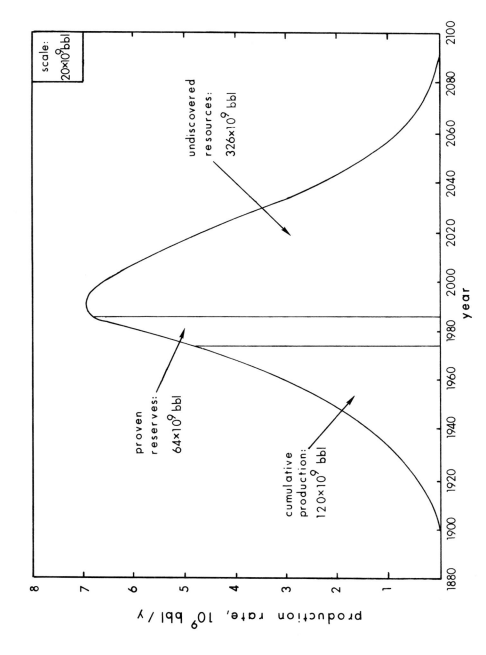

Fig. 2.5-1 Complete cycle of production of total petroleum liquids in the United States and adjacent continental shelves, exclusive of Alaska; the curve refers to the crude-oil producibility data shown in Fig. 2.2-2 and the NGL data shown in Fig. 2.4-1.

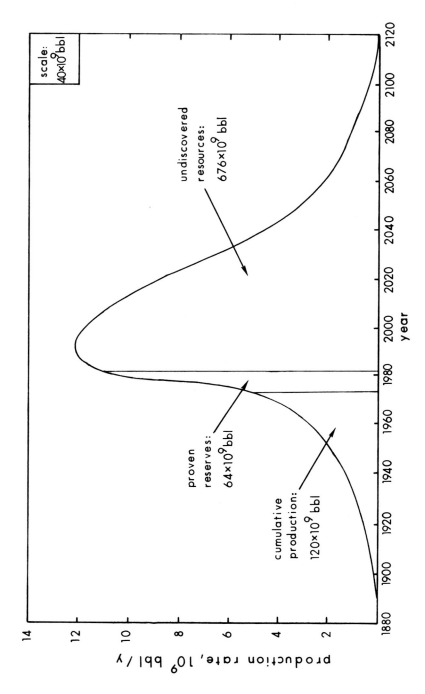

Fig. 2.5-2 Complete cycle of production of total petroleum liquids in the United States and adjacent continental shelves, exclusive of Alaska; the curve refers to the crude-oil producibility data shown in Fig. 2.2-3 and the NGL data shown in Fig. 2.4-1.

vey[2] in mid-1973, is shown in Table 2.5-1. Disagreements concerning

proper reserve estimates are briefly noted in Section 2.7.

Table 2.5-1 Total petroleum liquids resources in the United States and adjacent continental shelves; based on the data of the U.S. Geological Survey.[2]

Known reserves		Additional resources, 10^9 bbl	Total resources, 10^9 bbl
Original total petroleum liquids in place, 10^9 bbl	Proven recoverable reserves, 10^9 bbl		
455.5	48.8	372.2	827.7

2.6   Alaskan Reserves

Hubbert[1] (1969) has estimated the Alaskan crude-oil reserves at 25×10^9 bbl, the NGL at 5×10^9 bbl, and the NG at 150×10^{12} SCF. Later writers have presented crude-oil reserve estimates for Alaska as high as 100×10^9 bbl. Estimates of the total Alaskan petroleum liquids and natural-gas reserves by Theobald, Schweinfurth, and Duncan[2] are listed in Tables 2.6-1 and 2.6-2. We refer to the following Section 2.7 for divergent views on the magnitude of reserves of Alaskan oil, natural-gas liquids, and natural gas.

---

[1]Ref. [1] in Section 2.1.

[2]P. K. Theobald, S. P. Schweinfurth, and D. C. Duncan, Energy Resources of the United States, U.S. Geological Survey Circular 650, Washington, D.C., 1972.

Table 2.6-1 Total petroleum liquids reserves in Alaska and adjacent
            continental shelves as of year-end 1970; based on the
            data of Theobald, Schweinfurth, and Duncan.[2]

Feasibility of recovery	Identified resources, 10^9bbl	Undiscovered resources, 10^9bbl
recoverable	11	100
submarginal	20	450

Table 2.6-2 Natural-gas reserves in Alaska and adjacent continental
            shelves as of year-end 1970; based on the data of
            Theobald, Schweinfurth, and Duncan.[2]

Feasibility of recovery	Identified resources, 10^{12}SCF	Undiscovered resources, 10^{12}SCF
recoverable	31	480
submarginal	8	860

2.7   Summary Remarks on U.S. Reserves of Oil, Natural-Gas Liquids,
      and Natural Gas

As of July 1974,[1] a considerable controversy had developed about the
proper magnitude of the remaining recoverable but as yet undiscovered resources of petroleum liquids and natural gas in the U.S. According to a
Mobil Oil Company estimate, as supported by a number of oil company execu-
tives and by Hubbert, the recent U.S. Geological Survey estimates were far

---

[1]"Oil and Gas Resources: Did USGS Gush too High?", Science 185, 127-
129 (1974).

too optimistic. The magnitude of the discrepancy is illustrated by the data listed in Table 2.7-1 for oil and natural-gas liquids and for natural gas.

It is interesting to observe that the USGS estimates are substantially higher than the Mobil Oil Co. estimates for all locations, except for the offshore Pacific Coast region.

Table 2.7-1 Comparison of mid-1974 reserve estimates for oil and natural-gas liquids; reprinted with permission from the Mobil Oil Company and the U.S. Geological Survey.

Location	Recoverable but as yet undiscovered oil and natural-gas liquids, 10^9 bbl		Recoverable but as yet undiscovered natural-gas reserves in the U.S., 10^{12} SCF	
	USGS estimates	Mobil Oil Co. estimates	USGS estimates	Mobil Oil Co. estimates
On-Shore				
Alaska	25 to 50	21	105 to 210	104
Lower 48 States	110 to 220	13	500 to 1,000	65
Subtotal	135 to 270	34	605 to 1,210	169
Off-Shore				
Atlantic	10 to 20	6	55 to 110	31
Alaska	30 to 60	20	170 to 340	105
Gulf of Mexico	20 to 40	14	160 to 320	69
Pacific Coast	5 to 10	14	10 to 20	69
Subtotal	65 to 130	54	395 to 790	274
Total U.S. recoverable but as yet undiscovered reserve estimates	200 to 400	88	1,000 to 2,000	443

2.8 Hubbert's 1969 and Later Estimates of World Crude-Oil Reserves

Hubbert's 1969 summary for world crude-oil production is reproduced in Fig. 2.8-1.[1] Later estimates correspond to substantially larger values of $Q_{d, \infty}$.

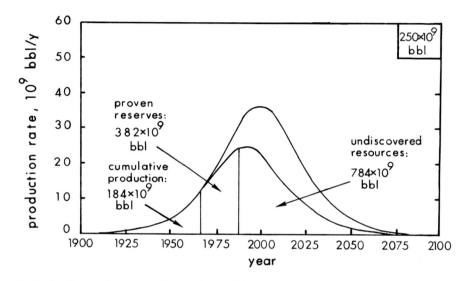

Fig. 2.8-1 Complete cycles of world crude-oil production for two values of $Q_{d, \infty}$. The upper envelope corresponds to $Q_{d, \infty} = 2,100 \times 10^9$ bbl, while the lower envelope represents $Q_{d, \infty} = 1,350 \times 10^9$ bbl. Reproduced from M. King Hubbert, Chapter 8 on "Energy Resources" in Resources and Man, Committee on Resources and Man, National Academy of Sciences - National Research Council, Publication 1703, Fig. 8.23, p. 196, W. H. Freeman and Co., San Francisco, California, 1969.

A recent estimate of the non-Communist world's crude-oil production is given in Fig. 2.8-2. In Fig. 2.8-2, it is assumed that both reserves and production of oil increase to 1985. However, the production rate grows rel-

[1]Ref. [1] in Section 2.1.

atively more rapidly so that the reserve life decreases from 40 years in 1960 to about 20 years in 1985. A compendium of oil reserves published in <u>Time Magazine</u> (November 19, 1973, p. 95) is indicative of how much is likely to be left out of an incomplete popular resource display: all of the entries shown in Fig. 2.8-3 were simply omitted.

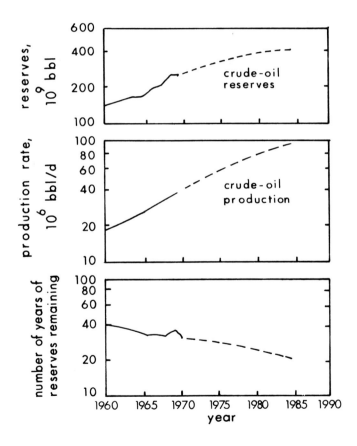

Fig. 2.8-2 Crude-oil production and reserve estimates for the non-Communist world to 1990; reproduced from S. H. Clark, <u>World Energy</u>, Stanford Research Institute, Menlo Park, California, 1972.

KNOWN OIL RESERVES THAT WERE OMITTED:

1. ALASKA NORTH SLOPE: $\sim 50 \times 10^9$ bbl.

2. OFFSHORE RESERVES in GULF, ATLANTIC, and PACIFIC: perhaps as much as $1,000 \times 10^9$ bbl (<200 m depth).

3. ALBERTA'S ATHABASCA TAR SANDS: 285×10^9 bbl recoverable with current technology; 625×10^9 bbl total.

4. SHALE OIL (in rock assaying > 25 gallons/ton): 600×10^9 bbl (480×10^9 bbl on federal land, 120×10^9 bbl on private land); $1,000 \times 10^9$ to $2,000 \times 10^9$ bbl, including lean reserves.

MAJOR SUSPECTED RESERVES:

1. CHINESE MAINLAND ON-SHORE AND OFF-SHORE (< 200 m deep): ? bbl.

2. OCEAN BOTTOM, > 200 m depth: ? bbl.

Fig. 2.8-3 A listing of potential oil reserves omitted in a popular display of resources (see Time Magazine, November 19, 1973, p. 95).

We conclude this discussion on world oil resources with the observation that the values given for $Q_{d,\infty}$ are all highly uncertain. It is interesting to note that the annual rates of discovery have consistently exceeded the annual rates of consumption for five-year intervals extending from 1920 to 1970 (see Fig. 2.8-4); with incremental fuel-price increases, this trend may well continue for some time. A map of the world drawn to size in such a manner as

to indicate the known recoverable oil reserves as of December 1972 is repro-

duced in Fig. 2.8-5. Oil deliveries from many producing countries have in

recent years been coordinated and controlled by OPEC, the Organization of

Petroleum Exporting Countries. During mid-1974, the North Sea oil re-

serves were estimated to yield three to four million barrels per day by the

early nineteen eighties, with three-quarters of the total going to the United

Kingdom.

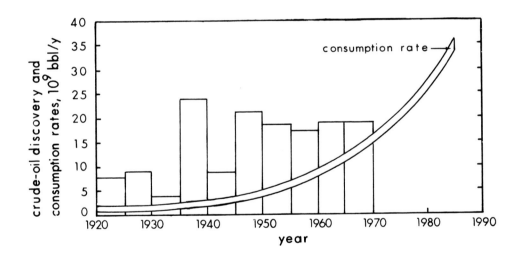

Fig. 2.8-4 Crude-oil discovery and consumption rates for Western countries.
            Oil discoveries until recently have exceeded consumption. Most
            experts agree that future discoveries are unlikely to keep pace
            with consumption. The five-year averages of approximate total
            discoveries are indicated by vertical bars. Reproduced from an
            EXXON advertisement in Time Magazine, December 3, 1973.
            Reprinted with permission from the EXXON Company.

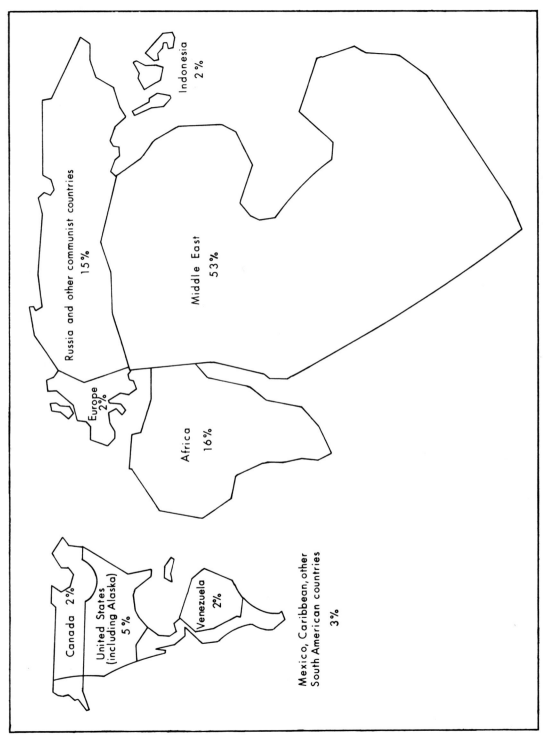

Fig. 2.8-5   The world of known oil reserves. The percentages given correspond to the shares of the world's known extractable oil reserves in each region. Reproduced from an EXXON advertisement in Time Magazine, December 3, 1973. Reprinted with permission from the EXXON Company.

2.9   Hubbert's 1969 and Later Estimates of Ultimate World Production of Natural-Gas Liquids, Total Petroleum Liquids, and Natural Gas

Hubbert's 1969 estimates,[1] for two values of ultimate crude-oil production, are listed in Table 2.9-1. Some later estimates are substantially higher.

Table 2.9-1   Estimates of ultimate world production of crude oil, natural-gas liquids, total petroleum liquids, and natural gas, based on two estimates of the ultimate production of crude oil; reproduced from M. King Hubbert, Chapter 8 on "Energy Resources" in Resources and Man, Committee on Resources and Man, National Academy of Sciences - National Research Council, Publication 1703, Table 8.3, p. 197, W. H. Freeman and Co., San Francisco, California, 1969.

Ultimate world crude-oil production, 10^9 bbl	Ultimate natural-gas liquids production 10^9 bbl	Ultimate total petroleum liquids production, 10^9 bbl	Ultimate natural-gas production, 10^{12} SCF
1,350	250	1,620	8,000
2,100	420	2,520	12,000

2.10   Estimates of Oil Reserves in the Tar Sands of Alberta, Canada, and the United States

The estimates of Pow, Fairbanks, and Zamora[1] of the recoverable oil from the tar-sand deposits in Alberta, Canada, are listed in Table 2.10-1.

---

[1] Ref. [1] in Section 2.1.

---

[1] J. R. Pow, G. H. Fairbanks and W. J. Zamora, "Descriptions and Reserve Estimates of the Oil Sands of Alberta" in Athabasca Oil Sands, K. A. Clark, editor, Research Council of Alberta, Edmonton, Alberta, Canada, Information Paper No. 45, 1963.

Table 2.10-1   Tar-sand deposits of Alberta, Canada; reproduced from Pow et al. [1]

Area	Evaluated reserves, 10^9 bbl
Athabasca	266.9
Bluesky-Gething	20.6
Grand Rapids	13.3
total	300.8

The U.S. Geological Survey[2] has indicated that the potential total re-coverable oil from tar sands in the United States is 15×10^9 bbl. A comparison of these two appraisals shows that the U.S. tar-sand deposits are only 5% as large as the deposits in Alberta, Canada.

2.11   United States and World Shale-Oil Resources

A 1965 estimate of the world shale-oil resources by Duncan and Swanson[1] appears in Table 2.11-1.

A 1972 estimate of the United States shale-oil resources is given in Table 2.11-2.

A mid-1973 estimate by the U.S. Geological Survey[2] indicates that the total potential recoverable oil from known U.S. oil-shale deposits yielding at

[2]Ref. [2] in Section 2.2.

[1]D. C. Duncan and V. E. Swanson, Organic-Rich Shales of the United States and World Land Areas, U.S. Geological Survey Circular 523, Washington, D.C., 1965.

[2]Ref. [2] in Section 2.2.

Table 2.11-1   Estimates of shale-oil resources of world land areas (in 10^9 bbl); reproduced from Duncan and Swanson[1] (g/t stands for gallons of shale oil recoverable per ton of shale).

Continent	Known resources				Possible extensions of known resources			Undiscovered and unappraised resources			Total resources		
	10-100 g/t*	25-100 g/t	10-25 g/t	5-10 g/t	25-100 g/t	10-25 g/t	5-10 g/t	25-100 g/t	10-25 g/t	5-10 g/t	25-100 g/t	10-25 g/t	5-10 g/t
Africa	10	90	small	small	ne[a]	ne	ne	4,000	80,000	450,000	4,000	80,000	450,000
Asia	20	70	14	ne	2	3,700	ne	5,400	106,000	586,000	5,500	110,000	590,000
Australia and New Zealand	small	small	1	ne	ne	ne	ne	1,000	20,000	100,000	1,000	20,000	100,000
Europe	30	40	6	ne	100	200	ne	1,200	26,000	150,000	1,400	26,000	140,000
North America	80	520	1,600	2,200	900	2,500	4,000	1,500	45,000	254,000	3,000	50,000	260,000
South America	50	small	750	ne	ne	3,200	4,000	2,000	36,000	206,000	2,000	40,000	210,000
total	190[b]	720	2,400	2,200	1,000	9,600	8,000	15,000	313,000	1,740,000	17,000	325,000	1,750,000

*   Recoverable under 1965 conditions.

a. ne = no estimate.

b. Of the approximately 2×10^{15} bbl here indicated, 190×10^9 bbl were considered recoverable under 1965 conditions, corresponding to the sum of the resource estimates given in the first column.

least 15 gallons per ton is 1×10^{12} bbl. This appraisal is based on a 50% recovery factor.

Table 2.11-2   Estimates of shale-oil resources in the United States; based on the data of Theobald, Schweinfurth, and Duncan.[3]

Feasibility of recovery	Identified resources, 10^9 bbl	Undiscovered resources	
		Extension of known resources, 10^9 bbl	Undiscovered or unappraised, 10^9 bbl
recoverable[a]	0	0	0
paramarginal[b]	160-600	850	500
submarginal[c]	1,600	2,500	20,000

a.   Recoverable with existing 1972 technology.

b.   Recoverable deposits yielding at least 30 gallons per ton.

c.   Recoverable deposits yielding less than 30 gallons per ton.

2.12   United States and World Coal Resources

The world's coal resources, as estimated by Averitt in 1969,[1] are summarized in Table 2.12-1 and in Fig. 2.12-1. Hubbert's[2] cycles of U.S. coal production refer to $Q_{d,\infty} = 0.74 \times 10^{12}$ mt and 1.486×10^{12} mt; his world coal-production cycles correspond to $Q_{d,\infty} = 4.3 \times 10^{12}$ mt and 7.6×10^{12} mt. A complete cycle for U.S. coal production with $Q_{d,\infty} = 2.9 \times 10^{12}$ mt is shown

---

[3]Ref. [2] in Section 2.6.

---

[1]P. Averitt, Coal Resources of the United States, U.S. Geological Survey Bulletin 1275, Washington, D.C., 1969.

[2]Ref. [1] in Section 2.1.

in Fig. 2.12-2. As estimate of the U.S. coal reserves by grade, compiled

in mid-1973 by the U.S. Geological Survey, [3] is given in Table 2.12-2.

Table 2.12-1   Estimates of total original coal resources of the world by continents[a]
(in billions of short tons); reproduced from Averitt. [1]

Continent	Resources determined by mapping and exploration	Probable additional resources in unmapped and unexplored areas	Estimated total resources
Asia and European U.S.S.R.	7,000[b]	4,000	11,000[c]
North America	1,720	2,880	4,600
Europe	620	210	830
Africa	80	160	240
Oceania	60	70	130
South and Central Americas	20	10	30
total	9,500[b]	7,330	16,830[c]

a.   Original resources in the ground in beds 12 inches thick or
     more and generally less than 4,000 feet below the surface,
     but includes small amounts between 4,000 and 6,000 feet.

b.   Includes about 6,500 billion short tons in the U.S.S.R.

c.   Includes about 9,500 billion short tons in the U.S.S.R.

[3]Ref. [2] in Section 2.2.

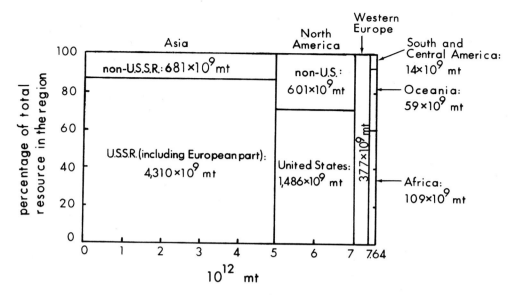

Fig. 2.12-1 Estimates of world resources of minable coal and lignite;
data from Averitt.[1]

Table 2.12-2 Estimates of coal resources in the United States; based on
the data of the U.S. Geological Survey.[4]

Coal type	Known reserves		Additional resources, 10^9 tons	Total resources, 10^9 tons
	Original coal in place, 10^9 tons	Proven recoverable reserves,[a] 10^9 tons		
anthracite	12.7	6.35	8.7	21.4
bituminous	259.5	129.75	1,090.4	1,349.9
subbituminous	77.8	38.90	1,071.0	1,148.8
lignite	50.8	25.40	653.4	704.2
total	400.8	200.40	2,823.5	3,224.3

a. An overall recovery factor of 50% is assumed.

_____

[4]Ref. [2] in Section 2.6.

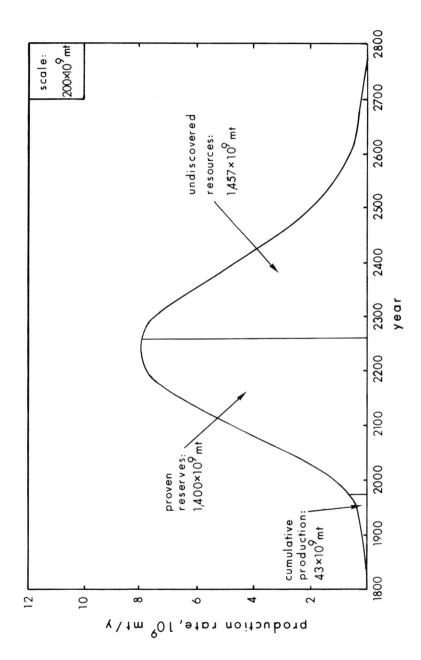

Fig. 2.12-2 Complete cycle of U.S. coal production for $Q_{d,\infty}$ = 2,900 × 10^9 mt (using Averitt's[1] estimate and assuming complete recovery). Note: earlier authors have presented curves of this type assuming 50% recovery.

2.13   Summary Remarks on Fossil-Fuel Exploitation

Hubbert's[1] fossil-fuel production-rate curves lead to the conclusions
summarized in Table 2.13-1. It is, of course, evident that the time scales
given in Table 2.13-1 are applicable only if past and future utilization and
discovery rates lie on fixed logistics curves. A drastic shift to coal as the
principal fossil fuel would invalidate the time scales, allowing longer use of
fossil fuels other than coal at diminished utilization rates and shorter-term
availability for coal at increased utilization rates.

Table 2.13-1 Final resource estimates for the U.S. and the world; based
on the 1969 data of Hubbert.[1]

| Resource | Approximate time in years remaining after 1970 for 80% depletion of resources in the | |
	U.S. (exclusive of Alaska)	World
crude oil	21	50 for $Q_{d,\infty} = 1.35 \times 10^{12}$ bbl; 60 for $Q_{d,\infty} = 2.10 \times 10^{12}$ bbl
natural gas	45	- - - -
natural-gas liquids	35	- - - -
total petroleum liquids	28	- - - -
coal	380 for $Q_{d,\infty} = 0.74 \times 10^{12}$ mt	370 for $Q_{d,\infty} = 4.3 \times 10^{12}$ mt
coal	570 for $Q_{d,\infty} = 1.486 \times 10^{12}$ mt	620 for $Q_{d,\infty} = 7.6 \times 10^{12}$ mt

---

[1] Ref. [1] in Section 2.1.

2.14   Epoch of Fossil-Fuel Exploitation

A summary of known recoverable and of as yet undiscovered but probably recoverable world fossil-fuel resources has been given by McKelvey and Duncan.[1] The known 22.5 Q of recoverable (1967) fossil-fuel resources, in units of Q, were given as 17 for coal, 1.7 for crude oil, 2.0 for natural gas, 0.21 for natural-gas liquids, 0.23 for oil from tar sands, and 0.87 for shale oil.   The potentially recoverable 450 Q given by McKelvey and Duncan[1] are distributed as follows: 320 for coal, 23 for oil, 20 for natural gas, 3.2 for natural-gas liquids, 6.3 for oil from tar sands, and 77 for oil from shale.

A historical perspective of fossil-fuel exploitation is shown in Fig. 2.14-1, which is reproduced from Hubbert.[2] Another view of the same type, but covering a much longer time scale and including energy sources other than fossil fuels, is shown in Fig. 2.14-2.

[1] V. E. McKelvey and D. C. Duncan, "United States and World Resources of Energy," Proceedings of the 3rd Symposium on the Development of Petroleum Resources of Asia and the Far East, UNECAFE, Mineral Resource Development Series, Volume 2, No. 26, 1967.

[2] M. King Hubbert, "Energy Resources, A Report to the Committee on Natural Resources," National Academy of Sciences - National Research Council, Publication 1000-D, Washington, D.C., 1962.

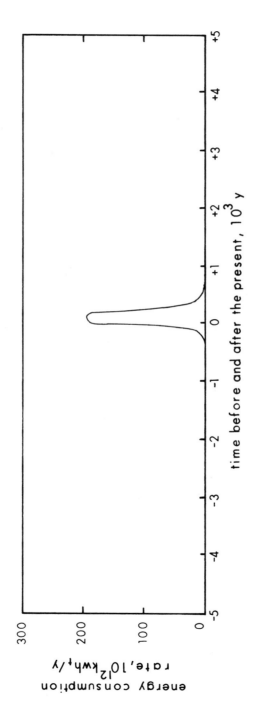

Fig. 2.14-1 Epoch of exploitation of fossil fuels in historical perspective, from minus to plus 5,000 years from the present; reproduced from M. King Hubbert, "Energy Resources, A Report to the Committee on Natural Resources," National Academy of Sciences - National Research Council, Publication 1000-D, modified version of Fig. 54, p. 91, Washington, D.C., 1962.

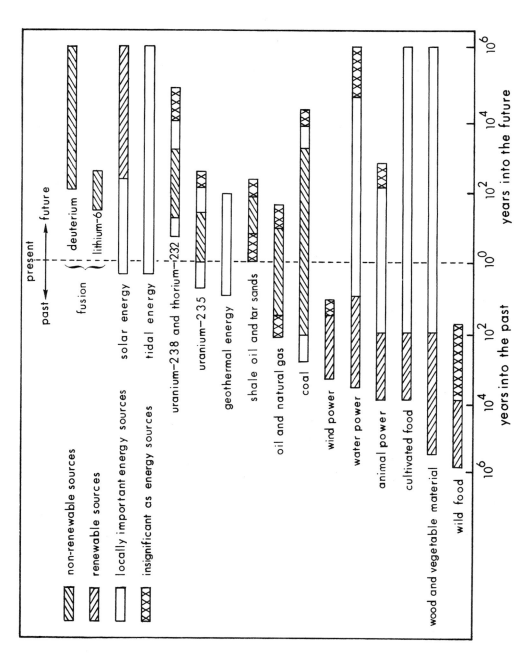

Fig. 2.14-2   An energy-resource utilization history from a long-term historical perspective; reproduced from E. Cook, "Energy for Millenium Three," Technology Review 75, 16-23, December 1972.

2.15   Nuclear-Fission Fuels

Since the magnitude of the energy derivable from uranium depends on the manner in which the uranium is used, a fission-fuel resource estimate is meaningful only in conjunction with specification of reactor type, whether it is a burner or a breeder reactor and at what conversion efficiency the fissile material is utilized. This approach may be contrasted with the procedure used in fossil-fuel evaluation, where the tacit assumption of 100% combustion efficiency is generally implied. The evaluation of fission-fuel resources is restricted, for present practical applications, to their use in nuclear reactors for the generation of electricity.

The isotope $^{235}_{92}U$ undergoes the following fission reaction on capture of slow neutrons:

$$^{235}_{92}U \rightarrow \text{fission products + neutrons} + 2 \times 10^2 \text{ Mev.} \qquad (2.15\text{-}1)$$

Referring to Table 1.2-2, we recall that 200 Mev correspond to 3.21×10^{-11} joule or 3.04×10^{-14} Btu or 5.23×10^{-21} bbl of petroleum equivalent. Since 1g of uranium - 235 contains 2.56×10^{21} atoms, it follows that fission of 1g of this atomic species releases the energy-equivalent of 13.4 bbl of petroleum = 2.8 mt of coal = 0.94 Mw-d. Current power stations for electricity production have power outputs of about 10^3 Mw$_e$. A plant of this size with a 33% conversion efficiency to electrical energy, burning only uranium-235, would consume $(1/0.33) \times (10^3/0.94)$ g/d = 3.22 kg/d. As was noted in Section 1.4, natural uranium contains only 7.11×10^{-3} parts of uranium-235 per part of uranium. Hence the uranium-235 extracted at 100% efficiency from 4.5×10^2 kg of uranium is required per day at 33% efficiency in order to provide the power for a 1,000-Mw$_e$ plant. We note that 10^3 Mwd$_e$ correspond to about 42,400 bbl/d at 33% conversion efficiency to electrical energy. The preceding numerical values refer to the conversion efficiency of the uranium-235 burner reaction and do not allow for the occurrence of some breeding of uranium-238.

In summary, a utility plant with an energy output of 10^3 Mwd$_e$ per day operating at 33% conversion efficiency will burn either 42,400 bbl/d of petroleum or all of the uranium-235 extracted from 4.5×10^2 kg of naturally-occurring uranium. The U_3O_8 contains $100 \times (3 \times 238)/(3 \times 238 + 8 \times 16) \simeq$ 85% of uranium. Hence 5.3×10^2 kg/d of U_3O_8 must be processed to provide nuclear burner fuel for the 10^3 Mw$_e$ power plant each day. One short ton (2,000 lb) of U_3O_8 has the energy-equivalent (see Table 1.2-2) of 7.32×10^4 bbl of petroleum when we consider only the uranium-235 content used in a nuclear burner. U.S. reserves (see Table 2.15-1) of 3.4×10^5 t of U_3O_8 at \$10/ (lb U_3O_8) are thus equivalent to about 25×10^9 bbl of petroleum.

The following relations are examples of reaction steps occurring in breeder reactors:

$$^{238}_{92}U + n \rightarrow {}^{239}_{92}U \rightarrow {}^{239}_{93}Np \rightarrow {}^{239}_{94}Pu , \qquad (2.15-2)$$

$$^{232}_{90}Th + n \rightarrow {}^{233}_{90}Th \rightarrow {}^{233}_{91}Pa \rightarrow {}^{233}_{92}U . \qquad (2.15-3)$$

The uranium-239 formed by neutron absorption of uranium-238 has a short life before it decays by β-emission to neptunium-239, from which plutonium-239 is produced by emission of another β-particle; in this manner, the fissile atom plutonium-239 is formed by breeding uranium-238 with neutrons. Similarly, thorium-232 absorbs a neutron to form thorium-233 which decays to protoactinium-233 with β-emission and then, with another β-emission, to the fissile product uranium-233.

Thus, when natural uranium becomes critical, uranium-235 fissions and releases neutrons, some of which may be used to make more fissionable material with uranium-238 or thorium-232 in a breeder reactor. As a rough rule, the energy yield from a practical nuclear reactor per unit mass of uranium is increased more than 40- to 50-fold for a breeder reactor, as compared with uranium fuel-utilization in a pure fission reactor.

We have presented in Section 1.4 some estimates for U_3O_8 supplies in the U.S. as a function of price. In addition, values of the U.S. U_3O_8 and ThO_2 deposits, compiled in mid-1973 by the U.S. Geological Survey,[1] are listed in Tables 2.15-1 and 2.15-2. Hubbert[2] estimated in 1969 that non-Communist world supplies of 0.835×10^6 tons of U_3O_8 were reasonably assured and that an additional potential of 0.740×10^6 tons existed. These numbers are easily translated to energy-reserve figures.

U.S. fuel resources of all types are listed in Table 2.15-3.

---

[1]Ref. [2] in Section 2.2.

[2]Ref. [1] in Section 2.1.

Table 2.15-1 Estimates of uranium resources in the United States; based on the data of the U.S. Geological Survey.[1]

Region	Known reserves		Additional resources	
	Maximum recovery costs,[a] $/lb U_3O_8	Quantity recoverable, 10^3 tons U_3O_8	Maximum recovery costs,[a] $/lb U_3O_8	Quantity recoverable, 10^3 tons U_3O_8
Western Interior	10	20	10	79
Northern Great Plains-Rocky Mountains	10	123	10	180
Southern Great Plains-Rocky Mountains	10	185	10	395
Pacific Coast	10	9	10	46
subtotal	10	337	10	700
Western Interior	15	34	15	110
Northern Great Plains-Rocky Mountains	15	194	15	290
Southern Great Plains-Rocky Mountains	15	279	15	515
Pacific Coast	15	13	15	85
subtotal	15	520	15	1,000
total		857		1,700

a. Recovery costs include premining, mining, transportation, and milling costs and are given in 1972 dollars.

Table 2.15-2 Estimates of thorium resources in the United States; based on the data of the U.S. Geological Survey.[1]

Region	Known reserves		Additional resources	
	Maximum recovery costs,[a] $/lb ThO_2	Quantity recoverable, 10^3 tons ThO_2	Maximum recovery costs,[a] $/lb ThO_2	Quantity recoverable, 10^3 tons ThO_2
Piedmont Province and Atlantic Coastal Plain	10	6.6	10	n.a.
Northern Great Plains	10	47.0	10	335
Rocky Mountains	10	11.0	10	n.a.
total	10	64.6	10	335

a. Recovery costs include premining, mining, transportation, and milling costs and are given in 1972 dollars.

n.a. = not available.

Table 2.15-3 Estimated U.S. fuel resources of all types in units of Q(= 10^{18} Btu); reproduced from the Cornell Work-shop on Energy and the Environment, U.S. Govern-ment Printing Office, Washington, D.C., 1972.[1]

Fuel	Known recoverable	Undiscovered recoverable	Known marginal or submarginal	Undiscovered marginal or submarginal	Total
coal	4.6	----	29	55	89
petroleum	0.28	1.16	0.23	1.71	3.4
natural gas	0.28	1.21	----	0.88	2.4
natural-gas liquids	0.03	0.14	----	0.28	0.4
oil in bituminous rocks	0.01	----	----	0.06	0.07
shale oil	0.29	----	11.6	23.2	35.1
total, fossil fuels	5.5	2.6	41	81	130
uranium[2]	0.22[3]	0.28-0.51[3]	1.4[4]-8.6[5]	0.25[4]-10.0[5]	20

1. From data by H. Perry, "Fuels for Electricity Generation," unpublished manuscript dated Jan. 25, 1972.

2. Uranium resources are given in terms of energy available to water-moderated reactors.

3. Minable at \$5 to \$10 per lb of U_3O_8.

4. Minable at \$10 to \$30 per lb of U_3O_8.

5. Minable at \$30 to \$100 per lb of U_3O_8.

If only the uranium-235 were used, the conversion factor to energy would be 3.04×10^{-14} Btu per uranium-235 atom or $3.04 \times 10^{-14} \times 2.56 \times 10^{21} = 7.78 \times 10^{7}$ Btu per g of uranium-235 or $7.78 \times 10^{7} \times 7.11 \times 10^{-3} = 5.53 \times 10^{5}$ Btu per g of natural uranium or $5.53 \times 10^{5} \times 0.85 = 4.7 \times 10^{5}$ Btu per g of U_3O_8. Thus, using the data of Table 1.4-3, the available supply from U.S. resources of 1.534×10^{5} mt of U_3O_8 at a 1972 price of \$10/lb or less corresponds to an energy-equivalent for the uranium-235 of 0.072×10^{18} Btu = 0.072 Q. Actually, the overall efficiency of a fissile-burner for uranium use is larger than about 1.5% (because of some breeding of the uranium-238), while we have used in effect an efficiency of 0.711%. Hence, the preceding number for U.S. resources should be increased to at least 0.15 Q. This value is somewhat smaller than the estimate of 0.22 Q given in Table 2.15-3. The more recent uranium-reserve estimates listed in Table 2.15-1 correspond to substantially larger energy resources: a value of 1.7×10^{6} t of U_3O_8 yields an energy-equivalent of about 1.5 Q.

Calculations similar to those described for U.S. reserves may be made for world reserves. The results for the nuclear fuels are contrasted with those for the fossil fuels in Table 2.15-4. A January 1973 compilation[3] of world uranium resources is reproduced in Table 2.15-5; world thorium reserves[4] are listed in Table 2.15-6.

[3]Nuclear News 16, 96, November 1973.

[4]Panel on the Utilization of Thorium in Power Reactors, pp. 10-11, Technical Reports Series No. 52, International Atomic Energy Agency, Vienna, Austria, 1966.

Table 2.15-4 Estimated world fuel resources of all types
in units of $Q(= 10^{18}$ Btu); reproduced from the
Cornell Workshop on Energy and the Environment, U.S. Government Printing Office,
Washington, D.C., 1972.[1]

	Known recoverable	Probable total
coal	300^2	350
petroleum	3.3-12.1	36
natural gas	1.2	8.2-12.5
natural-gas liquids	----.	1.1- 1.9
oil in bituminous rocks	----	----
shale oil	1.1	$2,100^3$
total, fossil fuels	~310	2,500
uranium	0.58	2.17^4

1. After H. Perry, "Fuels for Electricity Generation," unpublished manuscript dated Jan. 25, 1972.

2. Determined by mapping.

3. Includes resources with ten gallons or more per ton of shale.

4. Minable at $10 to $30 per pound of U_3O_8 and in terms of energy
obtainable by water-moderated reactors.

We must conclude that the availability of high-grade ore is limited and
its use in low-efficiency burners represents a wasteful application of a
valuable resource. At the estimated year 2000 energy-use rate in the U.S.
of 0.16 Q, our own high-grade reserves of uranium ore of 0.22 Q (see Table
2.15-3) would supply all of our energy needs for only about 1.37 years in
water-moderated nuclear reactors. Somewhat more efficient use of reserves
is made in gas-cooled nuclear reactors and much more efficient use (by
factors of about 40 to 50) in breeder reactors.

Table 2.15-5 Estimated world resources of uranium in 10^3 t of U_3O_8, as of
January 1973; reproduced from Ref. [3] and based on data from
the International Atomic Energy Agency, Vienna, Austria, and
from "Uranium Resources, Production & Demand," Organisa-
tion for Economic Cooperation and Development, Paris, France,
1973.

Country	Price Range <$10/lb U_3O_8		Price Range $10-15/lb U_3O_8	
	Reasonably assured resources (reserves)	Estimated additional resources	Reasonably assured resources (reserves)	Estimated additional resources
Argentina	12	18	10	30
Australia	92	102	38.3	38
Brazil	-	3.3[1]	0.9	-
Canada	241	247	158	284
Central African Republic	10.5	10.5	-	-
Denmark (Greenland)	7.0	13	-	-
Finland	-	-	1.7	-
France	47.5	31.5	26	32.5
Gabon	26	6.5	-	6.5
India	-	-	3	1
Italy	1.6	-	-	-
Japan	3.6	-	5.4	-
Mexico	1.3	-	1.2	-
Niger	52	26	13	13
Portugal (Europe)	9.3	7.7	1.3	13
(Angola)	-	-	-	17
South Africa	263	10.4	80.6	33.8
Spain	11	-	10	-
Sweden	-	-	351	52
Turkey	2.8	-	0.6	-
USA	337	700[2]	183	300
Yugoslavia	7.8	13	-	-
Zaire	2.3	2.2	-	-
total	1,126	1,191	884	821

1. Plus 70,000 t U by-product from phosphates.

2. Plus 70,000 t U by-product from phosphate and copper production.

Table 2.15-6 World thorium reserves; reproduced from Ref. [4].

Country	Type of deposit	Reserves of ThO$_2$, tons	Reserves of monazite, tons	Remarks	Source references
Africa					
Madagascar	placers uranothorianite masses	-	50,000 - 100,000	no figures available	Roubault (1958)
Nigeria	placers and granite	15,000	-		Bowie (1964)
Nyasaland	placers	15,000	-		Bowie (1964)
South Africa	veins	15,000	-		Poane (1960)
UAR	placers	371,060	-		El Shazly
Asia					
Ceylon	placers	-	9,000 - 12,000		Wadia, Fernando (1945)
India	placers	450,000	-		Bhola et al. (1964)
Taiwan	placers	-	8,800		Shen (1956)
Australasia					
New South Wales and Queensland, Australia	placers	-	34,000		Webb (1954)
Australia	placers	50,000	-		Poane (1960)

Table 2.15-6, continued.

Country	Type of deposit	Reserves of ThO_2, tons	Reserves of monazite, tons	Remarks	Source references
North America					
Canada	conglomerate	250,000	-	reserves	Griffith Roscoe (1964)
	mainly conglomerate	700,000	-	reserves and prognosticated resources	
USA	normally mined placers	362,380	-	resources at $5-10/lb ThO_2	
	Th disseminated placers	181,440	-	resources at $10-30/lb ThO_2	
	Conway granite	9,072,000	-	resources at $30-50/lb ThO_2	Faulkner, McVey (1964)
	granites	22,630,000	-	resources at $50-100/lb ThO_2	
	granites	2,721,600,000	-	resources at $100-500/lb ThO_2	
South America					
Brazil	placers	15,000	-	proven	Santos et al.
	pyrochlore deposits	130,000	-	estimated	
	bastanite deposits	37,000	-	-	

The data summarized in Table 2.15-4 should be compared with another estimate summarized in Table 2.15-7. We note the usual wide spread in resource evaluation made by different investigators. Interesting work on the estimation of mineral deposits, in general, and on uranium reserves (leading to larger values than those listed in the preceding tables), in particular, has been published by J. Brinck in a series of Euratom publications.[5, 6, 7]

We conclude this discussion with a brief comment on uranium needs for electricity production.

Industrial uranium requirements corresponding to four cases of projected nuclear-generating capacity, according to NPC (1972) estimates, are shown in Fig. 2.15-1. The nuclear-fuel-energy-to-electricity conversion efficiency is assumed to be 33%, as in conventional water-moderated reactors. We note that cumulative uranium requirements to the year 1985 amount to an appreciable fraction ($\simeq$ 25 to 40%) of the high-grade ore estimated to be potentially available in 1974 at a 1972 cost of less than \$15/lb of U_3O_8 (see Table 2.15-1).

2.16   Nuclear-Fusion Fuels

Energy-resource estimates for fusion reactors are given in the last two lines of Table 2.15-7. We shall now indicate briefly the origin of these values.

[5] J. W. Brinck, "Note on the Distribution and Predictability of Mineral Resources," European Atomic Energy Community (EURATOM), Brussels, Belgium, May 1967.

[6] J. Brinck, "Calculating the World's Uranium Resources," Euratom 6, 109-114, No. 4, 1967.

[7] J. Brinck, "Mimic," Eurospectra 10, 46-52, No. 2, June 1971.

Table 2.15-7 Fossil, fissile, and fusion world energy resources; reproduced from L. A. Booth, Central Station Power Generation by Laser-Driven Fusion, LA-4858-MS, Vol. 1, Los Alamos, N.M., February 1972.

Energy source	Available energy in Q		Years of supply at a utilization rate of 2.8 Q/y	
	known	estimated values of discoverable reserves	known	estimated values of discoverable reserves
fossil				
coal	19	270	6.8	96
oil and natural gas	5.1	90	1.8	32
fissile				
burners (1.5% efficient)				
rich ore (<$20/kg)	7.5	20	2.7 (rich-ore burners)	7.1
low-grade ore (>$20/kg)	2.8×10^4	8×10^4	1.0×10^4 (low-grade ore burners)	3×10^4
breeders (60% efficient)				
rich ore (<$20/kg)	300	950	107 (rich-ore breeders)	340
low-grade ore (>$20/kg)	9.5×10^5	3×10^6	3.4×10^5 (low-grade breeders)	10^6
			110 (total rich-ore)	347
			3.5×10^5 (total low-grade ore)	10^6
fusion (50% efficient)				
deuterium	4×10^9	4×10^9	$\sim 10^9$	$\sim 10^9$
lithium	3×10^6	3×10^6	$\sim 10^6$	$\sim 10^6$

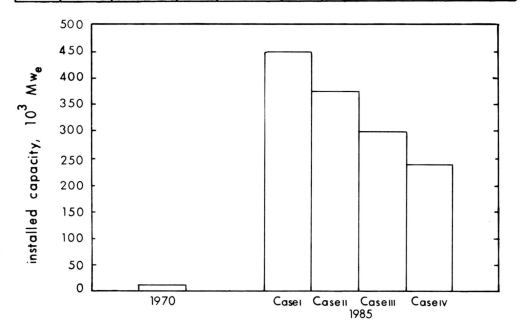

Uranium requirements from industry, 10^3 t of U_3O_8								
	Case I		Case II		Case III		Case IV	
year	annual	cumulative	annual	cumulative	annual	cumulative	annual	cumulative
1975	19	58	19	58	19	58	12	31
1980	51	240	46	230	37	200	29	140
1985	109	700	89	600	71	500	60	400

Fig. 2.15-1   Uranium requirements and Mw_e of installed electricity-generating capacity for various supply cases; reproduced from U.S.
Energy Outlook, National Petroleum Council, Washington D.C.,
1972.

It was stated in Section 1.4B that $1m^3$ of liquid water contains 34.4g of D
(deuterium) while Li occurs in sea water at 1 part in 10^7 with 7.42% of the Li
being $^6_3$Li, while minable deposits of Li_2O amount to 5 to 10×10^6 mt.

Fusion reactions with deuterium as primary fuel are the following, about
equally-probable, reaction steps:

$$^{2}_{1}D + ^{2}_{1}D \rightarrow ^{3}_{2}He + n + 3.2 \text{ Mev,} \qquad (2.16\text{-}1)$$

$$^{2}_{1}D + ^{2}_{1}D \rightarrow ^{3}_{1}T + H + 4.0 \text{ Mev.} \qquad (2.16\text{-}2)$$

The tritium formed according to Eq. (2.16-2) will subsequently react with deuterium according to the process

$$^{2}_{1}D + ^{3}_{1}T \rightarrow ^{4}_{2}He + n + 17.6 \text{ Mev.} \qquad (2.16\text{-}3)$$

The total energy released per deuterium atom is $(1/5) \times (3.2 + 4.0 + 17.6)\text{Mev} = 4.96 \text{ Mev}$.

On exposure to an adequate neutron flux, lithium-6 undergoes the fission reaction

$$^{6}_{3}Li + n \rightarrow ^{4}_{2}He + ^{3}_{1}T + 4.8 \text{ Mev.} \qquad (2.16\text{-}4)$$

The tritium-3 may then fuse with deuterium-2 according to Eq. (2.16-3) so that the overall reaction becomes

$$^{6}_{3}Li + ^{2}_{1}D + n \rightarrow 2^{4}_{2}He + n + 22.4 \text{ Mev.} \qquad (2.16\text{-}5)$$

We note that 1m^3 of water will release $(4.96 \text{ Mev/D-atom}) \times [(6.023 \times 10^{23}/2)\text{D-atoms/g of D}] \times (34.4 \text{g of D/m}^3 \text{ of } H_2O) = 5.14 \times 10^{25} \text{ Mev/m}^3 \text{ of } H_2O = 7.8 \times 10^{9} \text{ Btu/m}^3 \text{ of } H_2O$ if 4.96 Mev are released per atom. The total amount of water on the earth is about $1.5 \times 10^{18} \text{ m}^3$. Hence, the potential energy available by deuterium-fusion of the deuterium contained in the oceans is about $1.2 \times 10^{28} \text{ Btu} = 1.2 \times 10^{10} Q$ for a 100% energy-conversion efficiency.

The total energy derivable from lithium-6 has been estimated by Hubbert[1] to be about $2.4 \times 10^2 Q$; the much larger values listed in Table 2.15-7 apply when energy release according to the reaction (2.16-5) is properly prorated.

2.17   Solar Energy

According to the compilation given in Table 1.2-2, the total daily input of solar energy at the outer atmospheric boundary of the earth is $(0.949 \times 10^{-3} Btu/6.7 \times 10^{-23} d) = 1.42 \times 10^{19} Btu/d = 5.2 \times 10^{21} Btu/y$. Since the area of the diametral plane of the earth is approximately $1.27 \times 10^{18} cm^2$, this solar input of $(1.42 \times 10^{19} Btu/d) \times (2.78 \times 10^{-4} wh/0.949 \times 10^{-3} Btu) \times (1 d/24 h) = 1.73 \times 10^{17} w$ corresponds to an average flux density of $0.136 w/cm^2$.* Of this input, only $2.4 \times 10^{-2} w/cm^2 \simeq 500 cal/cm^2$-d or about 18% are actually received at the surface of the earth. The distribution of the solar energy received by our planet is shown in detail in Fig. 2.17-1, which contains a description of some energy flows to and from the earth.

Although the sun is an enormous energy source, the energy density at the surface of the earth is relatively low. For example, a conventional 10^3-Mw$_e$ electrical-generating station would require all of the solar-energy input

---

[1]Ref. [1] in Section 2.1.

---

*A flux density of $0.136 w/cm^2$ corresponds to 1,360 w incident per m^2 of pro-jected area of the illuminated half of the earth. The corresponding value per m^2 of surface area for the entire earth is $1,360 w/m^2 \div 4 = 340 w/m^2$ (compare Section 6.3) since the total surface area of the earth is $4\pi r_o^2$ (r_o = radius of the earth) while the projected area of the illuminated half is πr_o^2.

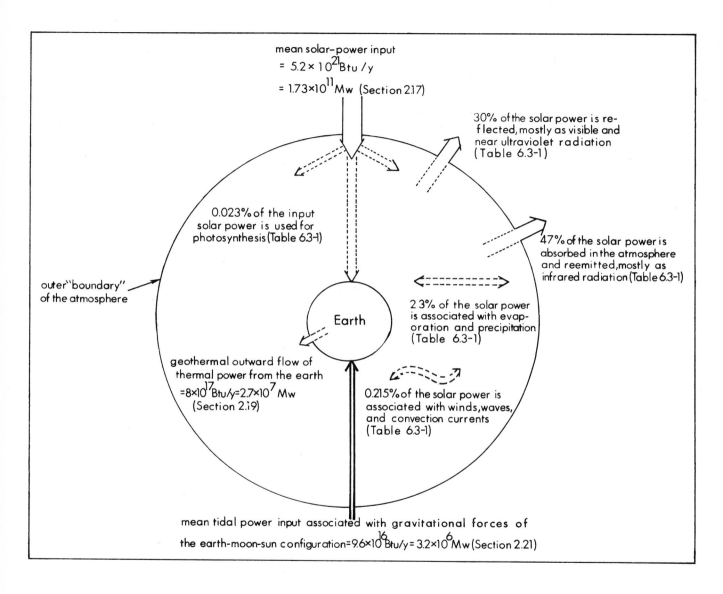

mean solar-power input
= 5.2×10^{21} Btu /y
= 1.73×10^{11} Mw (Section 2.17)

30% of the solar power is re-
flected, mostly as visible and
near ultraviolet radiation
(Table 6.3-1)

0.023% of the input
solar power is used for
photosynthesis (Table 6.3-1)

47% of the solar power is
absorbed in the atmosphere
and reemitted, mostly as
infrared radiation (Table 6.3-1)

outer "boundary"
of the atmosphere

Earth

2 3% of the solar power
is associated with evap-
oration and precipitation
(Table 6.3-1)

geothermal outward flow of
thermal power from the earth
= 8×10^{17} Btu/y = 2.7×10^{7} Mw
(Section 2.19)

0.215% of the solar power is
associated with winds, waves,
and convection currents
(Table 6.3-1)

mean tidal power input associated with gravitational forces of
the earth-moon-sun configuration = 9.6×10^{16} Btu/y = 3.2×10^{6} Mw (Section 2.21)

Fig. 2.17-1   Some aspects of energy flows (expressed as equivalent continuous power in-
puts) to and from the earth are shown. The solar power input is seen to be
far greater than the tidal or geothermal power. Not explicitly indicated are
man-made power sources, which are discussed in Chapter 6. The Section
and Table numbers following the descriptive titles refer to the location in
the text where more complete discussions of the entries may be found.

received on an average surface area of about $4.2 \times 10^6 m^2 = 4.2 \ km^2$. Even assuming a conversion efficiency from solar energy to electricity as high as 10%, the required average collection area for a 10^3-Mw$_e$ station becomes $42 km^2$.

It is the effective utilization of the energy input into large areas that presents the essential problem in the realization of useful large-scale solar-power engineering. Certainly the sun as an energy source is sufficiently large to accommodate our needs comfortably. As an example, the total estimated year 2000 world energy use of 2.1×10^{18} Btu/y is somewhat less than the daily received energy of $0.18 \times 1.42 \times 10^{19}$ Btu/d $= 2.56 \times 10^{18}$ Btu/d.

Solar-energy utilization will be considered more extensively in Chapter 14.

2.18 Hydrothermal Energy

By hydrothermal energy, we shall mean only that component of potential geothermal energy which is associated with natural (as distinct from man-made) storage of superheated steam without (dry hydrothermal energy) or with (wet hydrothermal energy) liquid water in underground reservoirs called thermal springs. Wet steam is about twenty times more abundant than dry steam. When a well is extended into a thermal spring, dry or wet steam exhausts to the surface, where it may be used for electric-power generation in a conventional steam-electric power plant. This energy source is characterized by the ease with which progressively larger generating stations may be constructed economically in stages.

Application of hydrothermal power generation was begun at Larderello in Tuscany, Italy, in 1904. This installation has been expanded until it reached a 1969 power output of 370 Mw_e. In addition, a number of smaller plants has been installed nearby.

The 1969 hydrothermal power-plant development around the world is shown in Table 2.18-1. In order to place these electricity-generating capacities on a suitable scale for comparison with oil and coal exploration, we note that a 1,000 Mw_e station would use about 3.8×10^4 bbl of petroleum/d or 8×10^3 mt of coal/d at a 90% use rate if the chemical (thermal)-to-electricity conversion efficiency is 33%.

An authoritative earlier (1965) estimate was made by White[1] of the amount of hydrothermal heat stored above surface temperatures to depths of either 3 or 10 km. White studied selected regions of the earth in detail and then extrapolated these estimates to the entire world surface. Of the total, White estimated that 5 to 10% was available in the Western United States. White's estimates for the world are 8×10^{21} joules $\simeq 2.5 \times 10^8$ Mwy to a depth of 3 km and 4×10^{22} joules $\simeq 1.25 \times 10^9$ Mwy to a depth of 10 km. Not all of this stored hydrothermal energy is available for electric-power generation. White's conservative estimate is that 1% of the hydrothermal energy stored to a depth of 10 km is readily usable. This estimate and an assumed exhaustion schedule of 50 years at an average conversion efficiency of 25% to

---

[1] P. E. White, Geothermal Energy, U.S. Geological Survey Circular 519, Washington, D.C., 1965.

Table 2.18-1   Hubbert's 1969 compilation of developed and planned hydrothermal-energy utilization; reproduced from M. King Hubbert, Chapter 8 on "Energy Resources" in <u>Resources and Man</u>, Committee on Resources and Man, National Academy of Sciences - National Research Council, Publication 1703, Table 8.9, p. 216, W. H. Freeman and Co., San Francisco, California, 1969.

Country and locality	Installed capacity in 1969, Mw_e	Planned additional capacity, Mw_e	Total capacity during the early seventies, Mw_e	Date of earliest installation
Italy[a]				
Larderello	370	-	370	1904
Monte Amiata	19	-	19	1962
total	389	-	389	
United States[b]				
The Geysers, Calif.	82	100	182	1960
New Zealand[b]				
Wairakei	290	-	290	1958
Mexico[b]				
Pathé	3.5	-	3.5	1958
Cerro Prieto (Mexicali)		75	75	1971
total	3.5	75	78.5	
Japan[b,c]				
Matsukawa	20	40	60	1966
Otake	13	47	60	1967
Goshogate		10	10	
total	33	97	130	
Iceland[d]				
Hveragerdi	(geothermal energy for house and greenhouse heating)	17	17	1960
U.S.S.R.[e]				
Kamchatka				
Pauzhetsk	5	7.5	12.5	1966
Paratunka	0.75	-	0.75	1968
Bolshiye Bannyye	25	-	25	1968
total	30.75	7.5	38.25	
grand total	828.25	296.5	1,124.75	

Sources: [a]Facca and Ten Dam, 1964; [b]Donald E. White, U.S. Geological Survey, June 1969; [c]Julian W. Feiss, 1968; [d]Icelandic Embassy, Washington, D.C., July 1969; [e]Donald C. Alverson, Foreign Geology Branch, U.S. Geological Survey, July 1969.

electricity show a steady generating capacity of $0.25 \times 1.25 \times 10^9 \times 10^{-2}/50 =$ 6.25×10^4 Mw$_e$ for the entire world for 50 years and 3.13 to 6.25×10^3 Mw$_e$ in the U.S. for 50 years. The 6.25×10^4 Mw$_e$ at 33% thermal energy-to-electricity conversion efficiency correspond to an oil-use rate of 2.62×10^6 bbl/d, which is not an inconsiderable contribution. If the higher limit estimated by White for U.S. hydrothermal resources could be developed, the electricity output at 33% conversion efficiency would be equivalent to an oil-use rate of 2.62×10^5 bbl/d or about 1.5% of the petroleum-energy consumed in the U.S. during 1973.

There are significant technical and environmental problems associated with hydrothermal power-generation development, which will be discussed in Chapter 18.

Mention should also be made of deep (more than two miles) sedimentary deposits containing trapped hot water, steam, and natural gas. These geo-pressurized zones are found off the Gulf Coast and represent an unexplored energy resource. Because the geopressurized zones are typically found at depths more than twice those from which hydrothermal energy is usually re-covered, drilling and exploitation will be very costly.

2.19 Geothermal Energy

The total outward heat flow from the interior of the earth through the surface of the earth averages 1.25×10^{-6} cal/sec-cm^2 or 39.4 cal/y-cm^2. The surface area of the earth is 5.1×10^{18} cm^2. Hence the total geothermal heat flux is 8×10^{17} Btu/y. Much of this heat flow occurs under the oceans.

If one percent of this power could be utilized for electricity production with a 25% conversion efficiency, the total generating capacity would be 6.7×10^4 Mw$_e$ and is thus seen to be comparable with the 50-year hydrothermal generating capacity estimated in the preceding Section 2.18.

An enormous amount of energy is stored in the core and mantle of the earth. It has recently been proposed to utilize this heat reservoir by drilling deep holes into the outer hot earth-mantle, injecting water for the production of steam, and using the steam as a clean power source for electricity production. The critical technological problem upon which the successful resolution of the economic viability of this proposal depends is the successful self-propagation into heated rock by fissuring of the drilled exposure holes, in order to assure continued heating of very large masses of water after providing access to the hot mantle through a single narrow well. This proposal is further discussed in Chapter 19.

2.20 Hydroelectric Energy

Water has been used for the production of some forms of power since Roman times. Many hydroelectric power-generation stations exist today with capacities well in excess of 10^3 Mw$_e$. The ultimate world capacity for energy production from this source has been estimated[1] to be 2.857×10^6 Mw$_e$ with 0.780×10^6 Mw$_e$ in Africa, 0.577×10^6 Mw$_e$ in South America, and $0.161 \times$

---

[1] Ref. [2] in Section 2.14.

10^6 Mw$_e$ in the U.S. It is interesting to observe that the fossil-fuel poor

regions in Africa and South America have the richest sources of hydroelectric-

power potential. Summaries of the world water-power potential and the 1969

installed capacity are given in Tables 2.20-1 and 2.20-2. The past and po-

tential U.S. capacity to the year 2060 is shown in Fig. 2.20-1. An estimate

of the ultimate U.S. hydroelectric capacity, compiled by the U.S. Geological

Survey, [2] is given in Table 2.20-3. The ultimate U.S. capacity is estimated

from stream-flow records collected for many years by the U.S. Geological

Survey.

Table 2.20-1   Hydroelectric water-power capacity for the world; reproduced
from M. King Hubbert, "Energy Resources, A Report to the
Committee on Natural Resources," National Academy of Sciences-
National Research Council, Publication 1000-D, Table 8, p. 99,
Washington, D.C., 1962.

Region	Potential capacity, 10^3 Mw$_e$	Percentage of world total	Developed capacity, 10^3 Mw$_e$	Percentage of potential developed
North America	313	11	59	19
South America	577	20	5	0.87
Western Europe	158	6	47	30
Africa	780	27	2	0.25
Middle East	21	1	-	-
Southeast Asia	455	16	2	0.44
Far East	42	1	19	45
Australasia	45	2	2	4.5
U.S.S.R., China, and satellites	466	16	16	3.4
total	2,857	100	152	

[2]Ref. [2] in Section 2.2.

Table 2.20-2   Installed 1969 hydroelectric-generation capacity of the world; based on the data of the U.S. Federal Power Commission.[3]

Region	1969 installed hydroelectric capacity, 10^3 Mw$_e$	Percentage of total installed electrical generating capacity
North America	83.9	22.1
Central America	0.5	41.7
West Indies	0.2	4.5
South America	13.4	50.0
Europe, including U.S.S.R.	126.4	26.4
Africa	6.1	29.7
Asia	37.6	32.1
Oceania	6.6	35.4
World	274.7	26.3

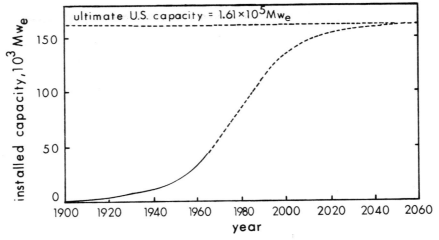

Fig. 2.20-1   Past and projected hydroelectric-power generation in the U.S.; reproduced from M. King Hubbert, Chapter 8 on "Energy Resources" in Resources and Man, Committee on Resources and Man, National Academy of Sciences - National Research Council, Publication 1703, Table 8.9, p. 216, W. H. Freeman and Co., San Francisco, California, 1969.

[3]World Power Data, U.S. Federal Power Commission, Washington, D.C., 1972.

Table 2.20-3 Hydroelectric water-power capacity for the United States;
based on the data of the U.S. Geological Survey.[2]

Region	Ultimate capacity, 10^3 Mw$_e$	1972 installed capacity, 10^3 Mw$_e$	Gross theoretical annual generation, 10^9 kwh$_e$
New England	4.8	1.51	13.4
Middle Atlantic	16.5	4.25	37.9
East North Central	2.2	0.94	9.7
West North Central	7.1	2.73	28.3
South Atlantic	14.5	5.47	34.3
East South Atlantic	9.1	5.22	28.4
West South Central	5.3	2.10	11.2
Mountain	32.4	6.22	119.9
Pacific	62.2	24.86	245.2
Alaska	32.6	0.08	172.7
Hawaii	0.1	0.02	0.3
total	186.8	53.40	701.3

In 1969, the installed hydroelectric capacity in the entire world amounted[3]
to 0.275×10^6 Mw$_e$ or about 9.6% of the total hydroelectric capacity, while total
world electrical capacity amounted to 1.05×10^6 Mw$_e$ (which equals 36.8% of
the total potential world hydroelectric capacity). The U.S. installed capacity
in 1972 was only about 28.6% of the total potentially available. We note from
Fig. 2.20-1 that rapid development of hydroelectric-generating capacity was
projected (in 1969) to occur in the U.S. at least until the year 2000 or, with an
accelerated schedule, at least until 1990, while the total potential (see Table
2.20-3) corresponds to about 95% of the 1971 total U.S. used capacity (includ-

ing electricity production from fossil-fuel and nuclear generating plants) of 0.196×10^6 Mw$_e$ (corresponding to 1.718×10^9 Mwh$_e$ produced).

2.21 Tidal Energy

The total rate of tidal-energy dissipation on the earth corresponds to the Munk-MacDonald limit and amounts to 3.2×10^6 Mw.[1] Munk and MacDonald arrived at this result by noting that tidal energy is derived from the potential and kinetic energies of the earth-moon system. As tidal energy is dissipated, the rotational energy of the earth, as well as the kinetic energy associated with orbital motion of the moon around the earth and of the earth-moon system around the sun, must all decrease. After three centuries of observations of these parameters, it appears that the length of the day on earth has increased by about 10^{-3} sec per 10^2 years, with corresponding changes in the rotational speed of the earth and in the moon orbital motion. Munk and MacDonald used these astronomical data to arrive at the estimate of 3.2×10^6 Mw for the total tidal energy. Later authors have given values for the rate of tidal-energy dissipation as high as 6.3×10^6 Mw[2] and as low as 2.7×10^6 Mw.[3] A recent

[1] W. H. Munk and G. J. F. MacDonald, The Rotation of the Earth, a Geophysical Discussion, p. 219, Cambridge Monographs on Mechanics and Applied Mathematics, Cambridge University Press, Cambridge, England, 1960.

[2] C. L. Pekeris and Y. Accad, "Solution of Laplace's Equations for the M$_2$ tide in the World Oceans," Phil. Trans. Roy. Soc. 265A, 413-436 (1969).

[3] M. C. Hendershott, "The Effects of Solid Earth Deformation on Global Ocean Tides," Geophys. J. Roy. Astron. Soc. 29, 389-402 (1972).

summary has been published by Jeffreys which appears to verify a value of about 3×10^6 Mw.[4]

Following earlier work by Taylor[5] and Jeffreys,[6] Munk and MacDonald (Ref. [1], pp. 209-221) have also estimated the total energy dissipation in shallow seas as 1×10^6 Mw.

A summary of maximum power obtainable from tidal sources, based on compilations by Treholm[7] and Bernshtein,[8] is reproduced in Table 2.21-1. Also listed in Table 2.21-1 are average potential power and maximum energy dissipation (for unit efficiency η in conversion of tidal energy to electricity) per year, the meaning of which will now be discussed.

The maximum possible energy dissipation during a tidal cycle is

$$E_{max} = \eta \rho g R^2 S, \qquad (2.21-1)$$

where ρ = sea density, g = gravitational acceleration, R = tidal range, S = surface area of the tidal basin, and η = conversion efficiency to electricity for tidal energy. The corresponding average power for the tidal basin is

---

[4] H. Jeffreys, "Tidal Friction," Nature 246, 346 (1973).

[5] G. I. Taylor, "Tidal Friction in the Irish Sea," Phil. Trans. Roy. Soc. London 220A, 1-33 (1919).

[6] H. Jeffreys, "Tidal Friction in Shallow Seas," Phil. Trans. Roy. Soc. London 229A, 239-264 (1920).

[7] N. W. Trenholm, "Canada's Wasting Asset - Tidal Power," Elect. News Eng. 70(2), 52-55 (1961).

[8] L. B. Bernshtein, Tidal Energy for Electric Power Plants, translation of the 1961 Russian Edition, Jerusalem, Israel, 1965.

Table 2.21-1 Tidal power: location, average potential power, and potential annual energy; based on data taken from Refs. [7] and [8]. Reproduced with modifications from M. King Hubbert, Chapter 8 on "Energy Resources" in Resources and Man, Committee on Resources and Man, National Academy of Sciences - National Research Council, Publication 1703, Table 8.8, pp. 212-213, W. H. Freeman and Co., San Francisco, California, 1969.

Location	Average range R, m	Basin area S, km^2	Average potential (total) power $\bar{P}$, 10^3 kw	Potential annual (total) energy E, 10^6 kwh$_t$
North America				
Bay of Fundy				
Passamaquoddy	5.52	262	1,800	15,800
Cobscook	5.5	106	722	6,330
Annapolis	6.4	83	765	6,710
Minas-Cobequid	10.7	777	19,900	175,000
Amherst Point	10.7	10	256	2,250
Shepody	9.8	117	2,520	22,100
Cumberland	10.1	73	1,680	14,700
Petitcodiac	10.7	31	794	6,960
Memramcook	10.7	23	590	5,170
subtotal			29,027	255,020
South America				
Argentina				
San José	5.9	750	5,870	51,500
Europe				
England				
Severn	9.8	70	1,680	14,700
France				
Aber-Benoît	5.2	2.9	18	158
Aber-Wrac'h	5.0	1.1	6	53
Arguenon & Lancieux	8.4	28.0	446	3,910
Frênaye	7.4	12.0	148	1,300
La Rance	8.4	22.0	349	3,060
Rothéneuf	8.0	1.1	16	140
Mont Saint-Michel	8.4	610	9,700	85,100
Somme	6.5	49	466	4,090
subtotal			11,149	97,811
U.S.S.R.				
Kislaya Inlet	2.37	2.0	2	22
Lumbovskii Bay	4.20	70	277	2,430
White Sea	5.65	2,000	14,400	126,000
Mezen Estuary	6.60	140	1,370	12,000
subtotal			16,049	140,452
grand total			63,775	559,483

obtained from the relation

$$\overline{P} = E_{max}/T, \qquad\qquad (2.21-2)$$

where T = half-period of the lunar day = 4.46×10^4 sec (= 12 hours and 24.4 minutes).

The efficiency for conversion of tidal power to electricity generally lies between 10 and 20%, although 25% has been achieved at La Rance, France. Reference to Table 2.21-1 shows that, at 25% conversion efficiency, utilization of the combined tidal power in all of the listed tidal basins will lead to the production of 16×10^3 Mw$_e$ of electrical power, or about 0.6% of the corresponding estimate for the hydroelectric resources. Nevertheless, tidal-power utilization will lead to important supplementary energy sources in selected regions of the world.

2.22 Wind Energy

A mature technology for wind power existed nearly sixty years ago. In 1915, 100 Mw$_e$ of electricity were being generated by wind power in Denmark. A 1.25-Mw$_e$ wind-powered generator, built in 1941, has been the only substantial effort to utilize wind energy in the United States.

Palmén and Newton[1] have estimated the instantaneous flux of momentum in the atmosphere of the northern hemisphere to be 10^{11} Mw in the winter

---

[1] E. H. Palmén and C. W. Newton, Atmospheric Circulation Systems: Their Structure and Physical Interpretations, Academic Press, New York, 1969.

season. During the summer season, the value drops by approximately 40%.
This momentum flux is created by a number of physical processes, all of
which are either initiated or driven by solar energy.

In 1954, the World Meteorological Organization[2] estimated that at least
2×10^7 Mw could be extracted from atmospheric winds. A 1972 study of the U.S.
wind-power potential made by Heronemus[3] led to the conclusion that the maximum annual electrical-energy production from the wind by the year 2000 is $1.5 \times$
10^9 Mwh$_e$. Table 2.22-1 lists the regions of the U.S. where wind-power
utilization appears to be most attractive. Estimates of the annual electrical-
energy production and the corresponding installed generating capacity for each
region are included in Table 2.22-1.

2.23 Selected Compendia of Energy-Resource Estimates

We present in Tables 2.23-1 and 2.23-2 two recently-published compilations of non-renewable (fossil, fissile, and fusion) and renewable (solar,
hydroelectric, tidal, and wind) energy resources, as well as estimates for
hydrothermal and geothermal energy (which may be partially renewable).
We note the usual wide variations in the estimates of energy-resource magnitudes.

---

[2]Energy from the Wind, World Meteorological Organization, Technical Note
No. 4, Geneva, Switzerland, 1954.

[3]W. E. Heronemus, "Power from the Offshore Winds," Proceedings of the
8th Annual Marine Technology Conference, Washington, D.C., 1972.

Table 2.22-1   Maximum energy extractable from the winds in the U.S. by the
year 2000; based on data from Heronemus [3] and reproduced
with modifications from <u>Solar Energy as a National Resource</u>,
NSF/NASA Solar Energy Panel, University of Maryland, College Park, Md., 1972.

Region	Annual potential electrical energy production, 10^9 kwh$_e$	Approximate potential installed generating capacity,[a] 10^3 Mw$_e$
offshore, New England	318	52
offshore, Eastern Seaboard, along the 100-meter contour, from the Ambrose shipping channel south to Charleston, South Carolina	283	46
along the E-W Axis, Lake Superior (320 m)	35	6
along the N-S Axis, Lake Michigan (220 m)	29	5
along the N-S Axis, Lake Huron (160 m)	23	4
along the W-E Axis, Lake Erie (200 m)	23	4
along the W-E Axis, Lake Ontario (160 m)	23	4
through the Great Plains from Dallas, Texas, North in a path 300 miles wide W-E, and 1,300 miles long, S to N; wind stations to be clustered in groups of 165, at least 60 miles between groups (sparse coverage)	210	34
offshore on the Texas Gulf Coast, along a length of 400 miles, from the Mexican border, eastward, along the 100-meter contour	190	31
along the Aleutian Chain, 1,260 miles, on transects each 35 miles long, spaced at 60-mile intervals, be-tween 100-meter contours	402	65
total	1,536	251

[a] An average load factor of 70% is assumed.

Table 2.23-1 Some estimates of resource and consumption rates; reproduced from M. R. Gustavson, <u>Dimensions of World Energy</u>, The Mitre Corporation, 1820 Dolley Madison Blvd., McLean, Virginia 22101, 1971. The estimates given in this compilation tend to be close to those of Hubbert (1969).

A. Fossil-fuel resources

	Amount	$Q(10^{18} Btu)$ equivalent[*]
coal and lignite	7.6×10^{12} mt	190
natural gas	1×10^{15} SCF	10
petroleum liquids	2×10^{12} bbl	11
Alberta, Canada, tar sands	3×10^{11} bbl	1.7
shale oil	1.9×10^{11} bbl	1.1

[*]Using 1 bbl of oil = 5.6×10^6 Btu, 1 SCF of natural gas = 1.0×10^3 Btu, 1 metric ton of coal = 2.5×10^7 Btu.

B. Renewable resources

	Q/y or Q
solar input to earth	5.3×10^3
solar input used in photosynthesis	1.2
solar input per 10^6 acres on earth	2.1×10^{-2}
total geothermal heat flux outward	8×10^{-1}
heat stored in geothermal systems to 10 km depth (in units of Q)	40
useful geothermal heat from hydrothermal areas (for a 100 y utilization period)	4×10^{-3}
tidal dissipation on earth	9×10^{-2}
usable tidal energy	1.9×10^{-3}
power corresponding to total hydrologic run-off	2.7×10^{-1}
useful hydroelectric power	8.6×10^{-2}

Table 2.23-1 continued.

C. Nuclear-energy resources

	Q
fission without breeding using \$10/lb U_3O_8 (about 2.335×10^6 t)	4.3
fission with breeding (for 10×10^6 t)	6.1×10^2
fusion of 1 ppm of oceanic D	1.1×10^4
complete conversion to energy of 10^6 t of matter	7.8×10^4

D. Earth characteristics

approximate heat capacity of the oceans	5.4×10^3 Q/$^{\circ}$C
power absorbed in global evaporation	9.8×10^2 Q/y
energy released in condensation of atmospheric water	3×10 Q
approximate heat capacity of the atmosphere	5 Q/$^{\circ}$C
heat release associated with the production of all of the atmospheric CO_2 from fossil fuels	3×10 Q
heat release associated with the production of all of the atmospheric CO_2 that is exchanged between the atmosphere and the oceans	3 Q/y

E. Energy-use rates

	Q/y
metabolic processes for 3.592×10^9 people in 1970 at an average of 2.350×10^3 kcal/day	1.2×10^{-2}
U.S. 1970 energy consumption rate	6.8×10^{-2}
world 1970 consumption rate	1.9×10^{-1}
world use rate compounded at 3%/y to the year 2000	4.6×10^{-1}
world use rate in the year 2000 if the per capita use rate equals the U.S. 1970 per capita use rate of 3.8×10^{-10} Q/y	2.1

Table 2.23-2 U.S. energy-output potential by the year 2000 for an
intermediate level of supply in 1985; reproduced from
U.S. Energy Outlook, National Petroleum Council,
Washington, D.C., 1972.

	Units	1985	2000
oil, total domestic liquid production	10^6bbl/d	14	10-18
natural gas production	10^{12}SCF/y	27	15-25
coal, traditional uses only	10^6t/y	863	1,200-1,700
hydroelectric energy	10^9kwh$_e$/y	316	340-380
nuclear energy	10^9kwh$_e$/y	2,463	7,500-9,500
oil, total domestic liquid production	10^{15}Btu/y	29	21-37
natural-gas production	10^{15}Btu/y	28	15-26
coal, traditional uses only	10^{15}Btu/y	21	30-42
hydroelectric energy	10^{15}Btu/y	3	4
nuclear energy	10^{15}Btu/y	25	61-102
total		106	131-211

CHAPTER 3

ENERGY CONSUMPTION BY SECTOR

Energy uses are reasonably well defined in terms of application requirements. Although a multiplicity of subdivisions is possible in terms of end
use, the following compilation of data is indicative of important types of
energy applications.

3.1   Energy Sources and Uses

A late 1973 estimate of the principal energy sources and current applications (see Fig. 3.1-1) shows 43% of the energy allocated to industrial
applications, 14% for commercial use, 24% for transportation systems, and
19% to satisfy residential demand.

In 1972, a barrel of refined oil was distributed, as is shown in Fig. 3.1-2,
between gasoline (37.7%), distillate fuel oil (17.96%), residual fuel oil (15.46%),
natural-gas liquids (13.78%), lubricants (0.88%), kerosene (1.4%), naphtha-
type jet fuel (1.48%), kerosene jet fuel (4.9%), and other uses (4.9%). The
commercial utilization of these crude-oil products is also shown in Fig. 3.1-2.
We note that gasoline was the primary refinery product, although reference
to Table 3.1-1 shows that the demand for some other crude-oil derivatives
was expected (in 1972) to increase relatively more rapidly during future
years. This emphasis on other refinery products was accelerated under the
impact of dwindling crude-oil supplies in late 1973 and early 1974.

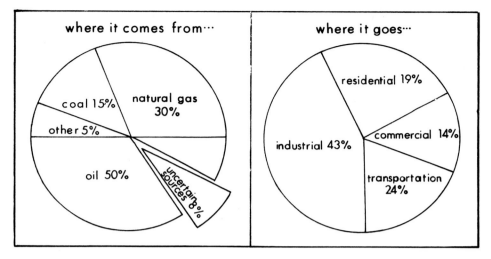

Fig. 3.1-1 Energy sources and their uses, winter 1973-74; reprinted with permission from Chemical and Engineering News 51, 13-14, November 13, 1973. Copyright by the American Chemical Society.

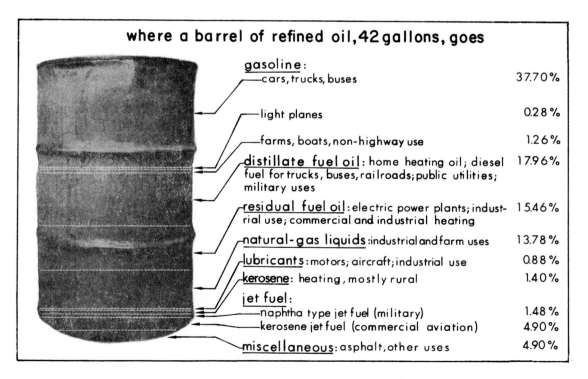

Fig. 3.1-2 End uses of a barrel of oil in 1972; reproduced from the American Petroleum Institute, Washington, D.C., 1973.

Table 3.1-1 Petroleum-product demands in 10^6 bbl/d; reproduced
from U.S. Energy Outlook, National Petroleum
Council, Washington, D.C., 1972.

	1972	1973	1974	1975	1976	1977	1978
motor gasoline	6.3	6.6	6.9	7.3	7.7	8.1	8.5
jet fuel	1.0	1.1	1.2	1.3	1.4	1.5	1.6
distillate	2.9	3.0	3.1	3.2	3.3	3.4	3.5
residual	2.7	3.7	4.6	5.4	6.4	7.0	7.5
other	3.3	3.5	3.7	3.9	4.1	4.3	4.5
total	16.2	17.9	19.5	21.1	22.9	24.3	25.6

The anticipated (in 1972) evolution of energy use to the year 1990 is shown in
in Fig. 3.1-3. Here the application range is broken down in a manner different
from that employed in Fig. 3.1-1. Thus, energy consumption by utilities,
which leads to electrical-energy production for all types of end uses, is
treated as a separate entry. Reference to Fig. 3.1-3 shows that energy
conversion to electricity is expected to represent the most-rapidly growing
component of the energy industries.

3.2 Some Examples of Industrial Energy Use

Every manufactured, agricultural, or service product carries an energy
price.

Some examples of 1968 energy costs for basic-materials processing
are listed in Table 3.2-1. The steel industry, which consumed 6.20% of the
total energy used in 1968, used 11,700 kwh of thermal energy (kwh_t) per ton

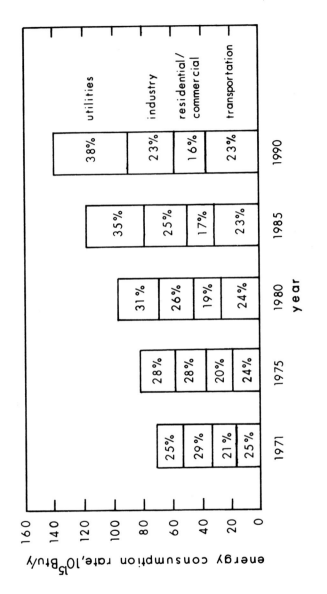

Fig. 3.1-3 The year 1971 energy consumption and estimated future energy consumption in the United States by consuming sector; reproduced from The Potential for Energy Conservation, U.S. Government Printed Office, Washington, D.C., 1972.

Table 3.2-1 Energy consumption in basic-materials processing during 1968; reproduced from A. B. Makhijani and A. J. Lichtenberg, "Energy and Well-Being," Environment 14, 10-18, June 1972.

Material	Energy for unit production, kwh_t/t	Machinery depreciation[a], kwh_t/t	Transportation[b], kwh_t/t	Total, kwh_t/t	1968 material consumption t	Total energy, kwh_t	Percentage of total 1968 energy consumption
steel (rolled)	11,700	700	200	12,600	90×10^6 (excluding alloys)	1.13×10^{12}	6.20
aluminum (rolled)	66,000	1,000	200	67,200	4.07×10^6	2.74×10^{11}	1.49
copper (rolled or hard drawn)	20,000	800	200	21,000	2×10^6	4.2×10^{10}	0.23
silicone, metal, and high-grade steel alloys	58,000	1,000	200	59,200	2×10^6	1.19×10^{11}	0.65
zinc	13,800	700	200	14,700	1.5×10^6	2.2×10^{10}	0.12
lead	12,000	700	200	12,900	0.467×10^6	6.05×10^9	0.04
miscellaneous electrically processed metal	50,000	1,000	200	51,200	2×10^6	1.02×10^{10}	0.06
titanium (rolled)	140,000	1,000	200	141,200	16×10^3	2.24×10^9	0.01
cement	2,200	50	50	2,300	74×10^6	1.7×10^{11}	0.93
sand and gravel	18	1	2 (short distance hauling)	21	918×10^6	1.83×10^{10}	0.10
inorganic chemicals	2,400	100	200	2,700	67×10^6	1.8×10^{11}	0.98
glass (plate finished)	6,700	300	200	7,200	10^7	7.2×10^{10}	0.39
plastics	2,400	300	200	2,900	6×10^6	1.74×10^{10}	0.10
paper	5,900	300	200	6,400	50.7×10^6	3.24×10^{11}	1.77
lumber	1.47 per board foot	0.02 per board foot	0.02 per board foot	1.51 per board foot	3.75×10^{10} board feet	5.66×10^{10}	0.31
coal	40	2	---	42	556.7×10^6	3.3×10^{10}	0.20

[a] These are approximate numbers derived as follows: the steel calculations refer to one ton of installed equipment (excluding buildings) per annual ton of steel production. Depreciation is calculated on a 30-year, straight-line basis. For non-electrically processed metals, the depreciation is taken to be equal to that for steel. Production facilities involving predominantly electrical equipment are amortized over 20 years and therefore the depreciation/t is 1.5 times that for steel. For non-metals, the depreciation/t allocation is about 5% of the energy required for producing one ton of product.

[b] These figures are based on the sum of the average railroad shipping distance (286 miles, i.e., the average distance between major stops) plus 200 miles truck freight (this is an approximate value, based on the fact that truck freight is in general comparable to train freight).

of product; in addition, 700 kwh_t/t were used for machinery depreciation and 200 kwh_t/t for transportation. Disregarding lumber, the lowest energy cost per ton of product listed occurs for sand and gravel (18 kwh_t/t); the highest energy cost per ton of finished product (141,200 kwh_t/t) went into the processing of rolled titanium.

In terms of energy conservation objectives, we must address ourselves to the problem of possible improvements in energy for manufacturing efficiency. A question of this type can only be answered after intimate familiarity has been obtained with all aspects of the procedures and technologies involved in the manufacturing processes.

The distribution of energy in the transportation sector is shown in Table 3.2-2 for the year 1968. Car use accounted for about 37% of all of the energy consumed in the transportation sector, while jets were responsible for a little more than 8%. Secondary transportation activities used up about 25% of the energy allocated to the transportation sector.

A breakdown of energy consumption for a variety of activities is given in Table 3.2-3 in $kwh_t/unit$ product. This compilation includes data for such items as food, beverage, and textiles, as well as for transportation and a variety of basic materials; it may be obtained from selected government publications.[1] Energy use for food has been examined in a separate study.[2]

---

[1] 1972 Census of Manufactures, Special Report Series on Fuels and Electric Energy Consumed, U.S. Department of Commerce, Report MC72(SR)-6, Washington, D.C., July 1973.

[2] E. Hirst, "Energy Use for Food in the United States," Report ORNL-NSF-EP-57, Oak Ridge National Laboratory, Oak Ridge, Tennessee, October 1973; see also Science 184, 134-138 (1974).

Table 3.2-2   Energy used for transportation in 1968; reproduced from
              D. P. Grimmer and K. Luszczynski, "Lost Power," Envi-
              ronment 14, 14-22, 56, April 1972.

Sector	Use	Energy consumption, 10^{15} Btu
primary transport (propulsion)	automobile	7.60
	truck and bus	3.06
	jet	1.63
	railroads	0.72
	marine	0.55
	all other propulsion	1.59
subtotal		15.15
secondary transport (related activities)	fuel refining, asphalt and road oil energy	2.42
	primary metals used in transport manufacture	1.02
	manufacturing	0.53
	other activities	1.05
subtotal		5.02
total		20.17

The soft-drink energy costs are detailed in Tables 3.2-4a to 3.2-4c.
Energy savings per gallon of beverage of about two-thirds may be accomplished by using 16-ounce returnable bottles and refilling these, on the
average, eight times. The savings are reduced for larger containers (see
Table 3.2-4c).

Table 3.2-3 Breakdown of U.S. energy consumption in 1968: the average hourly rate of energy use per person in the U.S. during 1968 is given in column 5; reproduced with modifications from A. B. Makhijani and A. J. Lichtenberg, "Energy and Well-Being," Environment 14, 10-18, June 1972.

Finished product or user	Energy/unit product,[a] kwh_t/unit	Product consumption	Total energy, kwh_t	Per capita energy per hour,[b] kwh_t/h	Comments
food (excluding beverages)	1,600/t	2×10^8 t	3.2×10^{11}	0.185	Excluding containers.
beverages					
carbonated	3/gallon	5×10^9 gallons	1.5×10^{10}	0.009	
distilled	15/gallon	2×10^8 gallons	3×10^9	0.002	
textiles (including leather goods)	c	-	6×10^{10}	0.035^d	Chlorine gas used in artificial fabric manufacture. Manufacture of chlorine gas is the major cause of mercury pollution.
construction					
residential[e]	-	-	3.02×10^{11}	0.175	
non-residential[e]	-	-	8.7×10^{11}	0.495	
roads[e]	-	-	1.85×10^{11}	0.107	Includes street lighting.
trucks					
manufacture	$89,000^f$	1.896×10^{11} t	1.69×10^{11}	0.098	Excluding transportation for basic materials.
operation	-	-	1.01×10^{12}	0.575	
passenger autos					
manufacture	$31,000^g$	10.5×10^6 t	3.26×10^{11}	0.189	
operation	-	-	2.67×10^{12}	1.545	
ships					
civilian					
manufacture	4,500/gross t[h]	0.44×10^6 gross t	1.99×10^9	0.001	25% oil tankers.
operation[i]	-	-	1.7×10^{10}	0.010	
military					
manufacture[j]	4,500/gross t	5.52×10^6 t	2.5×10^{10}	0.015	Approximate values.
operation	-	-			

Table 3.2-3, continued.

Finished product or user	Energy/unit product,[a] kwh_t/unit	Product consumption	Total energy, kwh_t	Per capita energy per hour,[b] kwh_t/h	Comments
trains					
manufacture	$20,000$/t dead wt[k]	3.26×10^6 t dead wt	6.52×10^{10}	0.038	
operation	-	-	1.8×10^{11}	0.104	
aircraft					
civilian					
manufacture					
single-engine	2×10^6/unit	9,000 units	1.8×10^{10}	0.010	Very approximate; includes aluminum used.[1]
multi-engine	18×10^6/unit	1,500 units	2.7×10^{10}	0.015	Domestic traffic only.
operation	-	-	2.9×10^{11}	0.168	
military					
manufacture	18×10^6/unit	1,000 units	1.8×10^{10}	0.010	As above for civilian aircraft manufacture, except that titanium is included here.
operation	-	-	1.42×10^{11}	0.082	Approximately 80% for aircraft.
military vehicles operation	$20,000$/t	8.4×10^6 t	0.68×10^{11}	0.039	Steel (except high-grade alloys), lead, zinc used; total excludes basic materials-processing machinery.
industrial machinery	$62,000$/t	4×10^6 t	2.48×10^{11}	0.144	High-grade steel alloys and electrically processed metals (except aluminum).
	$75,000$/t	0.5×10^6 t	3.75×10^{10}	0.022	Electrical aluminum.
	$29,000$/t	2×10^6 t	5.8×10^{10}	0.034	Electrical copper.
household and commercial durables					
steel	$20,000$/t[k]	4.4×10^6 t	8.8×10^{10}	0.051	
aluminum	$75,000$/t[k]	0.4×10^6 t	3.0×10^{10}	0.017	
defense-related steel	$20,000$/t[k]	2.06×10^6 t	4.12×10^{10}	0.024	Direct production only.
miscellaneous steel	$20,000$/t[k]	26.6×10^6 t	5.32×10^{11}	0.310	Spare parts, nuts, bolts, etc.

Table 3.2-3, continued.

Finished product or user	Energy/unit product, a kwh$_t$/unit	Product consumption	Total energy, kwh$_t$	Per capita energy per hour, b kwh$_t$/h	Comments
agricultural implements steel cans and packaging	20,000/t 1.0/12-oz can (20,000/t)	1.38 × 10^6 t 7.8 × 10^6 t	2.76 × 10^{10} 1.56 × 10^{11}	0.016 0.090	55% cans and containers, 45% packaging, 10 cans/lb. Recycling energy: approximately 0.5 kwh$_t$/12-oz can or 5 kwh$_t$/lb.
aluminum cans and packaging	2.07/12-oz can (82,800/t)	0.4 × 10^6 t^m	3.3 × 10^{10}	0.019	Growth rate is 10% per year, 20 cans/lb. Recycling energy is approximately 0.5 kwh$_t$/12-oz can or 10 kwh$_t$/lb.
miscellaneous aluminum	70,000/t	1 × 10^6 t	7 × 10^{10}	0.041	
glass containers	4/lb	1 × 10^{10} lb	4 × 10^{10}	0.023	The recycling energy requirement is the same as for manufacture of new glass.
miscellaneous wooden crates	4/lb 1.51/bd-ft	2 × 10^9 lb 10.5 × 10^9 bd-ft	8 × 10^9 1.59 × 10^{10}	0.005 0.009	
plastics packaging and containers	3.5 × 10^3/t	1 × 10^6 t	3.5 × 10^9	0.002	Mercury pollution due to use of chlorine gas.
miscellaneous paper (average, including paper board)	3.5 × 10^3/t 6,400/t	3.7 × 10^6 t 46.2 × 10^6 t	1.3 × 10^{10} 2.96 × 10^{11}	0.008 0.172	43% in the form of paper board and 5.6% in the form of newsprint. This probably has no advantages in energy savings but obvious ones in forest conservation.
non-energy uses	—	—	1.2 × 10^{12}	0.7	Excluding coke used for pig-iron production. Includes carbon-black production (NG), lubricating oils (lubricating oils for transport = 4 × 10^{10} kwh$_t$; for industry, 4.9 × 10^{10} kwh$_t$), petrochemicals (1.73 × 10^{11} kwh$_t$).

Table 3.2-3, continued.

Finished product or user	Energy/unit product,[a] kwh$_t$/unit	Product consumption	Total energy, kwh$_t$	Per capita energy per hour,[b] kwh$_t$/h	Comments
inorganic chemicals	2,400/t	67 × 10^6 t	1.6 × 10^{11}	0.093	
commercial lighting and miscellaneous electricity (air conditioning)	-		5.18 × 10^{11}	0.3	
household lighting and miscellaneous electricity	-		8.64 × 10^{11}	0.5	
household space heating	-		1.97 × 10^{12}	1.14	Includes cooking.
miscellaneous household heat	-		5.7 × 10^{11}	0.33	
commercial space heat	-		2.24 × 10^{11}	0.13	
commercial miscellaneous heat	-		6.9 × 10^{11}	0.4	
miscellaneous space heat	-		1.2 × 10^{11}	0.07	
Atomic Energy Commission	-		3 × 10^{11}	0.174	Operation of nuclear reprocessing plants, gaseous diffusion plants, and weapons research and development.
petroleum refining	44.5/bbl	3.216 × 10^9 bbl	1.43 × 10^{11}	0.083	
coal processing	42/t	556.7 × 10^6 t	3.3 × 10^{10}	0.018	
miscellaneous industry	-		1.62 × 10^{12}	0.94	Electronic industry, rubber, paints, miscellaneous mining, fertilizers, toys, instruments, ceramics, stone and clay products, etc.
agricultural kerosene consumption			6.25 × 10^9	0.004	
public electricity consumption	-		8.3 × 10^{10}	0.048	Use by federal, state, and local governments, excluding defense, AEC, and street lighting.
natural-gas processing	-		1.59 × 10^{11}	0.092	3% of NG production (average).
pipeline losses	-		2.12 × 10^{11}	0.123	4% of NG production (average).
gases vented and wasted	-		1.85 × 10^{11}	0.107	3.5% of NG production (average).
pipeline power					
subtotal			17.2 × 10^{12}	9.98	
unaccounted for			1.1 × 10^{12}	0.62	
total consumption (1968)			18.3 × 10^{12}	10.60	

Table 3.2-3, continued.

[a] These figures are calculated by adding energy for manufacture and energy for processing the materials used. General accuracy limits: ±20%.

[b] On the basis of a U.S. population of 200 million.

[c] The data are too sparse to justify estimation of a significant figure.

[d] On the basis of a 1% per year increase since 1950, during which year the consumption per capita (total for the textile industry divided by the population in 1950) was $0.0294 \, kwh_t/h$.

[e] Total consumption of electrical power in construction $\simeq 0.7 \times 10^{12}$ kwht. This power has been distributed to residential and non-residential users according to the percentage of total construction money spent in the three sectors (43% residential; 47% industrial, commercial, and public; 10% highways). All construction aluminum, steel, cement, sand, and gravel was assumed to be included in non-residential construction and roads. Construction plastics are divided equally between residential and non-residential construction.

[f] On the basis of a 10,000-lb truck with material processing and energy approximately equal to that for steel, which constitutes about 80% of the weight of the truck.

[g] On the basis of a 3,300-lb automobile (average including imports) calculated as in note f above, except that 0.2×10^6 tons of aluminum (40 lb/car) have been added.

[h] One-sixth of a ton of dead weight per gross ton; assumed to be steel.

[i] Roughly the same tonnage carried as trucks at approximately 18 kwh_t/t-mile.

[j] About 10^6 tons of steel were used for ship construction. Of this, about 0.08×10^6 tons were for civilian ships (gross weight divided by 6; see note h above). The rest of this steel (0.92×10^6 tons) is assumed to be military construction and the gross weight is obtained by multiplying this number by 6. Probably an underestimate since the weight of other materials is neglected.

[k] Assuming the same energy/ton of steel as for car manufacture.

[l] Assumes that 50% of the aluminum used for transportation was used for aircraft. See Table A 9-4 in H. H. Landsberg, et al, Resources in America's Future, Johns Hopkins Press, Baltimore, Maryland, 1963.

[m] Including all containering and packaging; about 50% in cans.

Table 3.2-4a   Energy expended in Btu for one gallon of soft drink in 16-ounce returnable or throwaway glass bottles; reproduced from B. M. Hannon, "Bottles, Cans, Energy," Environment 14, 11-21, March 1972.

Operation	Returnable (8 fills)	Throwaway (8 bottles)
raw material acquisition	990	5,195
transportation of raw materials	124	650
manufacture of container	7,738	40,624
manufacture of cap (crown)	1,935	1,935
transportation to bottler	361	1,895
bottling	6,100	6,100
transportation to retailer	1,880	1,235
retailer and consumer	- - -	- - -
waste collection	89	468
separation, sorting, and return for processing; 30% recycle	1,102	5,782
total energy expended in Btu per gallon		
recycled	19,970	62,035
not recycled	19,220	58,100

A summary for the primary industrial energy consumers is given in Table 3.2-5. Reference to these data shows the following ordering of total industrial energy consumption for the most energy-intensive industry types: primary metals--21.2%, chemicals and allied products--19.8%, petroleum refining and related industries--11.3%, food and kindred products--5.3%, paper products--5.2%.

The fuel use for heat and power, the fuel use per dollar value of product shipped, and the average fuel cost per dollar value of product shipped, for the major manufacturing industries in the United States in 1971, are given in Table 3.2-6. Similar data for electrical energy use are given in Table 3.2-7.

Table 3.2-4b   Energy expended in Btu for one gallon of soft drink in 12-ounce
cans; reproduced from B. M. Hannon, "Bottles, Cans, Energy,"
Environment 14, 11-21, March 1972.

Operation	Btu per gallon
mining (2.5 lb of ore per lb of finished steel)	1,570
transportation of ore (1,000 miles by barge)	550
manufacture of finished steel from ore	27,600
aluminum lid (11.9% of total can weight; 4.7 times the unit steel energy)	12,040
transportation of finished steel (392 miles average)	230
manufacture of cans (4% waste)	3,040
transportation to bottler (300 miles average)	190
transportation to retailer	6,400
retailer and consumer	- - -
waste collection	110
total energy for can container system[a]	51,830
total energy for 12-ounce returnable glass system	17,820
ratio of total energy expended by can container system to that expended by 12-ounce returnable glass	2.91

[a]The aluminum can system consumes 33% more energy than the bi-
metal (steel and aluminum) can system.

The chemical and allied products, primary metals, and petroleum and coal
industries were the leading fuel users (see Tables 3.2-3, 3.2-5, and 3.2-6).
The most fuel-intense manufacturing involved production of stone, clay, and
glass (see Table 3.2-6); these products also had the highest fuel cost per
dollar value of product shipped.   Other industries with high fuel costs per
dollar value of product shipped were primary metals and paper and allied
products (see Table 3.2-6).

Reference to the data of Table 3.2-7 indicates that the primary metals
and the chemical and allied products industries were the largest consumers

Table 3.2-4c Energy ratios for various beverage container systems; reproduced from B. M. Hannon, "Bottles, Cans, Energy," Environment 14, 11-21, March 1972. The energy ratios are defined as the energy, per unit beverage, expended for a throwaway container system divided by the energy, per unit beverage, expended for a returnable container system. [a]

| Container type | | | | | Throwaway-to-returnable |
Throwaway	Returnable	Quantity	Beverage	Returnable fills	energy ratio
glass	glass	16 oz	soft drink	15	4.4
can	glass	12 oz	soft drink	15	2.9
glass	glass	12 oz	beer	19	3.4
can	glass	12 oz	beer	19	3.8
paper	glass	1/2 gal	milk	33	1.8
plastic[b]	plastic	1/2 gal	milk	50	2.4

[a] Without remelting loop (discarded bottles and cans are not returned for remanufacture).

[b] High-density polyethylene.

Table 3.2-5 Industrial consumers of energy in 10^{12} Btu in the U.S.; reprinted with permission from Chemical and Engineering News 50, 10, September 18, 1972, and based on an Office of Science and Technology Report released in January 1972. Copyright by the American Chemical Society.

Industry	Coal	Natural gas	Petroleum products	Thermal-equivalent of electrical energy	Total energy
primary metals	2,838	863	306	1,291	5,298
chemical and allied products	666	1,219	1,426	1,626	4,937
petroleum refining and related industries	na[a]	1,012	1,589	225	2,826
food and kindred products	263	593	134	338	1,328
paper and allied products	467	341	211	280	1,299
stone, clay, glass, and concrete products	406	449	87	280	1,222
all other industries	976		721	1,572	8,050
total	5,616	9,258	4,474	5,612	24,960

[a] Included in all other industries, na = not available.

Table 3.2-6 Fuel use, fuel intensity, and fuel costs per $-value of product
shipped for manufacturing industries in the United States in
1971; based on data from the U.S. Department of Commerce.

Manufacturing industry	Fuel use for heat and power,[a] 10^9 kwh$_t$	Fuel intensity, kwh$_t$/$-value of product shipped	Average dollar fuel cost per $-value of product shipped
food and kindred products	266.8	2.58	0.004
tobacco	4.6	0.83	0.008
textiles	81.6	3.40	0.007
apparel	13.9	0.56	0.001
lumber and wood	57.3	3.84	0.010
furniture and fixtures	14.2	1.46	0.003
paper and allied products	350.5	13.77	0.022
printing and publishing	21.0	0.78	0.002
chemicals and allied products	714.6	13.78	0.017
petroleum and coal	443.3	16.46	0.017
rubber and plastics	51.3	3.01	0.005
leather	8.3	1.59	0.003
stone, clay, and glass	357.5	19.29	0.031
primary metals	595.4	11.22	0.022
fabricated metals	82.8	1.97	0.004
machinery, except electrical	85.3	1.54	0.003
electrical equipment	56.6	1.15	0.002
transportation equipment	86.4	0.99	0.002
instruments	16.5	1.34	0.003
ordnance and miscellaneous	24.5	1.43	0.003
all industries	3,332.4	4.97	0.008

[a] The kilowatt-hour of thermal energy-equivalent for all purchased fuels.

Table 3.2-7 Electricity use, electricity intensity, and electricity cost per
$-value of product shipped for manufacturing industries in the
United States in 1971; based on data from the U.S. Department
of Commerce.

Manufacturing industry	Electricity use for heat and power, 10^9 kwh$_e$	Electricity intensity, kwh$_e$/$-value of product shipped	Average dollar electricity cost per $-value of product shipped
food and kindred products	35.4	0.34	0.004
tobacco	0.9	0.16	0.002
textiles	25.0	1.04	0.010
apparel	5.5	0.22	0.004
lumber and wood	9.3	0.62	0.009
furniture and fixtures	3.9	0.40	0.006
paper and allied products	35.0	1.37	0.012
printing and publishing	9.6	0.36	0.005
chemicals and allied products	99.6	1.92	0.015
petroleum and coal	23.7	0.88	0.007
rubber and plastics	16.4	0.96	0.011
leather	1.7	0.33	0.005
stone, clay, and glass	24.9	1.35	0.014
primary metals	122.4	2.31	0.018
fabricated metals	20.3	0.48	0.006
machinery, except electrical	22.3	0.40	0.005
electrical equipment	23.6	0.48	0.005
transportation equipment	27.5	0.32	0.004
instruments	3.6	0.29	0.004
ordnance and miscellaneous	7.1	0.42	0.005
all industries	517.7	0.77	0.008

of electricity in 1971. These two industries also had the highest electricity
intensity and the highest electricity cost per dollar value of product shipped.
Comparison of the bottom entries in Tables 3.2-6 and 3.2-7 indicates that
the industry average of the fuel intensity (4.97 kwh_t/$-value of product
shipped) was nearly 6.5 times the industry average of electricity intensity
(0.77 kwh_e/$-value of product shipped) in 1971. Because of the relatively
low cost of fuels as compared to electricity, the industry average fuel and
electricity costs per dollar value of product shipped ($0.008/$-value of product shipped) were equal in 1971 (see the last lines in Tables 3.2-6 and 3.2-7).

3.3 Energy-Consumption Changes Associated with Technological Changes, Especially in Transportation

Energy use for transportation has historically consumed about 25% of the
total energy. During 1970, automobiles accounted for about 54% of the energy
expended on transportation, trucks for 21%, and aircraft for 6% (not including military transport). A graphical representation of the 1970 distribution for transportation energy applications is given in Fig. 3.3-1.

Passenger transportation costs in passenger-miles per gallon of fuel and
freight transportation costs in cargo ton-miles per gallon are listed in Table
3.3-1. We note a very large decline in these measures of propulsion efficiency with speed: from 930 cargo ton-miles per gallon for a supertanker
travelling at 15 knots to 8.3 for cargo hauled by a Boeing 707 jet at speeds in
excess of 500 mph; from 200 miles per gallon for a passenger in a suburban
train averaging perhaps 30 mph to 22 miles per gallon for the same passenger

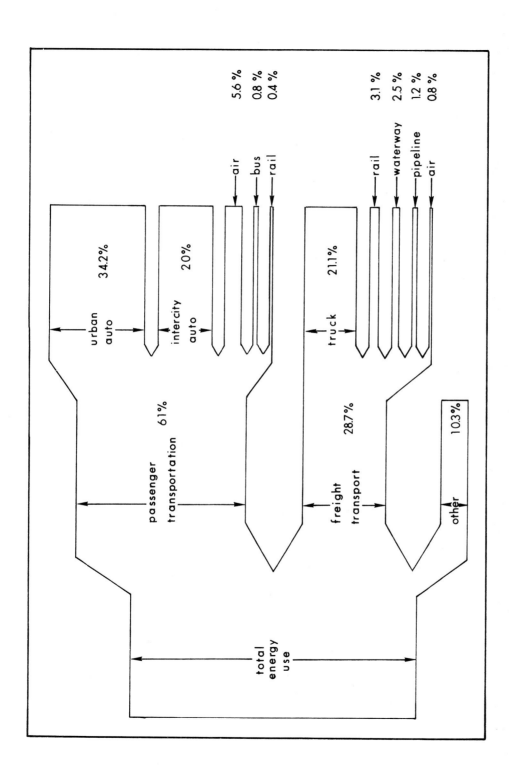

Fig. 3.3-1   The 1970 distribution for transportation energy applications.

Table 3.3-1   Transportation costs; reproduced with permission from R. A. Rice,
"System Energy as a Factor in Considering Future Transportation,"
ASME Paper 70-WA/ENER-8, 1970. Conversions are: 1 foot $\cong$ 0.305 m;
1 mile = 1.609 km; 1 hp = 746 watts; 1 knot $\cong$ 1.85 km/hr. Copyright
by the American Association of Mechanical Engineers.

Passenger		Freight	
Transport type	Passenger-miles per gallon	Transport type	Cargo ton-miles per gallon
large jet plane (Boeing 747)	22	one-half of a Boeing 707 (160 tons, 30,000 hp)	8.3
small jet plane (Boeing 707)	21	one-fourth of a Boeing 747 (360 tons, 60,000 hp)	11.4
automobile (sedan)	32	sixty 250-hp, 40-ton trucks	50.0
cross-country train[a]	80	fast 3000-ton, 40-car freight train	97.0
commuter train[b]	100	three 5000-ton, 100-car freight trains	250.0
large bus (40-foot)	125	inland barge tow, 60,000 gross tons	220.0
small bus (35-foot)	126	large pipeline: 100 miles, two pumps	500.0
suburban train (two-deck)[c]	200	100,000-ton supertanker, 15 knots	930.0

[a]One 150-ton locomotive and four 70-seat coaches plus diner lounge and baggage coach.

[b]Ten 65-ton cars and two 150-ton 2000-hp diesel locomotives.

[c]A ten-car gallery-car commuter train with 160 seats per car.

in a Boeing 747 jet travelling in excess of 500 mph.   The slight decrease in

energy cost associated with the largest jet planes, as compared with smaller

ones, if they are adequately loaded, is noteworthy.   A more detailed account

of related performance estimates is given in Table 3.3-2.

Additional information concerning the growth of energy consumption for

transportation with time is given in Table 3.3-3.   We note that, from 1950 to

1970, this application has consistently consumed from 24.0 to 25.5% of the

total energy used, corresponding to an average annual growth rate of 4.5%

in the energy used for transportation.

Table 3.3-4 shows the time evolution of total energy and of petroleum

usage in the U.S.   The last three columns are expressed, respectively, in

percentage of total petroleum supply derived from imports, in percentage of

total petroleum supply allocated for transportation use, and in percentage of

transportation energy derived from petroleum use.   We note from the data in

Table 3.3-4 that petroleum imports grew from 10.6% (in 1950) to 22.2%

(in 1970) of the total petroleum consumed, while the petroleum supply al-

located for transportation use was 50.3% in 1950 and 53.2% in 1970 of the

total petroleum consumed.   During the same time interval, the transportation

energy derived from petroleum rose from 77.8 to 95.5%.   Thus, by 1970, all

but 4.5% of the transportation energy was derived from petroleum.

The past (pre-1972) evolution and future projection (involving extrapo-

lation of pre-1972 trends and allowance for possible improvements in effi-

ciency) of energy consumption for passenger traffic are shown in Table 3.3-5.

Table 3.3-2 Efficiency of modes of passenger transport; reproduced with permission from R. A. Rice, "System Energy as a Factor in Considering Future Transportation," ASME Paper 70-WA/ENER-8, 1970. Copyright by the American Society of Mechanical Engineers.

Mode	Cruise power, hp	Speed, mph	Seat capacity, number	Assumed occupancy, %	Passenger-miles per gallon	Btu per passenger-mile
rail						
fast train[a]	2,400	100	360	55	133	980
commuter train[b]	4,000	40	1,000	50	100	1,300
cross-country train	2,400	60	360	55	80	1,600
10-car subway train[c]	4,000	30	1,000	50	75	1,700
road						
large bus	200	50	43	58	125	1,000
automobile (sedan)	50	67	4	25-50	16-32	8,100-4,100
air						
747 jet	60,000	500	360	55	22	5,900
707 jet	28,000	500	136	62	21	6,200
STOL plane (4-propellers)	10,000	200	99	55	18	7,200
SST (US)	240,000	1,500	250	60	13.7	9,500
helicopter (3-engine)	12,000	150	78	58	7.5	17,300

[a] 3-car, self-propelled, bi-directional double-deck, 67 tons per car.

[b] 10-car train with two diesel locomotives, 950 tons gross weight.

[c] Modern New York subway train during heavy, non-rush hour traffic.

Table 3.3-3 Past and total projected total energy consumption and
energy used for transportation in the U.S.; reproduced from E. Hirst, Energy Consumption for Transportation in the U.S., Report ORNL-NSF-EP-15, Oak
Ridge National Laboratory, Oak Ridge, Tennessee,
March 1972.[a]

Year	Total energy used, 10^{15} Btu	Energy used for transportation, 10^{15} Btu	Percent of total energy used for transportation
1950	34.1	8.7	25.5
1955	40.0	9.9	24.8
1960	45.0	10.9	24.2
1965	53.8	12.8	23.7
1970	68.8	16.5	24.0
1980	88.1	21.6	24.5
2000	168.6	42.9	25.4

[a]Data from the Bureau of Mines (1968, 1971).

The rapid increase in total passenger-miles, far in excess of population rise,

shows a growth from 3.88×10^{11} in 1950 to 9.87×10^{11} in 1970, while the use

of automobiles seemed headed for nearly total saturation of ground transpor-

tation. These trends were accompanied by increasing energy consumption,

reaching 4.88×10^{3} Btu per passenger-mile by 1970, a trend which appeared

barely reversible (see Future II projections in Table 3.3-5) in 1972. The

energy cost of automobile manufacture has been evaluated in a number of

studies (see Section 5.6 for details);[1] there are defined energy costs associ-

ated with emission abatement.[2]

[1]See for example, R. S. Berry and M. F. Fels, "The Energy Cost of Automobiles," Bulletin of the Atomic Scientists 29, 11-17, 58-60, December 1973.
[2]R. K. Prud'homme, "Automobile Emissions Abatement and Fuels Policy,"
American Scientist 62, 191-207 (1974).

Table 3.3-4 Past and projected total petroleum consumption and petroleum consumption for transportation in the U.S.; reproduced from E. Hirst, Energy Consumption for Transportation in the U.S., Report ORNL-NSF-EP-15, Oak Ridge National Laboratory, Oak Ridge, Tennessee, March 1972. [a]

Year	Total transportation energy use, 10^{15} Btu	Percentage of petroleum supply derived from imports [a]	Percentage of total petroleum allocated for transportation use	Percentage of transportation energy derived from petroleum use
1950	13.5	10.6	50.3	77.8
1955	17.5	11.5	52.0	92.0
1960	20.1	17.8	51.7	95.3
1965	23.2	21.4	52.5	95.5
1970	29.6	22.2	53.2	95.5
1980	36.0	--	57.6	96.1
2000	57.6	--	72.3	97.1

[a] Data from the Bureau of Mines (1968, 1971).

Table 3.3-5 Urban passenger traffic and energy consumption in the U.S.; reproduced from E. Hirst, Energy Consumption for Transportation in the U.S., Report ORNL-NSF-EP-15, Oak Ridge National Laboratory, Oak Ridge, Tennessee, March 1972. [a]

Year	Total traffic, 10^9 passenger-miles	Percentage of total passenger-miles			Total energy, 10^{15} Btu	Inverse efficiency, Btu/passenger-mile
		automobiles	buses	walking/ bicycles		
1950	388	89.6	10.4	-	1.81	4,670
1955	466	91.5	8.5	-	2.20	4,730
1960	585	92.6	7.4	-	2.79	4,770
1965	764	94.0	6.0	-	3.69	4,830
1970	987	95.4	4.6	-	4.82	4,880
Future I – Continuation of current trends [b]						
1980	1,410	97	3	-	6.97	4,950
1990	1,830	98	2	-	9.12	4,980
2000	2,250	98.5	1.5	-	11.25	5,000
Future II – Shift to greater energy efficiency						
1980	1,410	91	6	3	6.59	4,680
1990	1,830	89	8	3	8.42	4,600
2000	2,250	87	10	3	10.18	4,520

[a] Data from the Statistical Abstract of the United States (1970) and the Federal Highway Administration (1971).

[b] The transportation energy required for walking/bicycling is not included in this section because these energies are small relative to motor-vehicle energy requirements.

The energy-efficiency of various aircraft is detailed in Table 3.3.6. The entry for the proposed supersonic transport plane (SST) is pessimistic for very large aircraft. We note a progressive decrease in efficiency with new planes until the advent of the large B-747 transport planes.

Table 3.3-6 Energy-efficiency of various aircraft; reproduced from E. Hirst, Energy Consumption for Transportation in the U.S., Report ORNL-NSF-EP-15, Oak Ridge National Laboratory, Oak Ridge, Tennessee, March 1972.[a]

Type of craft	Years introduced	Inverse efficiency, Btu/seat-mile	Speed, mph
DC-3	forties	2,630	150
DC-6	fifties	3,130	270
DC-7	late fifties	3,030	330
Electra	sixties	3,330	400
DC-8	late sixties	4,000	525
B-747	seventies	2,700	575
SST(U.S.)	proposed	6,250	1,200

[a]Data from R. A. Rice, Chapter 9 on "Historial Perspective in Transport System Development," in Advanced Urban Transportation Systems, Carnegie-Mellon University, Pittsburgh, Pennsylvania, 1970.

Significant energy savings may be effected in the automobile-transportation sector by reducing the vehicle weight and lowering the operating speed.[3] If the 1971 car population (5% small cars with weights of 2,000 to 2,250 lb and yielding 21.5 to 24.4 miles/gallon; 10% compacts weighing from 2,500 to 2,750

[3]J. T. Dickinson, "Transportation and Energy Conservation in the Pacific Northwest," Physics Department and Environmental Research Center, Washington State University, Pullman, Washington 99163, February 1974.

lb and yielding 18.5 to 18.9 miles/gallon; 65% standard vehicles weighing

3,000 to 4,000 lb with a performance between 11.3 and 15.3 miles/gallon;

20% large cars weighing between 4,500 and 5,500 lb with a performance be-

tween 8.3 and 9.7 miles/gallon) had been changed to a mix of 50% small cars

and 50% compacts, 24% of the energy used for transportation in the Pacific

Northwest (Washington, Oregon, and Idaho) would have been saved.[3] A 100%-

shift from automobile to urban mass transit would save 20.6% of the total re-

gional transportation energy expended in 1971 at a mass-transit load factor of

20% and would save 34% at a mass-transit load factor of 100%. Replacement of

two-thirds of the automobile trips of 2 miles or less by human-powered modes

saves 1% of the regional transportation energy used for automotive fuel alone;

banning pleasure rides saves 0.4%; elimination of vacation trips to the region

saves 19%; reducing the average speed below a reference speed of 57.3 mph

saves 3.2% at 50 mph, 7.7% at 40 mph, 8.4% at 35 mph, and 9.2% at 30 mph

for passenger cars, while similar speed reductions for pickups and trucks

produce fuel-energy savings that are about 25% smaller.

3.4   Energy-Application Diagrams[1]

Energy sources, forms of application, end uses, and conversion efficien-

cies (in terms of useful and rejected energies) are shown for 1970 in Fig. 3.4-1

and projected to 1985 in Fig. 3.4-2. These figures are self-explanatory.

---

[1]Reproduced from Certain Background Information for Consideration when
   Evaluating the "National Energy Dilemma", Joint Committee on Atomic
   Energy, U.S. Government Printing Office, Washington, D.C., 1973.

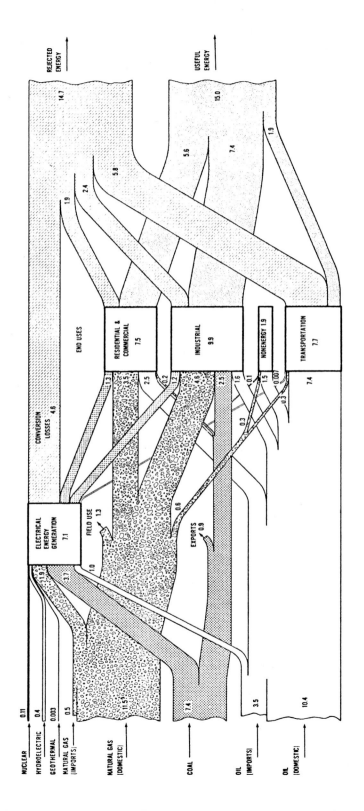

Fig. 3.4-1 The 1970 U.S. energy-flow diagram in units of $(10^6 \text{ bbl/d})_e$; reproduced from Ref. [1].

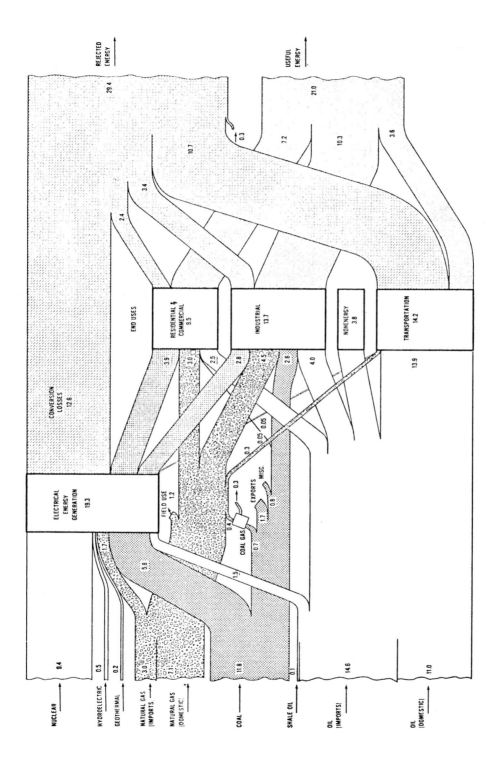

Fig. 3.4-2 The projected 1985 U.S. energy-flow diagram in units of $(10^6 \text{ bbl/d})_e$; reproduced from Ref. [1].

Charts of the type shown in Figs. 3.4-1 and 3.4-2 may be used to show the time evolution of energy-utilization efficiency (Fig. 3.4-3), end uses for energy application (Fig. 3.4-4), forms of use (Fig. 3.4-5), and energy source-type (Fig. 3.4-6). We note an increase in the projected total rejected energy to 1985 (Fig. 3.4-3), disproportionately rapid projected growth for transportation and industrial applications (Fig. 3.4-4), increasingly-rapid application of energy as electricity and in liquid forms (Fig. 3.4-5), and relatively rapid anticipated growth in the use of nuclear power and coal (Fig. 3.4-6).

3.5   <u>Energy Costs in Locomotion and Specific Power Requirements for Speed</u>

The energy costs of swimming, flying, and running have been examined by K. Schmidt-Nielsen.[1] He has prepared correlations between body weight and energy cost (C), which represents the energy consumed per unit mass per unit distance. A composite diagram showing the energy cost for all types of locomotion, as a function of body weight, is given in Ref. [1]. These curves show notably similar slopes. For a given body weight, swimming has a lower energy cost than flying which, in turn, is less costly than running; however, the differences in energy costs for different types of locomotion become smaller for larger body weights.[1]

A. Gold has suggested a simple physical model, on the basis of which it may be shown that the energy cost C varies approximately as the minus 1/3

[1]K. Schmidt-Nielsen, "Locomotion: Energy Cost of Swimming, Flying, and Running," Science <u>177</u>, 222-228 (1972).

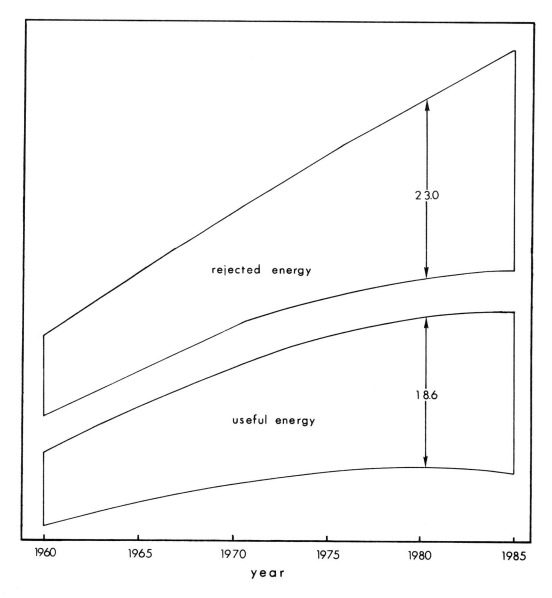

Fig. 3.4-3 Projected efficiency of energy use in units of $(10^6 \text{bbl/d})_e$; reproduced from Ref. [1].

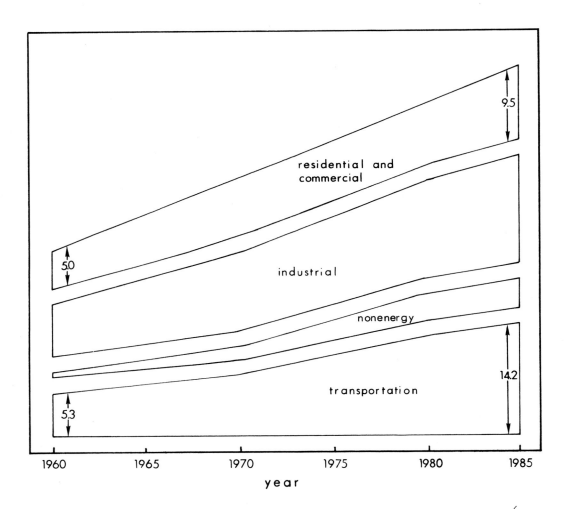

Fig. 3.4-4 Projected end uses for energy applications in units of $(10^6 \text{bbl/d})_e$; reproduced from Ref. [1].

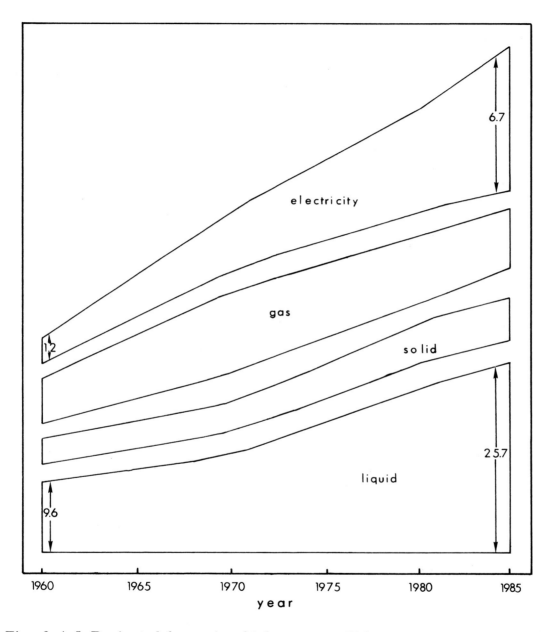

Fig. 3.4-5 Projected forms in which energy will be applied in units of $(10^6 \, bbl/d)_e$; reproduced from Ref. [1].

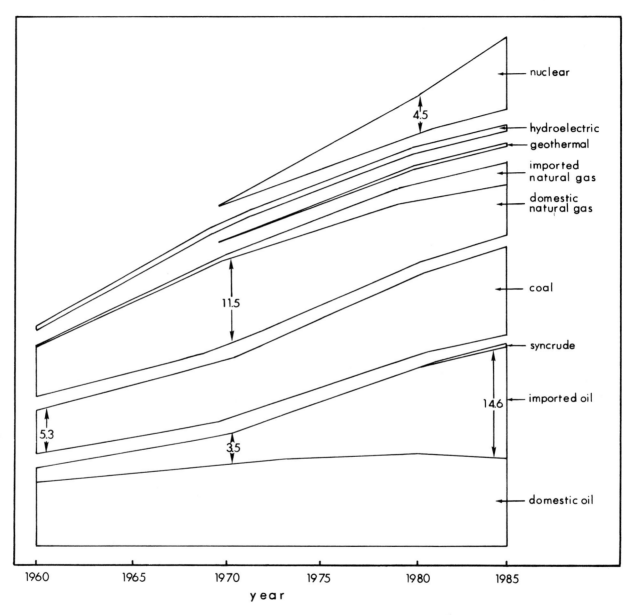

Fig. 3.4-6 Projected energy sources to 1985 in units of $(10^6 \text{bbl/d})_e$; reproduced from Ref. [1].

power of the body weight.[2] Gold's central assumption is the following: the

energy cost per unit mass per "step" is a constant c because a single con-

traction of an animal's propulsive muscle produces a "step". If W is the total

energy required per unit mass for an animal of mass m to go a distance corres-

ponding to N steps, then

$$W/m = cN = cd/\ell ,$$

where the number of steps $N = d/\ell$ if d is the total physical distance traversed

and ℓ equals the characteristic length per step. Here $c = W/mN$ is the energy

cost per unit mass per step (in cal/g).

The energy cost per unit mass per unit length (in cal/g-km) is $C = c/\ell$.

Also $m = k \ell^3$, where k is a constant, because the mass of an animal is

proportional to the cube of its characteristic length. Combining the two pre-

ceding relations leads immediately to the result

$$C = c/\ell = ck^{1/3} m^{-1/3} . \qquad (3.5\text{-}1)$$

Using the data of Ref. [1], Gold arrives at the following estimates (with

$k \approx 1$): $c = 3 \times 10^{-4}$ cal/g for running, 1×10^{-4} cal/g for flying, 4×10^{-5} cal/g

for swimming. The correlation given in Ref. [1] involves the energy per step as

a function of body weight and does not contain speed as an essential parameter.

Some justification for this type of approximation is given by Schmidt-Nielsen.[1]

---

[2]A. Gold, "Energy Expenditure in Animal Locomotion," Science 181, 275-276
    (1973).

A correlation between specific power (in horsepower per ton) and maximum speed (in mph) is reproduced in Fig. 3.5-1 from the work of Gabrielli and von Kármán.[3] Reference to Fig. 3.5-1 provides dramatic evidence of the increasing <u>power requirements</u> with increasing speed, from the horse to jet fighters and bombers. For fixed values of power applied to given times of locomotion, the energy and power requirements are, of course, simply proportional to each other.

The most remarkable feature of Fig. 3.5-1 is the apparent existence of a lower-bound envelope for the specific power as a function of speed. This lower bound corresponds to the limiting line in Fig. 3.5-1. All propulsion systems included in the compilation have higher specific-power requirements than correspond to this limiting line for given speeds. If the limiting line of Gabrielli and von Kármán identifies the lowest achievable specific power for a given maximum speed, then a location significantly above this line implies inefficient application of available specific power insofar as reaching maximum speed is concerned. Pedestrians, horses, destroyers, helicopters, and racecars are examples of inefficient specific-power users in this sense. Merchant ships travelling at speeds in excess of 25 mph become less efficient users of specific power for the production of speed than they are at lower speeds. A similar remark applies to an autorail above and below 80 mph, to a piston-powered commercial plane below 400 mph, to the bomber below about 500 mph, etc.

---

[3] G. Gabrielli and T. von Kármán, "What Price Speed?", Mechanical Engineering <u>72</u>, 775-781 (1950).

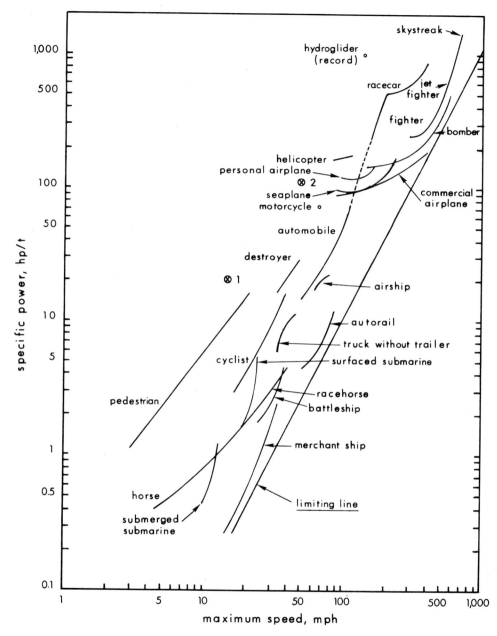

Fig. 3.5-1 Specific power, defined as the ratio of the maximum power available to the gross weight of the vehicle, plotted as a function of maximum speed. Reproduced from Ref. [3]. See the text for definitions of the points (⊗) labeled 1 and 2. Copyright by the American Society of Mechanical Engineers.

It is apparent that the correlation by Schmidt-Nielsen[1] and Gold[2] between body weight or characteristic length and energy cost C (in cal/g-km) does not relate directly to the correlation by Gabrielli and von Kármán[3] between specific power (in horsepower per ton, hp/t) and maximum speed V_{max} (in mph, mile/h) for pedestrians, horses, cyclists, and a wide variety of flying, ground-moving, surface-swimming, and underwater vehicles. The limiting line of Gabrielli and von Kármán corresponds, approximately, to the correlation

$$\text{specific power in hp/t} = 10^{-3}(V_{max} \text{ in mi/h})^2.$$

It is easily seen that the product 2.27 × (C in cal/g-km) × (V_{max} in mi/h) is, approximately, the specific power in hp/t.

If we use Schmidt-Nielsen's value of C = 0.6 cal/g-km for a body weight of 72.5 kg as corresponding to a man, we find a specific power of 1.36 × (V_{max} in mi/h) in hp/ton; at 3 mi/h, the specific power is about 4 hp/ton, as compared with the earlier estimate[3] of about 1.3 hp/t for the specified value of V_{max}; similarly, at 15 mi/h (corresponding to the 4-minute mile), the specific power is just over 20 hp/t (see point ⊗1 in Fig. 3.5-1), as compared with the earlier value of about 10 hp/t.

A flying animal with C = 1 cal/g-km (corresponding to a body weight of about 1kg) at 50 mi/h falls on the low-performance extrapolation of the specific power vs. V_{max}-curve for personal airplanes (see point ⊗ 2 in Fig. 3.5-1) of Gabrielli and von Kármán.

Gold's correlation between energy cost and (body weight)$^{-1/3}$ is seen to lead to the limiting line of Gabrielli and von Kármán only when (body weight)$^{-1/3}$ $\propto V_{max}$ for a given class of locomotion.

In view of the wide range of translational speeds accessible to animals and transportation devices of fixed weight, there appear to be good reasons for seeking correlations between specific power and maximum speed.

CHAPTER 4

THE ECONOMIC VALUE OF ENERGY UTILIZATION; PRICES FOR ENERGY RESOURCES; INVESTMENT COSTS; ELECTRICITY COSTS

Among the most difficult aspects of energy-utilization evaluation are economic-impact assessment, price forecasting, and investment-requirement predictions. We present in this Chapter 4 some facts and views on these elusive topics, as well as some historical data relating to electricity costs.

4.1 The Economic Value of Energy Use

On the basis of the numerical values listed in Table 1.2-2, we may conclude that the energy equivalent of 10^6 bbl/d of petroleum is 5.82×10^{12} Btu/d or 2.1×10^{15} Btu/y. Using a total energy-consumption rate for the U.S. in 1970 of 7×10^{16} Btu/y, we find that the 1970 energy-consumption rate was 33.2×10^6 bbl/d equivalent.* The 1970 value of the GNP** in the U.S. was about $\$900 \times 10^9$. If we assume that GNP in the U.S. is a linear function of energy utilization, then we may conclude that the GNP-equivalent of 10^6(bbl/d) equivalent of petroleum was $\$900 \times 10^9/33.2 \simeq \$27 \times 10^9/10^6$ (bbl/d) equivalent. Since the population of the U.S. changes rapidly with time, a more meaningful estimate involves the relation between income per person per year

---

* The terms total and thermal energy consumption are, of course, equivalent. For convenience, the subscript t is deleted where the meaning is clear from the context.

** Economic-value estimates such as GNP are subject to considerable uncertainties and provide, at best, only a statistical average indication of economic performance or well-being.

and per capita energy utilization. Proceeding on the assumption that the

postulated linearity continues to hold, we note that the 1970 U.S. population

was about 200×10^6 people and that, therefore [with (bbl/d) equivalent re-

placed by $(bbl/d)_e$],

$$\text{income/py} = (\$27 \times 10^9 / 200 \times 10^6) / 10^6 (bbl/d)_e$$

$$= \$135 / (10^6 \ bbl/d)_e \text{ in } 1970. \qquad (4.1\text{-}1)$$

There are other procedures for evaluating the relation between energy

consumption and personal income that have been used.

The 1970 income per person per year, or the GNP in \$/py, was about

$\$900 \times 10^9 / 200 \times 10^6$ py = \$4,500/py. The 1970 per capita energy consumption

was $(33.2 \times 10^6 \ bbl/d)_e \times (365 \ d/y) \times (5.82 \times 10^6 \ Btu/bbl) \div (200 \times 10^6 p) = 352$ in

$(10^6 \ Btu/py)_e$. Figure 4.1-1 shows a 1961 correlation between GNP in \$/py

with per capita energy consumption in $(10^6 \ Btu/py)_e$ for 44 different countries.

The personal U.S. energy consumption in 1970 may be expressed as $(33.2 \times$

$10^6 \ bbl/d)_e \times (365 \ d/y) \times (5.82 \times 10^6 \ Btu/bbl) \times (1 \ mt \ of \ coal/ \ 27.8 \times 10^6 \ Btu)$

$\times (10^3 \ kg \ of \ coal/mt \ of \ coal) \div (200 \times 10^6 p) = 12.7 \times 10^3 \ (kg \ of \ coal/py)_e$. A

1968 correlation of GNP in \$/py with energy consumption in $(kg \ of \ coal/py)_e$

is shown in Fig. 4.1-2 for 35 different countries.

We may also express the 1970 per capita energy consumption as $(33.2$

$\times 10^6 \ bbl/d)_e \times (365 \ d/y) \times (5.82 \times 10^6 \ Btu/bbl) \times (2.78 \times 10^{-7} \ kwh/0.949 \times$

$10^{-3} \ Btu) \div (200 \times 10^6 p) = 104$ in units of $(10^3 \ kwh/py)_e$. A correlation between

GNP in \$/py and per capita energy consumption in $(10^3 \ kwh/py)_e$ is shown in

Fig. 4.1-3 for five countries for the years 1958, 1961, 1963, 1966, and 1969.

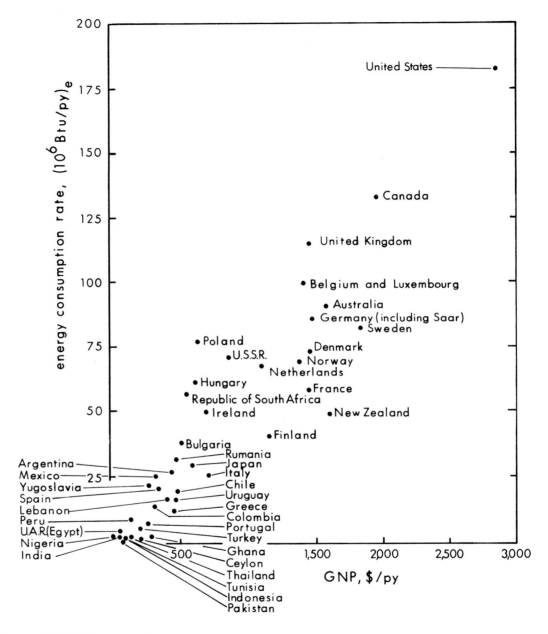

Fig. 4.1-1 Personal energy use and per capita Gross National Product for
           selected countries: 1961; reproduced from <u>Energy R and D and
           National Progress</u>, U.S. Government Printing Office, Washington
           D.C., 1964.

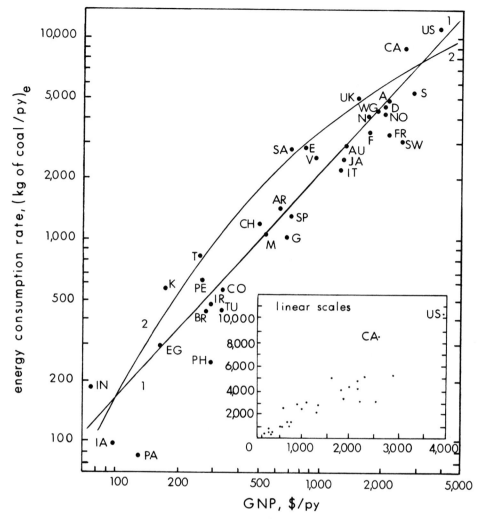

Fig. 4.1-2 The relation between yearly per capita income ($/py) in 1968 and
energy consumption in (kg of coal/py)$_e$ for different countries; reproduced from A. J. Surrey and A. J. Bromley, "Energy Resources," Futures 5, 90-107 (1973). The symbols in Fig. 4.1-2
identify the following countries:

A	= Australia	EG	= Egypt	K	= S. Korea	SP	= Spain
AR	= Argentina	F	= Finland	M	= Mexico	SW	= Switzerland
AU	= Austria	FR	= France	N	= Netherlands	T	= Taiwan
BR	= Brazil	G	= Greece	NO	= Norway	TU	= Turkey
CA	= Canada	IA	= Indonesia	PA	= Pakistan	UK	= United Kingdom
CH	= Chile	IN	= India	PE	= Peru	US	= United States
CO	= Colombia	IR	= Iran	PH	= Philippines	V	= Venezuela
D	= Denmark	IT	= Italy	S	= Sweden	WG	= W. Germany
E	= Eire	JA	= Japan	SA	= South Africa		

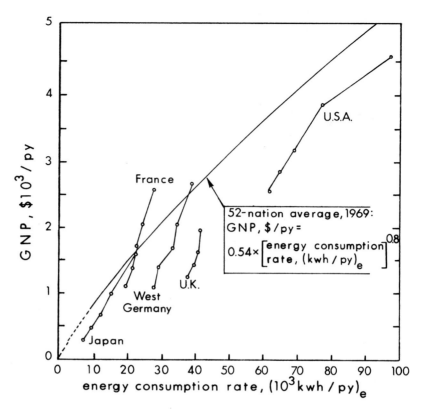

Fig. 4.1-3 World per capita GNP in 1969, in relation to energy consumption (heavy line) and a similar relation over an eleven-year period for Japan, France, West Germany, U.K., and the U.S. Encircled points represent data for 1958, 1961, 1963, 1966, and 1969, in sequence from the lower left, for five nations. Reproduced from H. C. Hottel, "Combustion and Energy for the Future," Fourteenth Symposium (International) on Combustion, p. 6, The Combustion Institute, Pittsburgh, Pa., 1973.

Study of Figs. 4.1-1 to 4.1-3 leads to the following conclusions:

a. Although personal income generally tends to increase with energy consumption, these two parameters are not simply related for different countries, nor does the same proportion hold for a given country in different years.

b. All of the correlations show that, during a given year, very large variations in energy consumption are compatible with the same personal income in different countries. For example (see Fig. 4.1-1), in 1961, a

GNP of about \$1,500/py required the use of $50 \times (10^6 Btu/py)_e$ for New Zealand

and, in the same energy-consumption units, about 60 in France, about 70 in

Denmark, about 93 in Australia, and about 115 in the United Kingdom; con-

versely, Poland had a somewhat higher energy consumption than Denmark

and yet achieved less than one-half of the per capita GNP of Denmark. In 1968

(see Fig. 4.1-2), Switzerland achieved about the same GNP in \$/py as

Canada while using about 3,000 $(kg of coal/py)_e$ as compared with Canada's

consumption of nearly 9,000 $(kg of coal/py)_e$; West Germany achieved a

higher per capita GNP at lower personal energy consumption than the United

Kingdom; Greece had nearly the same per capita income as Argentina while

using 40% less energy per person.

    c. With some imagination, one can draw a correlation curve for some

countries that shows a rising rate of change of personal energy consumption

with personal GNP (see curve 1 in Fig. 4.1-2) and another showing a falling

rate of change of personal energy consumption with rising personal GNP

(see curve 2 in Fig. 4.1-2).

    d. The growth rates of personal GNP with per capita energy consump-

tion may be greatly different in different countries (see Fig. 4.1-3). For

example, between 1958 and 1969, France achieved an average increase in

personal GNP with increased per capita energy consumption of about $(\$170/py)/(10^3 kwh/py)_e$, while the corresponding U.S. incremental ratio was only

about $(\$57/py)/(10^3 kwh/py)_e$. This difference is clearly related to the rapid development of relatively non-productive personal-service activities in the

United States with high personal energy consumption and low personal GNP

contribution. A decrease in the rate of rise of personal GNP with growth in

per capita energy consumption (see, especially, the curve for the U.S. in

Fig. 4.1-3) may be a sign not only of advanced technological development but

also of conspicuously-wasteful energy use such as excessive space heating,

air conditioning, and lighting, coupled with relatively inefficiently-functioning

consumer items such as cars, refrigerators, ovens, etc.

The data shown in Figs. 4.1-1 to 4.1-3 suggest that we need to develop

optimal strategies for maximizing the growth rate of personal GNP while

minimizing the growth rate of personal energy utilization. The recognition

of this need is not in conflict with the obvious result that a positive slope of the

personal-GNP divided by the personal-energy consumption curves vs. time shows

that energy is being used progressively more efficiently for income production.

This last idea is exemplified by the plots of per capita energy consumption,

per capita GNP, and the ratio of per capita GNP to per capita energy con-

sumption for the U.S., as functions of time (for the period 1870 to 1970)

given in Fig. 4.1-4. Optimal GNP growth per unit energy consumption is

a very sensitive function of the type of industrial activity involved. For ex-

ample, a perfume-wine-watch industry will necessarily appear more favorable

than a steel-car-service economy.

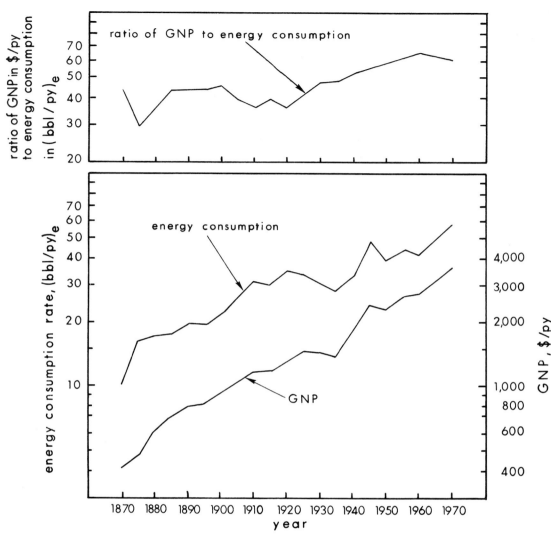

Fig. 4.1-4 Per capita GNP and energy consumption of the U.S. and their ratio as functions of time for the years 1870 to 1970; based on data of the U.S. Department of Commerce and the U.S. Department of Labor. The per capita GNP is given in constant (1958) dollars. The data are plotted for five-year intervals.

4.2 Costs of Natural Gas and Crude Oil*

In the publication FPC (FPC stands for Federal Power Commission) News,

---

* Energy costs have been highly time-dependent in recent years. This fact should be kept in mind. We have 1970, 1971, 1972, 1973, and 1974 estimates, which differ greatly, even after correction for inflation.

volume 6, number 43, for the week ended October 26, 1973, we find the following entries:

i. "The Federal Power Commission today ruled that a proposal by a natural-gas producer, affiliated with a distributor, to buy gas at 62.2 cents per thousand cubic feet under the Commission's optional pricing procedures for resale to its intrastate distributor parent was not in the public interest."

ii. "The average price received by the major interstate pipelines for natural gas sold for resale was 50.75 cents per thousand cubic feet in August 1973 compared to the August 1972 average of 47.24 cents."

iii. RATE SCHEDULE FILINGS BY INDEPENDENT PRODUCERS OF NATURAL GAS FOR CHANGES IN RATE LEVELS.

Line no.	Date of filing	Seller	Rate schedule no.	Buyer	FPC pricing area	Rates (cents per Mcf)[a] present	proposed	Pressure base (psia)	Estimated annual amount of increase or (decrease) in dollars
1	10-15-73	Amoco Production Company	494	El Paso National Gas Company	Permian Basin Texas RRD#8	22.21000	31.12000	14,650	10,157
3	10-15-73	Champlin Petroleum Company	72	Panhandle Eastern Pipe Line Company	Hugoton Anad'Ko. OKLA, Panhandle	14.14000	14.46000	14,650	77
14	10-15-73	Sohio Petroleum Company	99	West Lake Natural Gasoline Company	Permian Basin Texas RRD#7B	09.50000	15.00000	14,650	165

[a] $Mcf = 10^3$ SCF.

A glance at the preceding data shows a rather remarkable lack of uniformity between rate schedules and no reasonable relation between scheduled delivery prices and current costs. It is not difficult to understand how a discrepancy between supply and demand can develop when current contract costs exceed allowable rate schedules by factors of 2.3 to 5.4.

Fossil-fuel price predictions are a hazardous intellectual activity. For example, in a November 1972 publication, the Stanford Research Institute[1] published the data shown in Tables 4.2-1 and 4.2-2. According to these estimates, the cost of a barrel of crude oil delivered to the U.S. was not expected to reach $6.00 until about 1976 or 1977. However, late 1973 contract figures already exceeded $10.00/bbl. The data in Tables 4.2-1 and 4.2-2 are interesting only insofar as they show the applicable pricing and cost distribution for 1969 and 1971 and provide some idea on expected price differentials in different regions as of this date.

Table 4.2-1 Late 1972 crude-oil cost estimates per bbl; reproduced from Ref. [1].

	1969	1971	1975	1980
host country take	$0.80	$1.30	$2.15	$3.25
oil company production revenue	0.50	0.50	0.50	0.75
transportation	0.90	1.25	1.20	1.25
tariff, insurance port charges	0.15	0.15	0.25	0.25
delivered price of crude	2.35	3.20	4.10	5.50
refining costs	1.10	1.15	1.30	1.50
average price, all products, ex-refinery	3.45	4.35	5.40	7.00

Table 4.2-2 Late 1972 crude-oil cost estimates per bbl; reproduced from Ref. [1].

	1975	1980
Delivered price of crude oil per bbl		
U.S.	$4.10	$5.50
Western Europe	4.00	5.40
Japan	3.60	5.00
Average product price per bbl, ex-refinery		
U.S.	$5.40	$7.00
Western Europe	5.00	6.60
Japan	4.55	6.15

[1] S. H. Clark, World Energy, Stanford Research Institute, Menlo Park, California, 1972.

Another late 1972 price prognosis is shown in Table 4.2-3. Even the

post-1970 estimates for the relative costs of Middle East crude, low-sulfur

fuel oil (0.3 weight percent), and naphtha may be grossly in error. In partic-

ular, the energy cost for SNG made from naphtha may soon be no higher than

the energy cost of low-sulfur fuel oil made from Middle Eastern crude.

Table 4.2-3 Values assumed for Middle East crude oil and derivative fuels
at the U.S. East Coast (in 1972 dollars) per bbl. Reproduced
from S. Field, SNG and the 1985 U.S. Energy Picture, Stanford Research Institute, Menlo Park, California, 1972.

| Year | Imported Middle East crude oil, $/bbl | 0.3 weight percent sulfur no. 4 fuel oil[a] | | Naphtha | | SNG[b] from naphtha, $\text{¢}/10^6$ Btu |
		$/bbl	$\text{¢}/10^6$ Btu	$\text{¢}/\text{gal}$	$/bbl	
1970	3.00	4.40	71	9.7	4.07	106
1975	3.50	4.85	78	11.4	4.79	121
1980	4.00	5.30	86	13.0	5.46	135
1985	5.00	6.16	100	16.2	6.80	163
1990	6.00	7.05	114	19.5	8.19	193

[a]The processing of the high-sulfur fuel oil into 0.3 weight percent sulfur fuel
oil is expected to result in substantial "viscosity give-away" and to cause
no. 6 fuel oil to become no. 4 fuel oil. The gross heating value is assumed
to be 6.18×10^6 Btu/bbl.

[b]Calculated on the assumption that SNG is manufactured by a regulated utility
company.

The National Petroleum Council[2] used its (relatively low) estimates

for imported crude-oil prices in order to determine the long-term implica-

tions on the U.S. balance of trade. The numerical values (which should

be roughly doubled in view of prevailing prices in late 1973) are listed for

[2]U.S. Energy Outlook, National Petroleum Council, Washington, D.C., 1972.

1975 and 1985 in Table 4.2-4 with reference to four possible strategies (IV: extrapolation of current, i.e., late 1972 trends; I: low-import, high-domestic development option; II and III: intermediate cases; see Section 4.3 for discussion of the investment-cost implications of these options). Even at late 1972 prices, it was apparent that continuation of existing trends (option IV) was not a viable supposition. It is interesting to observe that oil exports were estimated to remain constant between 1975 and 1985 while oil imports (under option IV) nearly doubled. The entries in Table 4.2-4 can be simply scaled to newer price estimates by noting that trade deficits increase with the amounts and prices paid for foreign energy sources.

It is, of course, expected that an increase of prices will reduce the total energy demand, as will also be the case for a decrease of economic and population growth. The interplay between these factors is indicated in Fig. 4.2-1 for a particular set of postulated values for price increases and reduced growth rates. The most severe reduction considered in this study is seen to correspond to a savings of about 30% by the year 2000 in total energy expenditure.

The growth rates shown in curves A, B, and C of Fig. 4.2-1 refer to the following average annual percentage growth rates for population and GNP, respectively: curve A -- 1.1%, 3.1%; curves B and C -- steady decline from the early 1972 rate to zero in the second quarter of the next century, slow decrease to 2.5% by the end of the century. In addition, curve C is based on the assumption of a 50% increase in the cost of both electric power and fossil fuels by the year 2000, both attributable to environmental control expenditures and fuel scarcities.

Table 4.2-4 National Petroleum Council (December 1972) trade deficit estimates in 10^9 for energy fuels; reproduced from Ref. [2]. The
dollar costs of fuel refer to about \$4.15/bbl and \$0.417/10^3 SCF
in 1975 or \$0.831/10^3 SCF in 1985.

Balance of trade deficits* in energy fuels, 1975				
	Case I	Case II	Case III	Case IV
oil imports[a] (delivered)	10.9	11.1	12.9	14.6
natural gas and LNG imports	0.5	0.5	0.5	0.5
total energy fuels imports	11.4	11.6	13.4	15.1
oil exports	(0.4)	(0.4)	(0.4)	(0.4)
steam coal exports	(0.2)	(0.2)	(0.2)	(0.2)
metallurgical coal exports	(1.3)	(1.3)	(1.3)	(1.3)
total energy fuels exports	(1.9)	(1.9)	(1.9)	(1.9)
total energy fuel deficit	9.5	9.7	11.5	13.2

Balance of trade deficits* in energy fuels, 1985				
	Case I	Case II	Case III	Case IV
oil imports[a] (delivered)	5.4	13.1	20.4	29.1
natural-gas and LNG imports	4.9	5.0	5.3	5.4
total energy fuels imports	10.3	18.1	25.7	34.5
oil exports	(0.4)	(0.4)	(0.4)	(0.4)
steam coal exports	(0.3)	(0.3)	(0.3)	(0.3)
metallurgical coal exports	(2.1)	(2.1)	(2.1)	(2.1)
total energy fuels exports	(2.8)	(2.8)	(2.8)	(2.8)
total energy fuel deficit	7.5	15.3	22.9	31.7

*Case I refers to high domestic supply resulting from intensive exploration;
Cases II and III are, respectively, progressively lower intermediate supply
cases associated with intermediate increases in domestic exploration; Case
IV refers to continuation of exploration prevailing during the sixties and seventies, prior to December 1972. The cost bases used for both oil and LNG
are clearly too low.

[a]Including synthetic gas feedstocks.

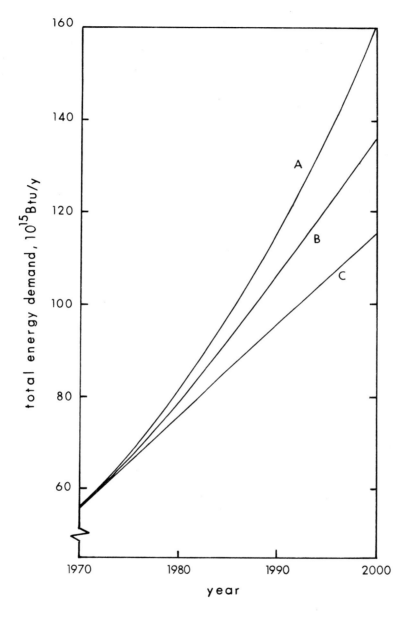

Fig. 4.2-1 Alternative estimates for total energy demand. The curves
labeled A, B, and C correspond, respectively, to an extrapolated
National Petroleum Council estimate, a reduced economic and
population growth scenario, and conditions of reduced growth and
energy-price increases. Reproduced from the Cornell Workshop
on Energy and the Environment, U.S. Government Printing Office,
Washington, D.C., 1972.

4.3   Capital Investment Costs

Although we shall generally try to assess technological development costs in connection with a particular technological-implementation program, it is of interest at this time to emphasize the enormity of the development programs associated with each of the options I to IV listed in Table 4.2-4. Some of the NPC[1] results are summarized in Table 4.3-1 for the cumulative time period 1971-1985. We note that the average yearly expenditures for the 15-year period were estimated to fall between 30×10^9 (option IV) and 36.5×10^9 (option I) in 1970 U.S. dollars. In option I there is greatly expanded domestic exploration and production of oil and gas, increased emphasis on the manufacture of synthetic gas and oil from coal, and expansion of nuclear power-plant development.

Capital investment costs for oil production vary greatly with the region and technology involved. This fact is illustrated by the data summarized in Table 4.3-2.

4.4   The Cost of Electricity

Figure 4.4-1 shows a summary of residential electricity costs, corrected for inflationary losses in currency values, from 1950 to 1973. In terms of 1967 U.S. $ values, the costs in $\cent/kwh_e$ decreased approximately 35 percent by 1973. This fact attests to the economic advantages associated with improved technology and to the economies resulting from increasingly large-scale use of a commodity. It is highly doubtful that similarly successful reductions are

---

[1]Ref. [2] in Section 4.2.

Table 4.3-1 A 1972 estimate of cumulative capital requirements for the U.S. energy industries from 1971 to 1985, in billions of dollars; reproduced from Ref. [1].

	Case I	Case IV
oil and gas		
exploration and production	171.8	88.0
oil pipelines	7.5	7.5
gas transportation	56.6	29.5
refining[a]	19.0	38.0
tankers, terminals	2.0	23.0
subtotal	256.9	186.0
synthetics		
from petroleum liquids	5.0	5.0
from coal (plants only)	12.0	1.7
from shale (mines and plants)	4.0	0.5
subtotal	21.0	7.2
coal[b]		
production	14.3	9.4
transportation	6.0	6.0
subtotal	20.3	15.4
nuclear		
production, processing, and enriching	13.1	6.7
total all fuels	311.3	215.3
electricity generation and transmission[c]	235.0	235.0
water requirements	1.1	0.7
total energy industries	547.4	451.0

[a]Based on maximum U.S. requirements, some of which may be spent outside of the U.S.

[b]Cases I and IV include capital requirements involved in using coal for synthetic fuels.

[c]See Ref. [1] for the conditions under which these numbers apply.

Table 4.3-2 A 1974 estimate of capital costs for oil production in different regions and for different technologies; based on data from A. Lovins, "World Energy Strategies", Bulletin of the Atomic Scientists 30, 14–32, May 1974. Reprinted by permission of Science and Public Affairs, Copyright 1974 by the Educational Foundation for Nuclear Science.

Source of energy	Capital cost, $/bbl-day
Persian Gulf	100 – 300
Nigeria	600 – 800
Venezuela, Far East, Australia	700 – 1,000
North Sea	2,500 – 4,000
Large deep-sea reservoirs	3,000
U.S. reservoirs on the North Slope of Alaska	3,000 – 4,000
Tar sands of Alberta, Canada	4,000 – 8,000
High-grade oil shales	4,500 – 9,000
Gas synthesized from coal	5,500 – 8,000
Liquid fuel synthesized from coal	6,000 – 9,500
Liquified natural gas delivered to U.S.	6,000 – 10,000

Note: The last four entries refer to undeveloped technologies and the cost estimates given in the table are therefore subject to large potential revisions.

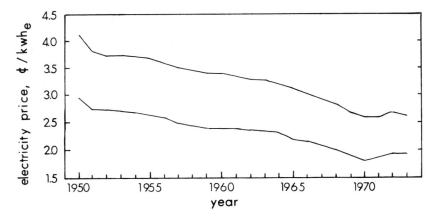

Fig. 4.4-1 Weighted average residential electricity prices for cities of 2,500 population or more. The upper curve corresponds to a monthly use of 250 kwh$_e$ while the lower curve represents a monthly use of 500 kwh$_e$. The 250 kwh$_e$/month use rate includes lighting, small appliance use, refrigeration, and cooking. The 500 kwh$_e$/month use rate includes water heating in addition to those uses specified for the 250 kwh$_e$/month use rate. The prices are given in constant 1967 dollars. Based on data from the U.S. Federal Power Commission and the U.S. Department of Commerce.

achievable in future years, except possibly through the creation of an entirely new large-scale technology such as electricity production using nuclear-fusion energy.

As fuel prices rise, the cost of electricity production tends to rise as well. However, the relation between fuel-input costs and electricity-output costs is not linear and depends, to a large extent, on the technology involved in energy conversion. We show in Table 4.4-1 an estimate for the incremental cost of electricity production in water-moderated fission reactors with increasing cost of U_3O_8. The electricity cost is expressed in the units of mills/kwh$_e$ = 10^{-3} \$/kwh$_e$ = 10^{-1} ¢/kwh$_e$.

A more explicit discussion of the effect of fuel costs on electricity costs is given in the following Sections 4.5 and 4.6 for all types of fuels.

Table 4.4-1 The effect of uranium price on the cost of electricity (the 1972 price was \$8/lb); reproduced from <u>Potential Nuclear Power Growth Patterns,</u> U.S. Atomic Energy Commission, WASH 1098, Washington, D.C., 1970. Reported by M. Benedict in "Electric Power from Nuclear Fission, "Bulletin of the Atomic Scientists <u>27,</u> 8-16, September 1971. Reprinted by permission of Science and Public Affairs. Copyright 1971 by the Educational Foundation for Nuclear Science.

Price in \$/lb of U_3O_8	Increase in electricity cost due to higher-priced uranium, mills/kwh$_e$
8	0.0
10	0.1
15	0.4
30	1.3
50	2.5
100	5.5

4.5 Overview of Electrical-Energy Costs Using Different Technologies

A 1973 version[1] of estimated installation costs in \$/kw$_e$ for electricity-generation plants is shown in Fig. 4.5-1. Established technologies are described by filled-in rectangles while new technologies are identified by open rectangles. The total electrical-energy cost per kwh$_e$ is the sum of the plant and fuel costs per kwh$_e$.

The plant cost per kwh$_e$ is related to the power-installation cost per kw$_e$ as follows:

$$\text{plant cost/kwh}_e = \frac{\text{(percentage per y of installation cost charged as fixed cost)}}{\text{(average yearly percentage load factor)}} \times \frac{\text{(installation cost/kw}_e)}{(8.76 \times 10^3 \text{ h/y})}.$$

[1] J. H. Anderson, "Statement on Energy Research Policy to the Senate Committee on Interior and Insular Affairs," July 16, 1973; reprinted by Sea Solar Power, Inc., 1615 Hillock Lane, York, Pa., 17403.

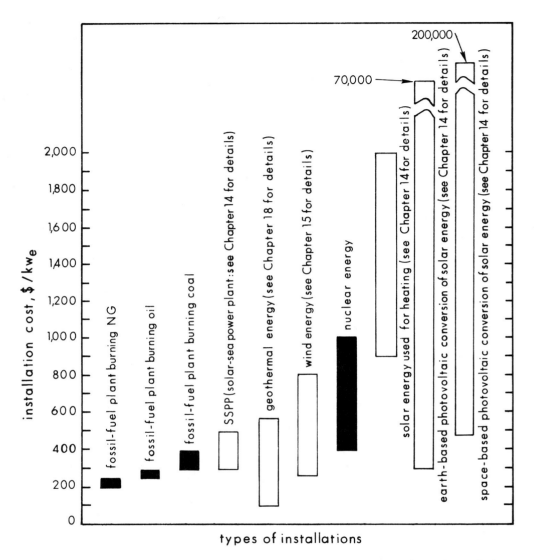

Fig. 4.5-1 Anderson's (1973) map of installation costs for electricity-generation plants. Filled-in rectangles represent established technologies while open rectangles identify developing technologies.
Mid-1974 costs for coal-fired power plants were about $400/$kw_e$
while quotations for conventional nuclear power plants were
about $800/$kw_e$. Reproduced with modifications from Ref. [1].

Fixed costs are computed by the utility companies at percentages varying from about 12% to 18%, with 15% representing a reasonable average value. Average yearly load factors for established technologies range from as low as 30% (for gas turbines used in peak-shaving) to about 75% for conventional fossil-fuel plants.

The fuel cost/kwh_e may be calculated from the following convenient relation:

$$\text{fuel cost/kwh}_e = \frac{[1 \times 10^6 \text{ Btu}/(2.78 \times 10^2/0.949)\text{kwh}_e]}{(\text{fractional fuel-utilization efficiency})} \times \left(\frac{\text{fuel cost}}{1 \times 10^6 \text{ Btu}}\right) .$$

In a diagram of electrical-energy cost as a function of percentage load factor, we may plot diagonal lines of constant (plant cost)/kwh_e. This parameter varies inversely with the load factor. Anderson's 1973 map of electrical-energy costs per kwh_e is shown in Fig. 4.5-2. Included in Fig. 4.5-2 is an estimate of about $0.34/kwh for a draft horse at 22.8% load factor for a horse yielding one horsepower, 8 hours per day, 250 days per year (1,490 kwh/y); the capital cost of the horse is taken as $300 and its "fuel cost" (food) is $1.25/day. It should be noted that the kwh/y of horse power is not really convertible into kwh_e/y.

4.6   Electricity Cost Calculations[1]

As an illustration of costing procedures in electricity generation, we consider the analysis of Anderson,[1] which refers to 1970 investments and charges. By mid-1974, these estimates were too low by perhaps 20 to 90%,

---

[1]R. T. Anderson, "Simplify Power-Plant Cost Calculations," Power 114, 39-41, July 1970.

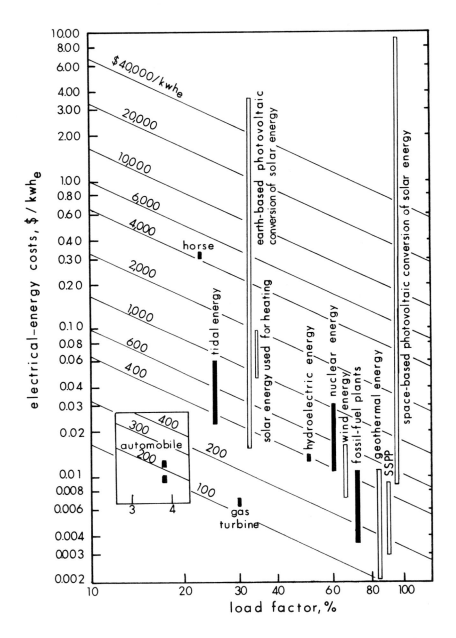

Fig. 4.5-2 Anderson's (1973) map of electrical-energy costs for different
energy sources as a function of operating load factor. The diagonal lines represent constant plant costs in $/kwh$_e$. Established
technologies are represented by filled-in rectangles while open
rectangles identify developing technologies. The entry for the
horse refers to kwh$_t$ and is not located on the proper diagonal line
since the "equivalent plant cost", for an eight-year working life
of the horse, is only about ($300/8y)/(1,490 \text{ kwh}_t/y) = \$0.025/\text{kwh}_t$.
Reproduced from Ref. [1].

depending on the technology involved. With capital construction costs changing rapidly, especially for new technologies, proper updating of the following
evaluation must be deferred for some time.

A.   Capital Costs and Fixed Charges

Curves showing capital costs and fixed charges are readily constructed
as follows.

With the installed plant cost in $/kw$_e$ treated as a variable parameter,
the installed capital cost is obtained by multiplying the installed plant cost
in $/kw$_e$ by the electricity-generating capacity expressed in kw$_e$. Thus at
$160/kw$_e$, the installed plant cost for an 800-Mw$_e$ plant is $160 \times 800 \times 10^3$ =
128×10^6. The curves in Fig. 4.6-1 are easily extended to include 1973
and later plant costs between $260/kw$_e$ and $450/kw$_e$. During 1970, the oil-
and gas-burning stations cost somewhat more than $120/kw$_e$ up to capacities
of about 700 Mw$_e$ and then decreased in cost per kw$_e$; the corresponding values
were about $190/kw$_e$ and $240/kw$_e$ for coal and nuclear plants, respectively
(see Fig. 4.6-1).

The right-hand lines in Fig. 4.6-1 show data for annual fixed costs corresponding to variable percentages of fixed charges. For example, at
annual fixed charges of 13.5% (typical for privately-owned utilities), the
128×10^6 installation requires an annual fixed expenditure of 17.3×10^6/y
(see Fig. 4.6-1).

B.   Fuel and Other Costs

For a 33% thermal- to electric-energy conversion efficiency and a

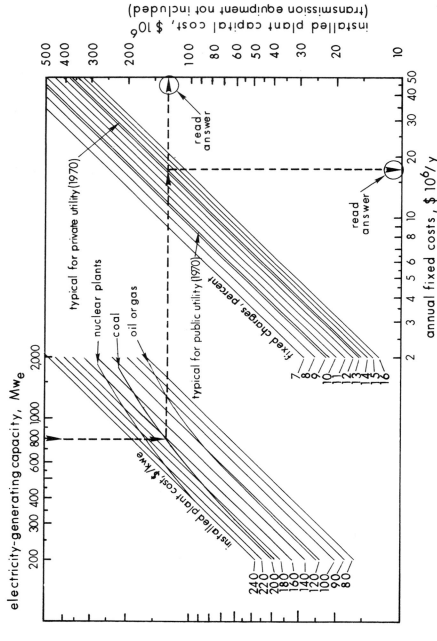

Fig. 4.6-1 Installed and fixed charges for power plants as a function of electricity-generating capacity; reproduced from Ref. [1]. Publicly-owned utilities have lower fixed charges because they are exempt from the payment of State income taxes. Reprinted with permission from Power, July 1970.

90% operating factor (plant factor), an 800-Mw$_e$ station requires 3 × 800 × 0.90 Mwy = 2,160 Mwy of thermal energy. At 27.8 × 10^6 Btu/mt (= 25.2 × 10^6 Btu/t), the annual coal requirement becomes (2,160 Mwy) × (10^{18} Btu/ 3.35 × 10^7 Mwy) × (1t/25.2 × 10^6 Btu) = 2.57 × 10^6 t/y of coal. For a 38% thermal- to electric-energy conversion efficiency and a 75% plant factor, the annual coal requirement is reduced to just under 2 × 10^6 t/y (see the dotted curve on the right-hand side in Fig. 4.6-2). Similar calculations may be performed for other heating values of coal, for oil and gas fuels, for other thermal- to electrical-energy conversion efficiencies, and for other plant factors. The results are shown in Fig. 4.6-2 and refer to a thermal- to electrical-energy conversion efficiency defined by the Btu/kwh$_e$ curves. Multiplication of the annual fuel requirements in Btu by the energy cost per Btu, then yields the annual fuel costs (see Fig. 4.6-2). Typical 1970 fuel costs in cents/10^6 Btu are shown in the lower part of Fig. 4.6-2. For example, an 800-Mw$_e$ coal plant requiring 1.99 × 10^6 t/y of coal has an average annual fuel cost of $11.35 × 10^6/y (see Fig. 4.6-2).

The annual operation and maintenance (O and M) cost in $/y is obtained by multiplying the O and M values in $/kwy$_e$ by the plant capacity in kw$_e$. Typical values are shown in Fig. 4.6-3 for generating stations using gas, oil, coal, or nuclear fuels. Reference to Fig. 4.6-3 indicates that an 800-Mw$_e$ plant requires an annual operation and maintenance expenditure of $2.24 × 10^6/y.

The preceding curves may finally be combined to determine the electricity generation cost in mills/kwh$_e$ by noting that electricity-generation

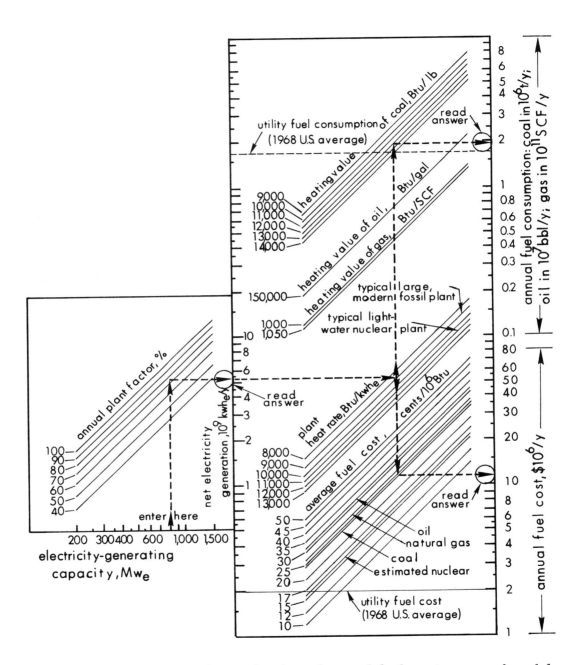

Fig. 4.6-2 Diagrams for the evaluation of annual fuel costs; reproduced from Ref. [1]. Reprinted with permission from Power, July 1970.

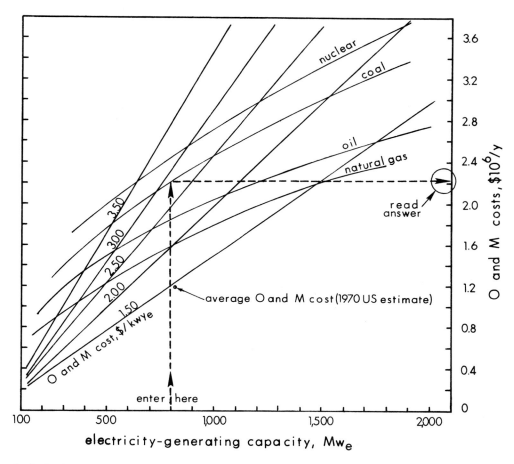

Fig. 4.6-3 Annual operating and maintenance costs for various O and M costs
in $/kwy$_e$; reproduced from Ref. [1]. Reprinted with permission
from Power, July 1970.

costs in mills/kwh$_e$ = 10^3 × (fixed costs in $/y + fuel costs in $/y + O and

M costs in $/y) ÷ electrical-energy generation in kwh$_e$/y. The nomogram

shown in Fig. 4.6-4 facilitates the evaluation of total electricity-generation

costs. For example, an 800-Mw$_e$ plant generating 5.26 × 10^9 kwh$_e$/y of

electricity with an annual plant cost of $30.89 × 10^6/y produces electricity

at a cost of 5.88 mills/kwh$_e$ (see Fig. 4.6-4).

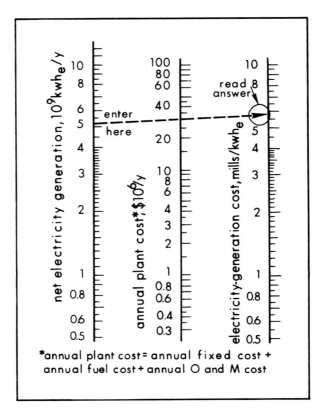

Fig. 4.6-4 Nomogram for the evaluation of electricity-generation costs; reproduced from Ref. [1]. Reprinted with permission from Power,
July 1970.

4.7   Energy-Cost Comparisons for Fossil Fuels and Foods; Some Examples of Future Energy Sources and Costs

E. Cook has published interesting energy-cost comparisons involving
fossil fuels, electricity, and food products.[1] He notes that about eight units
of fossil-fuel energy are required per unit of food energy produced, with energy measured in terms of combustion-energy release in a power plant.
About two units of energy are spent in the manufacture of farm machinery

[1]E. Cook, "Saving the Environment Goat and Economy Cabbage, " EXXON
U.S.A. , Second Quarter, 1974, pp. 11-15.

and for the fertilizers, herbicides and pesticides used; the remaining six units of energy are consumed in food processing, handling, storage, transportation, and refrigeration. This type of energy conversion to food is ultimately economical because of the relative ease and low cost of energy-resource recovery as compared with food production and distribution. Representative energy costs (as of February 1974) are summarized in Fig. 4.7-1.

The development of new technologies will provide us with new energy sources. An estimate of development times for these new sources, as well as anticipated costs, has been prepared by B. Rubin et al.[2] Some examples of this work are shown in Figs. 4.7-2 and 4.7-3. The time schedules (see Figs. 4.7-2 and 4.7-3) for utilization of such techniques as MHD power conversion using coal, or in situ recovery of shale oil, appear to be optimistic.

[2]B. Rubin, S. Winter, W. Ramsey, and G. Werth, "A Rationale for Setting Priorities for New Energy Technology Research and Development," Report UCRL-51511, Lawrence Livermore Laboratory, Livermore, California, 1974.

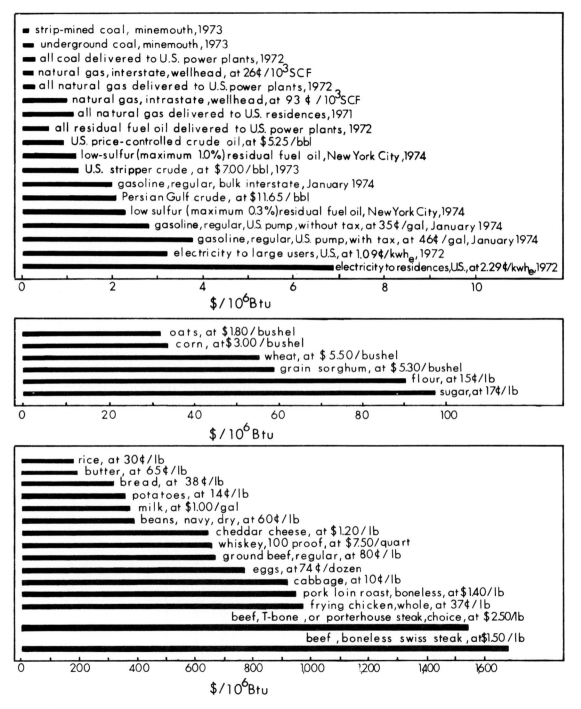

Fig. 4.7-1 Energy-cost comparisons for combustion in a boiler and use in a power plant; based on February 1974 data and reproduced from Ref. [1].

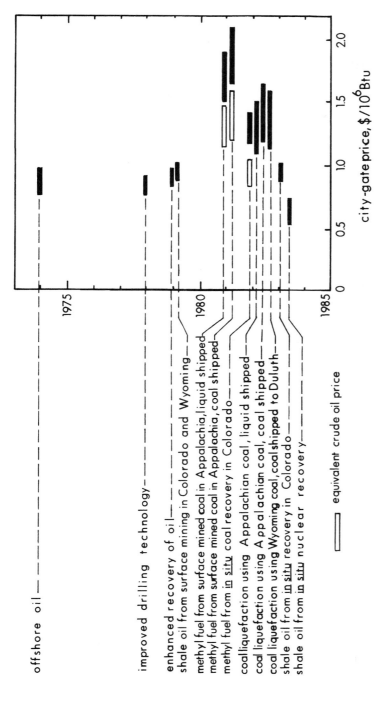

Fig. 4.7-2 Estimates of developing energy sources for transportation in New York City. The city-gate prices are based on 1973 pre-embargo costs and references available at that time and are given in 1973 dollars. The time scales represent estimated dates of demonstration plant operation assuming the initiation of vigorous R&D programs for each technology. In some cases, of course, this has not occurred. Reproduced with modifications from Ref. [2].

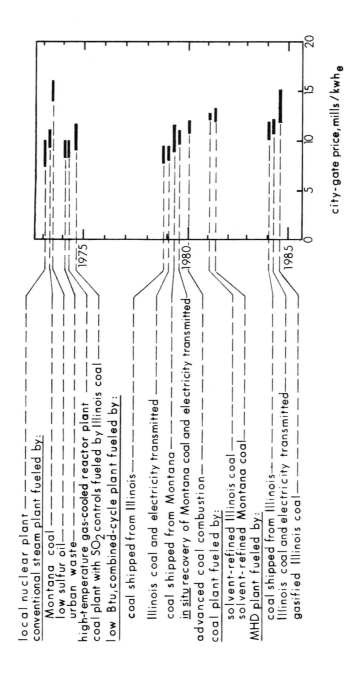

Fig. 4.7-3   Estimates of developing sources for electricity generation in Chicago.   The city-gate prices are based on 1973 pre-embargo costs and references available at that time and are given in 1973 dollars.   The time scales represent estimated dates of demonstration plant operation assuming the initiation of vigorous R&D programs for each technology.   In some cases, of course, this has not occurred.   Reproduced with modifications from Ref. [2].

CHAPTER 5

ENERGY-UTILIZATION EFFICIENCIES, WASTE RECOVERY,
AND RELATED TOPICS

In this chapter, we consider the following topics: increased efficiencies achieved by improved utilization of technology (Section 5.1), energy consumption associated with appliance use (Section 5.2), efficiencies of gas and electric appliances (Section 5.3), insulation and energy savings in the heating of buildings (Section 5.4), energy costs of intercity passenger and freight traffic (Section 5.5), energy requirements for the automobile (Section 5.6), urban transportation energy requirements for bicycles and automobiles (Section 5.7), slowing the growth rate of energy use in California (Section 5.8), recovery and utilization of municipal solid waste (Section 5.9), waste-oil re-refining (Section 5.10), and measures of energy-utilization efficiency (Section 5.11). In a society that has been oblivious to energy efficiencies, significant improvements in energy-utilization techniques are not difficult to define.

5.1 Increased Efficiencies in Energy Use Associated with Technological
Improvements

Although we have been called a nation of wastrels, our major industries have shown improved energy-utilization efficiencies with the introduction of

233

more sophisticated technologies. This point has been stressed by Hottel.[1] However, as we shall see, the past energy savings have been inadequate when viewed in the context of our social habits. Examples of energy savings are listed below.

a. The efficiency of electrical-power generation has increased significantly with time. For example, between 1925 and 1965, improved design of utility-generating stations has decreased the average thermal energy required for the production of electrical energy (which is referred to as the "heat rate") from 25,000 Btu/kwh$_e$ to 10,000 Btu/kwh$_e$.[1] Utility burner efficiencies are close to 90%.[1]

Overall thermal conversion efficiencies for coal burners have increased from 5% in 1900 to about 40% in 1973; oil and gas burners have overall conversion efficiencies for thermal-to-electrical energy of about 33%. Magnetohydrodynamic generators and high-temperature turbine generators should reach efficiencies of 50%.

b. What has been referred to as our most retrograde industry (the railroads) shows a decrease in energy consumption for freight hauling from 3,500 Btu/ton-mile in 1950 to 750 Btu/ton-mile in 1969.[1]

c. In 1950, the production of one ton of pig iron required 0.92 ton of coke; by 1970, only 0.63 ton of coke was required per ton of pig iron.[1]

d. Efficiencies expressed in terms of usable energy relative to the theoretical energy release for complete burning of household furnaces have

---

[1]H. C. Hottel, "Combustion and Energy for the Future," _Fourteenth Symposium (International) on Combustion_, p. 9, The Combustion Institute, Pittsburgh, Pa., 1972.

steadily improved with time and now fall between 50 and 60% for furnaces

using hand-fired bituminous coal, while reaching 60 to 75% for stoker-fired

furnaces burning bituminous coal and for hand-fired furnaces burning anthracite.

Efficiencies of gas and oil burners in the range 70 to 80% are easily achievable.[1]

Efficiency losses amount to 5 to 10% for badly-adjusted furnaces during con-

tinuous operation and up to 30% during start-up and shut-down.[1] If the

home-furnace and commercial-furnace efficiencies had been raised from

55 to 80% during 1973, about 3.6% of the total expended energy would have

been saved since about 21% of the total energy was spent on the residential/

commercial sector and about one-half of this energy was consumed by space-

heating units.

The distribution of energy consumption by end use in the residential,

commercial, industrial, and transportation sectors for 1960 and 1968 is

summarized in Table 5.1-1.

A summary of currently (1971) achievable energy efficiencies for

various applications is reproduced in Fig. 5.1-1. We note energy-con-

version efficiencies as high as 99% for large electrical generators re-

ferring to mechanical-to-electrical energy conversion and as low as 4 to

5% for incandescent bulbs converting electrical energy to radiant energy.

Aircraft gas turbines are seen to yield conversion efficiencies of 34 to

36% for chemical- to thermal- and thermal- to mechanical-energy conver-

sion (see Fig. 5.1-1); for these devices, improved efficiencies require

higher operating temperatures, which have been reached in time with the

development of improved high-temperature materials (see Fig. 5.1-2).

Table 5.1-1 Total fuel-energy consumption in the United States by end use.
Electric-utility consumption has been allocated to each end use.
Reproduced from Patterns of Energy Consumption in the United
States, U.S. Government Printing Office, Washington D.C., 1972.

End use	Consumption, 10^{12} Btu		Annual growth rate, %	Percentage of national total	
	1960	1968		1960	1968
residential sector					
space heating	4,848	6,675	4.1	11.3	11.0
water heating	1,159	1,736	5.2	2.7	2.9
cooking	556	637	1.7	1.3	1.1
clothes drying	93	208	10.6	0.2	0.3
refrigeration	369	692	8.2	0.9	1.1
air conditioning	134	427	15.6	0.3	0.7
other	809	1,241	5.5	1.9	2.1
total	7,968	11,616	4.8	18.6	19.2
commercial sector					
space heating	3,111	4,182	3.8	7.2	6.9
water heating	544	653	2.3	1.3	1.1
cooking	93	139	4.5	0.2	0.2
refrigeration	534	670	2.9	1.2	1.1
air conditioning	576	1,113	8.6	1.3	1.8
feedstock	734	984	3.7	1.7	1.6
other	145	1,025	28.0	0.3	1.7
total	5,742	8,766	5.4	13.2	14.4
industrial sector					
process steam	7,646	10,132	3.6	17.8	16.7
electric drive	3,170	4,794	5.3	7.4	7.9
electrolytic processes	486	705	4.8	1.1	1.2
direct heat	5,550	6,929	2.8	12.9	11.5
feedstock	1,370	2,202	6.1	3.2	3.6
other	118	193	6.7	0.3	0.3
total	18,340	24,960	3.9	42.7	41.2
transportation sector					
fuel	10,873	15,038	4.1	25.2	24.9
raw materials	141	146	0.4	0.3	0.3
total	11,014	15,184	4.1	25.5	25.2
national total	43,064	60,526	4.3	100.0	100.0

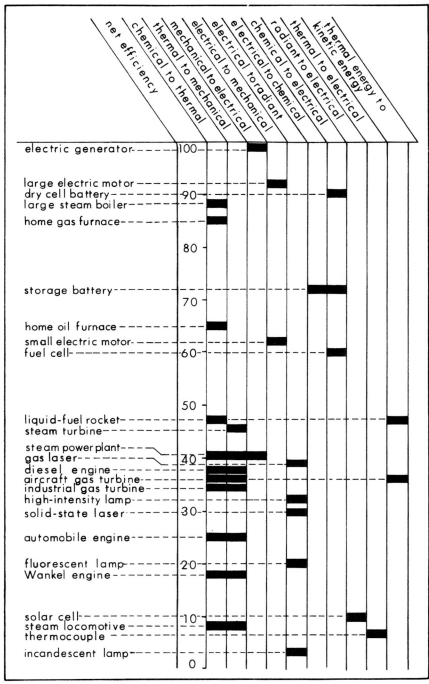

Fig. 5.1-1 A summary of optimal conversion efficiencies obtainable in 1971
for various applications; reproduced from "Conservation of Energy," prepared by H. Perry for the Committee on Interior and
Insular Affairs, U.S. Government Printing Office, Washington,
D.C., 1972.

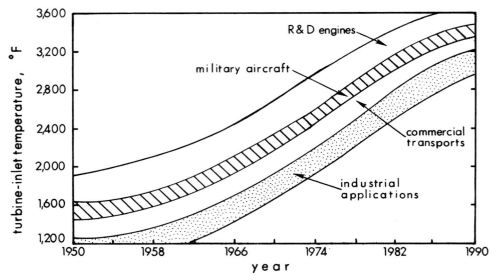

Fig. 5.1-2 The development of higher turbine-inlet temperatures with time
has led to improved operating efficiencies. The development of
improved military-aircraft turbines is followed in about two years
by corresponding improvements in commercial transports and by
about five years in industrial-power applications; reproduced from
F. L. Robson, A. J. Giramonti, G. P. Lewis, and G. Gruber,
"Technological and Economic Feasibility of Advanced Power Cycles and Methods of Producing Non-Polluting Fuels for Utility
Power Stations," prepared for the National Air Pollution Control
Administration by the United Aircraft Research Laboratory, East
Hartford, Connecticut, 1970.

5.2   Energy Consumption Associated with Electrical Appliance Usage

Annual consumer expenditures for appliances (in 1971) and residential
electrical-energy (in 1967) use for appliances are shown in Fig. 5.2-1. We
note that television sales commanded the principal consumer expenditure, followed by refrigerators and washing machines. However, refrigerators-
freezers and home water heaters were the principal energy users.

Power consumption, average annual use time, and yearly energy consumption for selected appliances are listed in Table 5.2-1, together with some
obvious recommendations for minimizing use rates. Efficiencies of room air

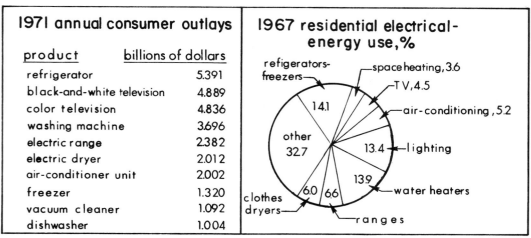

Fig. 5.2-1 A 1971 listing of consumer outlays for appliances and a 1967 compilation of residential electrical-energy use by home appliances. The consumer expenditures include the amortized acquisition cost and the annual service and energy consumption costs. Reproduced from The Productivity of Servicing Consumer Durable Products, Center for Policy Alternatives, M.I.T., Cambridge, Mass., 1974.

conditioners for thermal energy removal, in Btu removed per wh_e of electricity consumed, are shown in Fig. 5.2-2. We note an energy-efficiency variation of more than a factor of two for air conditioners.

5.3 Efficiencies of Gas and Electric Appliances

The utilization efficiency of an appliance is a measure of how effective the appliance is in using energy to accomplish its intended purpose. The utilization efficiencies for various appliances are calculated differently. For instance, the utilization efficiency of space heaters is defined as the ratio of the heat supplied to the total energy consumed. The utilization efficiencies of other appliances, such as ranges, water heaters, and clothes dryers, are functions of many factors such as load, appliance size, and daily use rate. Laboratory simulation and home-use monitoring are employed to derive these efficiencies.

Table 5.2-1 Power consumption, average annual use time, and average annual electrical energy consumption by appliances; based on data compiled by the Electric Energy Association (1974).

	Average power, w	Assumed use, h/y	Energy use per year, kwh_e/y	What to do in order to minimize energy use for a fixed duty cycle
FOOD				
blender	300	3	0.9	
broiler	1,140	75	85	
carving knife	95	8	0.8	
coffee maker				Avoid needless repetitive use.
brew cycle	600	150	90	
warm cycle	80	600	48	
deep fryer	1,448	56	83	
dishwasher	1,201	30	363	Use for a large number of dishes only.
freezer (frostless, 15 ft³)	440	4,000	1,761	Check door gasketing carefully and replace if worn. Open and close efficiently for access. Keep coils on rear clean.
frying pan	1,200	84	100	
hand mixer	80	13	1	
microwave oven	1,500	127	190	
self-cleaning oven	4,800	157	750	Do not preheat for more than 10 minutes. Cook as many dishes at one time as possible. Use available heat after turn-off for final heating of dishes. Use self-cleaning mode sparingly.
range	8,200	55	455	
refrigerator (frostless, 12 ft³)*	321	3,800	1,217	Check door insulation (a dollar bill should fit tightly in the door) and replace if worn. Change to standard models from frost-free models for 50% energy savings; remove ice before it interferes with efficiency in standard models. Know what you are going to take from the refrigerator before you open the door. Keep coils on rear clean.

Table 5.2-1, continued.

	Average power, w	Assumed use, h/y	Energy use per year, kwh_e/y	What to do in order to minimize energy use for a fixed duty cycle.
toaster	1,100	35	39	Do not prewarm and use with material at room temperature.
waffle iron	1,200	21	25	Do not prewarm and use with material at room temperature.
waste disposal	445	67	30	Use only when necessary.
LAUNDRY clothes dryer	4,856	204	993	Use on full loads only. Install in a sheltered part of the house.
iron (hand)	1,008	141	144	Avoid prolonged delays between ironing applications.
washing machine	512	200	103	Use warm (not hot) water. Use on full loads only, preferably during the day to avoid interference with peak electricity use.
water heater (standard)	2,475	1,700	4,219	Repair leaky hot-water faucets at once. Take showers, rather than baths, for a 33% saving of hot water. Do not set thermostat above 140°F. Place in sheltered location near to points of hot-water use.
COMFORT room air conditioner **	860	1,000	860	Eliminate leakage and blocking of ducts. Use at least 1.5 inches of insulation. Use units only where required. Draw cool night air in with an auxiliary fan (e.g., an oven-exhaust fan).
electric blanket	150	1,000	150	Avoid overheating; use dual controls for two people--or compromise at the lower comfort limit.
dehumidifier	257	1,462	377	

Table 5.2-1, continued.

	Average power, w	Assumed use, h/y	Energy use per year, kwh$_e$/y	What to do in order to minimize energy use for a fixed duty cycle.
fan (rollaway)	171	806	139	Use natural air circulation whenever possible.
heater (portable)	1,322	133	176	Reserve applications to emergency conditions.
heating pad	60	55	3	
humidifier	177	920	163	
HEALTH				
hair dryer	381	37	14	
shaver	15	30	0.5	
sun lamp	279	57	16	
toothbrush	7	71	0.5	
ENTERTAINMENT				
radio	71	121	86	Do not leave unattended units in operation; adjust sound levels to minimal requirements.
radio-record player	109	1,000	109	Schedule listening to programs as a family or group activity. Unplug instant turn-on sets
television				from the wall sockets to eliminate energy consumption when the sets are not in use.
black and white				
tube-type	160	2,200	350	
solid-state	55	2,200	120	
color				
tube-type	300	2,200	660	
solid-state	200	2,200	440	
HOUSEWARES				
clock	2	8,760	17	
floor polisher	305	49	15	
sewing machine	75	146	11	
vacuum cleaner	630	73	46	Do not use a vacuum cleaner when a sweeper will do.
light bulbs	40 to 300			Use fluorescent light bulbs of equivalent rating; turn off all but necessary lights.

Table 5.2-1, continued.

General recommendations at home and away from home:

1. Buy units of proper minimum size for the required application.

2. Avoid wasteful use on all utilities, including lights, heaters, air conditioners, record players, TV-sets, etc.

3. Use adequate insulation everywhere: in construction, at least 6 inches on ceilings below attics, at least 3.5 inches in walls. Install storm windows to reduce the heat loss by 50%.

4. To use available solar heat, open drapes during the day and close them at night. If sensitivity to sunlight prevents extended day-time use, closing the drapes at night in heated rooms still remains as a useful energy-saving device.

5. Remember that standard units (e.g., for refrigerators, hot-water heaters) are generally more energy-effective than deluxe models.

6. Clean home-heating units at least once per year.

7. Wood-burning fireplaces are very inefficient energy users, with at least 20% of the energy going up the chimney.

General remarks on home-electricity use:

1. The 1973 average cost to the homeowner for electricity was 23.8 mills/kwh$_e$ =2.38 cents/kwh$_e$.

2. The average U.S. household consumed 8,079 kwh$_e$ during 1973, as compared with about 1,900 kwh$_e$ in 1930.

_____

* Energy use by refrigerator/freezers: 661 kwh$_e$/y for a single-door, manual-defrost model (9 to 13 ft^3); 1,179 kwh$_e$/y for a two-door, cycle-defrost unit (12 to 15 ft^3); 1,810 kwh$_e$/y for a two-door, top-freezer, frost-free model (12 to 20 ft^3); 2,197 kwh$_e$/y for a side-by-side, frost-free unit (16 to 25 ft^3).

** Based on 1,000 hours of operation per year. This figure will vary widely depending on the area and the specific size of the unit. Look for air conditioners with high Btu/wh$_e$ or efficiency rating: a rating of 8 is good, 5 is poor; the most efficient units have ratings up to 11. See Fig. 5.2-2 for the wide spread in efficiencies of commercial air conditioners.

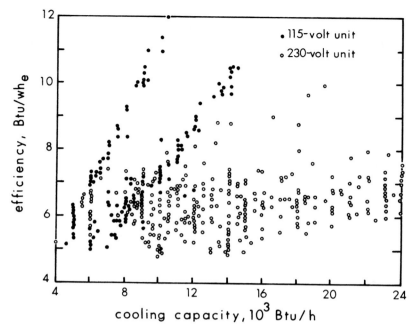

Fig. 5.2-2 Efficiency of room air conditioners as a function of unit size.
The solid circles correspond to 115-volt units and the open
circles represent 230-volt units. Reproduced from a statement
prepared by E. Hirst and J. C. Moyers for the Committee on
Science and Astronautics, U.S. House of Representatives, U.S.
Government Printing Office, Washington, D.C., 1972.

For ranges, the standard test for determining thermal efficiency involves heating of standard volumes of water. Monitoring of the useful output of hot water, while accounting for recovery efficiencies and standby
losses, is used to determine the utilization efficiency of water heaters.
The determination of clothes-drying efficiency is based on the energy input
required to dry a specified load of water-saturated test clothes.

Typical utilization efficiencies of gas and electric appliances are given
in Table 5.3-1. The data in Table 5.3-1 indicate that, with the exception of
clothes dryers, electric appliances have significantly higher utilization efficiencies than gas appliances (where, however, no allowance is made for
energy loss in making electricity from gas or another primary energy source).

Table 5.3-1   Utilization efficiencies of household appliances; based on the data of the Gas Engineers Handbook, The Industrial Press, New York, 1965.

Appliance	Energy-utilization efficiency, %	Efficiency ratio, electric/gas
space heater		1.3
electric-resistive	95	
gas	75	
water heater		1.4
electric	92	
gas	64	
range		1.9
electric	75	
gas	40	
clothes dryer		1.0
electric	65	
gas	65	

A more realistic measure of appliance energy-efficiencies is obtained when the energy losses that occur in the production, transportation, and distribution of energy are included.   The average efficiency of production of fossil fuels is 96%.   The average heat rate for U.S. electrical generating plants using fossil fuels is 10,000 Btu/kwh$_e$,[1] which corresponds to a thermal-to-electrical-energy conversion efficiency of 34.1%.   Transportation and distribution of natural gas and electric power result in additional energy losses: approximately 4% of the transported natural gas is used as compressor fuel and the electrical power lost during transmission and distribution averages about 9%.[2] Thus the overall efficiency of supplying natural gas to the consumer

---

[1]Ref. [1] in Section 5.1.

[2]Statistical Yearbook of the Electrical Utility Industry for 1970, Edison Electric Institute, New York, N.Y., 1971.

is $0.96 \times 0.96 = 0.92$. Similarly, the overall efficiency of supplying electrical energy to the consumer is $0.96 \times 0.341 \times 0.91 = 0.30$. These efficiency figures indicate that, on the average, supplying energy to the consumer in the form of electricity uses 3.1 times the primary energy required to supply the equivalent energy in the form of natural gas.

The overall efficiency of a household appliance is the product of the energy-supply efficiency and of the energy-utilization efficiency. The overall energy-efficiencies of electrical and gas appliances are shown in Table 5.3-2.

Table 5.3-2 Comparative energy-efficiencies of household appliances.

Appliance	Overall energy-efficiency, %	Ratio of primary energy consumed, electric unit/gas unit
space heater		2.4
electric-resistive	29	
gas	69	
water heater		2.1
electric	28	
gas	59	
range		1.6
electric	23	
gas	37	
clothes dryer		3.0
electric	20	
gas	60	

Although electric appliances generally have higher utilization efficiencies than gas appliances (see Table 5.3-1), Table 5.3-2 indicates that, when production, transportation, and distribution energy-efficiencies are included, gas appliances have substantially higher overall energy-efficiencies than electric appliances.

The 1970 U.S. average price for residential natural gas was $1.06/10^6 Btu[3] and the 1970 U.S. average price for residential electricity was $0.021/ kwh$_e$.[4] Thus, on an equivalent energy basis, the cost of residential electricity was 5.8 times the cost of residential gas in 1970. In 1970, the relative operating costs of electrical and gas appliances, based on the energy-utilization efficiencies listed in Table 5.3-1, are shown in Table 5.3-3.

Table 5.3-3 Relative operating costs of electrical and gas appliances in 1970.

Appliance	Operating cost ratio, electric/gas
space heater	4.5
water heater	4.1
range	3.1
clothes dryer	5.8

5.4 Energy Use for Space Heating, Air Conditioning, and Illumination

During 1968, 19.2% of the total energy was used in residences, 14.4% in commercial buildings, 41.2% by industry, and 25.2% for transportation.[1] More than one-half of the residential demand, corresponding to 11% of the total energy used in the U.S., was allocated to space heating; the space-heating contribution from the commercial sector amounted to 6.9% of the total U.S. energy demand.[1] Air conditioning in residential and commercial units required 2.5% of the total U.S. energy consumption during 1968.[1] Thus,

[3] Gas Facts, American Gas Association, Arlington, Virginia, 1970.

[4] Typical Electric Bills, Federal Power Commission, Washington, D.C., 1970.

[1] Patterns of Energy Consumption in the United States, U.S. Government Printing Office, Washington, D.C., 1972.

heating and cooling of residential and commercial buildings required 20.4%

of the total energy used in the U.S. during 1968(see Table 5.1-1).

A.   Reduction of Energy Use by Insulation

Builders are more likely to pay attention to insulation requirements in

all-electric homes than in gas- or oil-heated units. The Federal Housing

Authority (FHA) has provided minimum property standards (MPS) since 1965,

which roughly allowed thermal losses from residential units up to 2,000 Btu/

(10^3ft^3)-(degree-day). A 1970 property-standard requirement by the Office

for Housing and Urban Development (HUD), "Operation Breakthrough," re-

duced the allowable thermal-loss figure to essentially 1,500, while 1972 FHA

standards required a further reduction to roughly 1,000 Btu/(10^3ft^3)-(degree-

day).* Here the term degree-day ($^\circ$F-d) refers to a one degree difference in

temperature between the inside and outside of a house during a twenty-four

hour period.

For specified average external conditions, the heat losses from buildings

may be estimated as a function of insulation by using standard procedures.

Representative results for New York and Minneapolis are reproduced in

---

*The revised and unrevised MPS data given are oversimplified because the
actual MPS data refer to thermal-loss rates per unit area rather than the
volumetric measures indicated. The unrevised MPS for houses with gas
heating were actually 50 Btu/ft^2-h while the corresponding value for houses
with electric heating was 40 Btu/ft^2-h. The revised MPS data for both gas-
and electricity-heated houses cannot be expressed as constant heat-loss
rates per unit area because the slope of the curve of the heat loss as a function of floor-area requirements is not a constant.

Fig. 5.4-1 from an evaluation by Moyers.[2] As is explained in the extensive legend to Fig. 5.4-1, reductions of energy consumption for space heating by about 40% may be achieved by adding suitable ceiling and wall insulation, as well as storm windows. In order to show the relation between the data of Fig. 5.4-1 and current FHA regulations, we note that the model home used in Fig. 5.4-1 had a volume of 14.4×10^3 ft^3 and that the average inside and outside temperatures during the heating season were assumed to be $65°$F and $44°$F, respectively. Hence, a heat loss of 100×10^6 Btu/y corresponds to

$$100 \times 10^6 \text{ (Btu/y)} \times (1/241)(\text{y/heating season days}) \times (1/14.4 \times 10^3 \text{ft}^3) \times$$

$$(1/21°\text{F}) \simeq 1.4 \times 10^3 \text{ Btu}/(10^3 \text{ft}^3) - (°\text{F-d}).$$

Since field observations show similar leaks in commercial and residential units, energy savings should be similar for these two types of structures.[3] Air inflow is responsible for 25 to 50% of heating and cooling requirements[4] and exceeds required ventilation by a factor of four (Ref. [4], p. 337), except in areas of high pollution (toilets, kitchens, conference rooms).[3] Ultimately achievable losses have been estimated as about 700 Btu/$(10^3$ft$^3)$-(°F-d). As was noted in Section 5.2, considerable improvements may be obtained by using more efficient heating and cooling units and minimizing the use of intermittent operation.

---

[2] J. C. Moyers, "The Value of Thermal Insulation in Residential Construction: Economics and the Conservation of Energy," Report ORNL-NSF-EP-9, Oak Ridge National Laboratory, Oak Ridge, Tenn., 1971.

[3] G. A. Berg, "Energy Conservation through Effective Utilization," Science 181, 128-138 (1973).

[4] Engineers Handbook of Fundamentals, pp. 381-383, American Society of Heating, Refrigeration and Air-Conditioning Engineers, New York, N.Y., 1972.

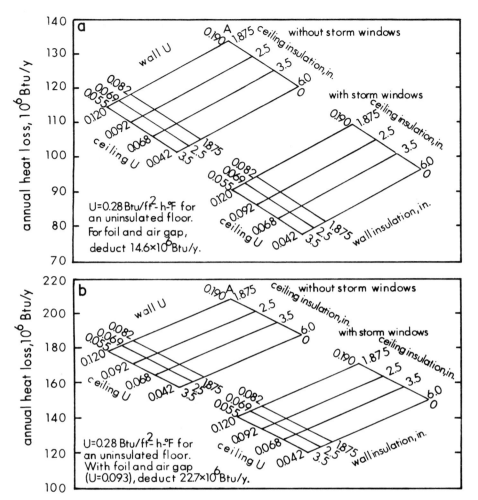

Fig. 5.4-1 The annual heat loss from model homes with various thicknesses
of insulation in (a) New York and (b) Minneapolis. A quantitative
estimate of the savings in energy for home heating, which are
technologically feasible, may be obtained as follows. The upper
point, A, in (a) and (b) may be assumed to represent the approximate state of insulation and storm-window sealing in approximately 90% of housing built prior to issuance of minimum property
standards. The heat losses from these houses can be reduced by
approximately 45% by application of heavy ceiling insulation, side-
wall insulation, and installation of storm windows. Thus, it would
not be unreasonable to assume that if installation of insulation and
storm windows on housing units now in service were feasible, the
present (1971) national demand for fuel consumed in space heating
of residences could be reduced by approximately 40%. The heat-
transfer coefficient U is expressed in Btu/ft^2-h-$^\circ$F. Reproduced
from Moyers.[2]

With the installation of proper insulation for energy savings, there will be continuous monetary savings. Moyers[2] has estimated both the energy and monetary savings for a New York residence in 1970 dollars for both the unrevised MPS and the revised MPS; his results are reproduced in Table 5.4-1. These data serve to emphasize the importance of installing adequate insulation expecially in homes using electric heating.

Of course, large energy savings can be effected by using building materials with low energy costs. According to R. G. Stein and Associates,[5] poor design has led to excessive use (by as much as 50%) of energy-intensive concrete and steel.[5] The World Trade Center in New York City has a power use of 8×10^4 kw$_e$, which was sufficient for more than 100,000 people in the U.S. during 1970.

B.   Illumination Costs

About 1.5% of the total energy consumed in the U.S. was expended on illumination; this corresponds roughly to 5% of the total electricity consumption. Actually-used illumination levels generally exceed requirements by a factor of 2 or more, with inadequate use being made especially of daylight. Recommended illumination levels for commercial buildings have more than tripled since 1955 and now correspond to 100 foot-candles = 1,076 lumen/m^2.

We refer to Berg's paper[3] for further elaboration of the topics considered in this Section 5.4.

---

[5]R. G. Stein, "Architecture and Energy," lecture delivered at a meeting of the American Association for the Advancement of Science, Philadelphia, Pa., December 29, 1971; quoted by A. L. Hammond, Science 178, 1080 (1972).

Table 5.4-1 Comparison of insulation requirements and monetary and energy savings for a New York residence; reproduced from Moyers.[2]

Insulation specification	Insulation for the unrevised MPS		Insulation for the revised MPS		Insulation for the economic optimum	
	gas	electric	gas	electric	gas	electric
wall insulation thickness, in.	0	1.875	1.875	1.875	3.50	3.50
ceiling insulation thickness, in.	1.875	1.875	3.50	3.50	3.50	6
floor insulation	no	no	yes	yes	yes	yes
storm windows	no	no	no	no	yes	yes
monetary savings, $/y	0	0	28	75	32	155
reduction of energy consumption, %	0	0	29	19	49	47

5.5 Energy Costs of Intercity Passenger and Freight Traffic

Energy costs associated with transportation expenses have been reviewed in Section 3.3. We emphasize here the obvious fact that, without technological improvement, significant energy savings may be accomplished by using slower modes of transportation for passenger and freight traffic (compare Tables 3.3-1, 3.3-2 and 3.3-5). Replacement of the automobile by buses or bicycles, as well as walking, leads to very substantial energy savings in urban transport, while either buses or railroads are significantly more energy-effective for intercity transport than automobiles or airplanes. Hirst's estimates[1] for these modes of passenger transportation are summarized in Table 5.5-1, where the

[1] E. Hirst, "Transportation Energy Use and Conservation Potential," Bulletin of the Atomic Scientists 29, 36-42, November 1973.

Table 5.5-1 Energy-efficiencies for passenger transportation; based on data from E. Hirst, "Transportation Energy Use and Conservation Potential," Bulletin of the Atomic Scientists 29, 36-42, November 1973, and from a statement prepared by E. Hirst and J. C. Moyers for the Committee on Science and Astronautics, U.S. House of Representatives, U.S. Government Printing Office, Washington, D.C., 1972. Data from the former source are reprinted by permission of Science and Public Affairs. Copyright 1973 by the Educational Foundation for Nuclear Science.

Method or vehicle used for transportation	Energy use for a 100% load factor, Btu/passenger-mile	Average load factor in 1970, %	Average energy use in 1970, Btu/passenger-mile
urban transportation			
bicycle	200	100	200
walking	300	100	300
mass transit			
bus	650	18	3,700
electric	1,100	26	4,100
average	760	20	3,800
automobile	2,300	28	8,100
intercity transportation			
bus	740	46	1,600
railroad	1,100	37	2,900
automobile	1,600	48	3,400
airplane	4,100	49	8,400

previously-discussed variabilities between somewhat different vehicles of the same type such as aircraft (compare Section 3.3) have been ignored. It is, of course, clear that the energy consumption per passenger-mile varies linearly with the fuel-consumption rate per mile. Thus, a large car yielding 8 miles/gallon will show three times the energy consumption of a small car yielding 24 miles/gallon which carries the same passenger load. It is also interesting to note (see Table 5.5-1) that, under average conditions, bicycling is a more efficient use of human energy than walking.

5.6   Total Energy Requirements for the Automobile in the United States

The direct energy consumption by automobiles was discussed in detail in Chapter 3 (see Tables 3.2-2, 3.3-2, and 3.3-5). In addition to the energy required to power automobiles, energy is used to produce gasoline, to manufacture and sell automobiles, to manufacture replacement parts, to provide automotive maintenance, to manufacture and sell tires, to insure automobiles, and to construct and maintain roadways.

An automobile is manufactured from steel, copper, aluminum, rubber, glass, plastics, and other materials. The industrial processes associated with these materials such as mining, conversion from raw ore to primary products, fabrication, and transportation to automobile assembly factories consume energy.

In 1970, 6.55×10^6 automobiles were manufactured in the U.S., repre-

senting a total wholesale value of 14.5×10^9.[1] The energy used for assembly of automobiles in 1970 was 4.01×10^3 Btu/$-value of automobile
shipped. The energy consumed in supplying the automobile manufacturers
with raw and fabricated materials in 1970 amounted to 5.13×10^4 Btu/$-value
of automobile shipped. The 1970 total primary energy coefficient for the manufacture of automobiles is obtained by adding the assembly and material energy
costs and was 5.53×10^4 Btu/$-value of automobile shipped.[2] The average
1970 automobile wholesale price was 2.22×10^3; thus, on the average, 1.23
$\times 10^8$ Btu were required for manufacturing one automobile in 1970. This estimate agrees well with a 1967 value of 1.27×10^8 Btu calculated by Berry
and Fels.[3] The energy consumed in the manufacture of an automobile in
1970 would have been sufficient to power the average automobile (at 13 miles/
gallon) in use in 1970 over a distance of approximately 1.2×10^4 miles.

The energy required for the manufacture of an average 1967 automobile
is shown in Table 5.6-1. The total energy requirements for automobiles in
the U.S. in 1960 and 1970 are shown in Table 5.6-2. A comparison of the
energy required for automobiles and the total U.S. energy consumption in
1960 and 1970 are given in Table 5.6-3.

[1] Statistical Abstract of the United States, U.S. Bureau of the Census, U.S.
Government Printing Office, 1971.

[2] E. Hirst and R. Herendeen, "Total Energy Demand for Automobiles,"
Paper 730065, SAE International Automotive Engineering Congress,
Detroit, Michigan, 1973.

[3] R. S. Berry and M. F. Fels, "The Energy Cost of Automobiles," Bulletin
of the Atomic Scientists 29, 11-17, 58-60, December 1973.

Table 5.6-1   Energy consumption during 1967 in the manufacture of one automobile; based on the data of Ref. [3].   Reprinted by permission
of Science and Public Affairs.   Copyright 1973 by the Educational
Foundation for Nuclear Science.

Process	Energy consumption, 10^8 Btu
manufacture of metallic materials	0.89
manufacture of other materials	0.03
fabrication of parts and assembling of the automobile	0.32
transportation of materials	0.02
transportation of assembled automobile	0.01
total	1.27

Table 5.6-2   Total U.S. energy requirements for automobile production and
use during 1960 and 1970; reproduced from Ref. [2].

Item	Energy requirements, 10^{15} Btu	
	1960	1970
gasoline consumption	5.60	8.94
gasoline refining and retail sales	1.28	2.07
oil consumption, refining, and retail sales	0.07	0.11
automobile manufacturing	0.86	0.80
automobile retail sales	0.17	0.21
repairs, maintenance, and parts	0.35	0.37
parking and garaging	0.22	0.44
tire manufacturing and retail sales	0.09	0.23
insurance	0.19	0.31
taxes (highway construction)	0.73	1.00
total	9.56	14.48

Table 5.6-3   U.S. total energy consumption and energy requirements for automotive use during 1960 and 1970; reproduced from Ref. [2].

Item	1960	1970
total automobile energy requirements, 10^{15} Btu	9.56	14.48
total automobile mileage, 10^{11} miles	5.90	9.01
total energy use for automobiles, 10^4 Btu/mile	1.62	1.61
total U.S. energy consumption, 10^{15} Btu	44.57	67.44
percent of total U.S. energy consumption devoted to automobiles	21.4	21.5

5.7   Urban Transportation Energy Requirements for Bicycles and Automobiles

In 1972, bicycle sales in the U.S. had grown to 13.9×10^6 units. Automobile sales in the U.S. during the same period were 11.3×10^6. In early 1974, there were 65×10^6 bicycles and 93×10^6 registered passenger cars in the U.S.

The human intake-energy requirements for bicycling (in a wind-free environment on a flat surface at about 10 mph) are about 400 kcal/h, which may be compared with a requirement of 120 kcal/h for sitting or standing.[1] Thus, in order to bicycle at an average speed of 10 mph, an incremental human energy input of about $(280 \text{ kcal/h})(0.949 \times 10^{-3} \text{ Btu}/0.24 \text{ cal}) \div 10$ mph $\simeq 110$ Btu/mile is required. For a person who bicycles, this additional energy input is ultimately supplied by increased food utilization. Since approximately 7.2 Btu of primary energy were required[2] to grow, process, transport, sell, and prepare each Btu of food in the U.S. in 1971, the additional primary energy requirement for the food needed to support a bicyclist is 790 Btu/mile. Accelerated food production through the use of organic fertilizers represents inefficient conversion of fuel energy to food energy.

The primary energy costs for bicycle manufacture, transport, sale, maintenance, tires, and bikeways have been estimated by Hirst[3] and are

[1]P.O. Astrand and K. Rodahl, Textbook of Work Physiology, McGraw-Hill, New York, 1971.

[2]Food: Consumption, Prices, Expenditures, Economic Research Service, U.S. Department of Agriculture, U.S. Government Printing Office, Washington, D.C., 1972.

[3]E. Hirst, Energy Use for Bicycling, Report ORNL-NSF-EP-65, Oak Ridge National Laboratory, Oak Ridge, Tenn., 1974.

given in Table 5.7-1.

Table 5.7-1   Total energy requirements per passenger-mile for bicycling in
the United States in 1971; reproduced from Ref. [3].

Item	Energy requirements, Btu/passenger-mile
food production	790
bicycle manufacture	150
transportation and retail sales	60
repairs and maintenance	90
tires	200
bikeways	50
total	1,340

The 1971 average total energy requirements (including manufacturing and other charges), for urban automobiles traveling 5 miles or less, were[4] 11,200 Btu/passenger-mile. Comparison of the energy requirements for transportation by automobile and bicycle for distances not greater than 5 miles, indicates that the potential saving for an average passenger load (~1.9) is 9,860 Btu/passenger-mile when the automobile is replaced by the bicycle. The 1971 cumulative urban automobile travel, for distances of five miles or less, was 2.95×10^{11} passenger-miles, of which 63% occurred during good weather and daylight conditions suitable for cycling.[3] If 10% of the 1971 urban trips of five miles or less, occurring during good weather and daylight hours (corresponding to 1.8% of the total 1971 urban automobile passenger-miles), had been shifted from automobiles to bicycles, an energy saving of approximately

---

[4] E. Hirst, Direct and Indirect Energy Requirements for Automobiles, Report ORNL-NSF-EP-64, Oak Ridge National Laboratory, Oak Ridge, Tenn., 1974.

(9,860 Btu/passenger-mile)(2.95 $\times$ 10^{11} passenger-miles)(0.63)(0.10) $\simeq$

1.8 $\times$ 10^{14} Btu or, equivalently, of 0.85 $\times$ 10^6 bbl/d would have been realized.

A shift from automobiles to bicycles offers additional potential benefits, including reduced parking problems, reduced noise and air pollution, improved health for cyclists, and the possibility of combining recreation, exercise, and transportation. The disadvantages of such a shift may include[3] increased travel times, cyclist safety problems in mixed traffic, bicycle security, cyclist exposure to concentrated air pollution, and low cargo capacity of bicycles.

5.8   Slowing the Electricity-Use Rate in California

The growth rate of energy use, in general, and of electricity use, in particular, has been examined in some detail for California.[1] In summary, the following obvious technological changes have been recommended for slowing the electricity-use rate in California: improved thermal insulation on all new structures; reduction of lighting requirements to reasonable minimum needs; increased efficiency in appliance design and utilization; replacement of electricity by gas for space heating, water heating, refrigeration, cooking, and air conditioning over the near term; introduction of solar units for space and water heating over the longer term.

---

[1]K. P. Anderson, _Some Implications of Policies to Slow the Growth of Electricity Demand in California_, Report R-990-NSF/CSA, The Rand Corporation, Santa Monica, California, 1972.

Some of the aspects of this study, which are of particular interest in the present context, will now be summarized briefly.

The value of economic activity in terms of electricity consumption (\$GSP/kwh_e) is the inverse of the electricity intensity (in kwh_e) per dollar of gross state product (\$GSP). Some typical entries, including the percentages sold to out-of-state customers, are reproduced in Table 5.8-1. Economic elasticity relating to electricity consumption was estimated on the assumption that

$$\text{quantity of electrical energy purchased (E)} = a$$

$$+ b \times (\text{natural logarithm of the unit price paid for electrical energy} = \ln P)$$

$$+ c \times (\text{natural logarithm of the value added by the use of electrical energy} = \ln VA)$$

$$+ \text{error term,} \qquad\qquad\qquad (5.8\text{-}1)$$

where a, b, and c are empirically-determined constants.

In the past, the utilities have charged preferentially-lower rates to heavy users of electricity. The 1967 electricity costs charged by various customer classes are shown in Table 5.8-2. As the result, large values of E with low values of P [see Eq. (5.8-1)] may reflect, in part, high purchases of electricity to produce large value added and, in part, large purchases E to achieve preferentially-low values for P. To avoid this type of distortion, a "typical average" value or "nominal price" was placed on electricity cost. The price elasticity of demand is then the coefficient b in Eq. (5.8-1). Table 5.8-3 contains a summary of U.S. and California electricity intensities and of price elasticities for actual and nominal electricity costs. It is interesting

Table 5.8-1 Estimates of electricity intensity in 1969 and percentage of
product sales to out-of-state customers in 1960 by sector in
California; reproduced from Ref. [1].

Sector	Estimated electricity intensity, kwh$_e$/$GSP	Estimated product sales to out-of-state customers, percent
agriculture	1.33	} 28.6
mining	2.11	
manufacturing	1.12	46.8
government	0.43	18.8
construction		1.6
transportation/com-munications/utilities		22.0
wholesale trade	} 0.82	2.5
retail trade		0.3
finance/real estate/ insurance		9.6
services		7.2
total	1.10	19.2[a]

Sources: Bank of California; Edison Electric Institute;
W. E. Mooz; U.S. Bureau of the Census.

[a] Individual sector percentages are weighted
by shares of total employment. A sales-
weighted average was not available.

to note that California products (except for petroleum, coal, stone, clay,
glass, lumber, and apparel) carry lower electricity costs than the corresponding country-wide figures. Price elasticities of demand are seen to vary
widely with product type; no simple correlation appears to be associated with
electricity intensity.

Table 5.8-2 Costs and revenue by major customer class for the Southern
California Edison Company in 1967; reproduced from Ref. [1].

Customer class	Average revenue, ¢/kwh$_e$	Average total cost, ¢/kwh$_e$	Marginal variable cost, ¢/kwh$_e$
domestic	2.32	2.46	0.45
lighting and small power	2.28	1.67	0.44
large power	1.12	1.16	0.41
very large power	0.75	0.85	0.40

The percentage of dollar value added by the U.S. manufacturing sector
and also the percentage of product sales to out-of-state customers are shown
in Table 5.8-4.

The improved energy-utilization efficiency associated with conversion of
electricity to gas for various home-use applications is summarized in Table
5.8-5. Since the thermal energy-equivalent of 1 kwh is 3,412 Btu, a conversion rate in the last column of Table 5.8-5 smaller than $3 \times 3,412$ Btu/
kwh$_e$ = 10,236 Btu/kwh$_e$ measures directly the energy savings associated
with gas use in different applications, if we assume a 33% conversion efficiency from thermal energy to electricity in electrical-power generation.
Reference to Table 5.8-5 shows that gas is a more economical direct energy
source than electricity for all applications other than refrigeration and some
types of air conditioning. The preceding statement might not apply if abundant and cheap nuclear energy were available.

Table 5.8-3 Electricity intensity in California and the United States during 1963 and estimated price elasticities of electricity demand based upon 1962-1963 data in 1958 dollars; reproduced from Ref. [1].

SIC code	Manufacturing sector	Electricity intensity, kwh_e/$-value added		Price elasticity of demand: b in Eq. (5.8-1)	
		U.S.	California	actual price	nominal price
33	primary metals	7.121	3.783	-1.13[a]	-1.00[a]
28	chemicals	6.408	3.542	-1.60[a]	-1.61[c]
26	paper and pulp	5.960	3.352	-1.64[a]	-1.89[a]
29	petroleum and coal	5.196	5.580	-0.69[a]	-0.85[c]
32	stone, clay, glass	2.789	3.042	-1.30[d]	-1.50[d]
22	textiles	2.747	0.665	-1.22[c]	-1.03[c]
30	rubber and plastics	1.650	1.575	-0.25	-0.23
24	lumber	1.636	2.043	-1.64[a]	-1.43[d]
20	food and beverages	1.097	0.895	-1.33[a]	-0.72[d]
37	transportation equipment	0.888	0.807	-1.01[a]	-0.53[c]
34	fabricated metals	0.865	0.734	n.a.[e]	n.a.
36	electrical machinery	0.850	0.631	-1.49[a]	-0.70[c]
35	nonelectric machinery	0.750	0.657	-1.16[a]	-0.33
19, 39	ordnance and miscellaneous	0.679	0.556	n.a.	n.a.
25	furniture	0.633	0.445	-0.97[d]	-0.10
38	instruments	0.586	0.422	n.a.	n.a.
31	leather	0.571	--	-0.76[d]	-0.69[f]
27	printing	0.431	0.423	-0.73[c]	+0.16
23	apparel	0.348	0.361	n.a.	n.a.
21	tobacco	0.301	--	n.a.	n.a.

Note: SIC is the standard industrial classification system, published by the federal government; n.a. means "not available."

[a] Statistically significant at the 0.001 level.

[c] Statistically significant at the 0.05 level.

[d] Statistically significant at the 0.01 level.

[e] A value of +0.55 was obtained by Fisher and Kaysen using 1956 data, but the result is not significant statistically.

[f] Statistically significant at the 0.10 level.

Table 5.8-4 The California share of U.S. value added during 1967 and the share
            of product sales to out-of-state customers during 1960; reproduced
            from Ref. [1].

SIC code	Manufacturing sector	Value added, 10^6	Share of U.S. value added, percent	Share of product sales to out-of-state customers, percent	
				private sector	government
37	transportation equipment	3,653.7	12.97	10.8	61.7
36	electrical machinery	3,012.5	12.30	26.2	41.8
20	food and beverages	2,986.4	11.22	21.5	2.3
35	nonelectric machinery	1,790.2	6.43	53.4	10.7
34	fabricated metals	1,552.0	8.60	18.3	12.5
27	printing	1,167.2	8.13	12.9	0.5
28	chemicals	1,116.8	4.74	37.6	3.7
33	primary metals	933.3	4.67	15.3	12.0
32	stone, clay, glass	662.6	7.95	25.2	0.7
23	apparel	561.6	5.58	40.1	3.7
29	petroleum and coal	554.2	10.21	17.5	5.8
24	lumber	532.8	10.71	21.6	2.5
30	rubber and plastics	523.0	7.69	32.3	12.4
26	paper and pulp	497.9	5.10	31.8	0.0
38	instruments	474.7	7.40	17.4[a]	56.9[a]
25	furniture	382.8	9.18	13.3	0.8
39	miscellaneous	374.7	8.15	40.7	0.9
22	textiles	111.3	1.37	31.5[b]	3.1[b]
19	ordnance	} 2,505.9	} 30.51	n.a.	n.a.
31	leather			n.a.	n.a.
--	all manufacturing	23,393.6	8.93	22.6[c]	24.2[c]

[a]Includes SIC 19, ordnance.

[b]Includes SIC 31, leather.

[c]Weighted by employment shares; sales shares are not available.

Table 5.8-5 Alternative estimates of typical conversion rates for gas and electricity in selected uses; reproduced from Ref. [1].

| | Estimated annual consumption by a typical household | | Estimated conversion rates,a Btu/kwh$_e$ | Estimated end use energy ratio,b Btu-gas/Btu | Theoretical conversion rates,b Btu/kwh$_e$ |
	gas, 10^6 Btu	electricity, 10^3 kwh$_e$			
cooking	10	1.2	8,300	2.00	6,800
refrigeration	12	1.2c	10,000	3.16c	10,800
water heating	28	4.8	5,800	1.45	5,000
clothes drying	5	1.0	5,000	1.04	3,500
central air conditioning	--	--	--	2.60-4.30d	8,900-14,700
central heating	--	--	4,900-6,800e	1.31	4,500

Sources: The Edison Electric Institute and the American Gas Association.

aWith the exception of central heating, the figures in this column are obtained by dividing column 1 by column 2. The central-heating estimate is obtained from efficiency rates published in Electrical World.

bThe figures in this column are obtained by multiplying the corresponding end-use energy ratios by the theoretical conversion rate of 3,412 Btu/kwh$_t$.

cUsing an electric pilot.

dThe low-end estimate of 2.6 applies only to relatively large units (e.g., apartment buildings or commercial establishments), where combined gas heating-cooling systems can be used.

eThe lower figure applies to commercial and industrial units; the upper to units in single-family detached houses. Apartment units are estimated to fall in between. Equal insulation standards are assumed for gas and electric applications.

The data summarized in this Section 5.8 are indicative of the type of input that is required in order to develop a State master plan for economic and technical activities that has as its primary purpose the maximization of $GSP per unit of energy consumed. It is, of course, not obvious that this type of optimization represents the best state of the State of California or of any other State.

5.9   Recovery and Utilization of Municipal Solid Waste

The term municipal solid waste refers to the mixed solid materials resulting from residential, commercial, and industrial garbage and trash collections. This definition excludes special industrial wastes, large demolition wastes, and specialty loads of like items such as rubber tires, junk automobiles, and sewage sludge.

The composition of municipal waste is a highly variable function of geographic location, climate, season, and socioeconomic characteristics of the contributing population. The definitions of municipal-waste components and their typical concentrations are given in Tables 5.9-1 and 5.9-2.

In 1969, more than 250×10^6 t of municipal solid waste were produced in the U.S.[1] This production rate is equivalent to the generation of 1.25 t of solid waste per person per year. Annual U.S. municipal-waste production is expected to grow to more than 500×10^6 t/y by the year 2000. This esti-

---

[1] Environmental Quality, Council on Environmental Quality, Washington, D.C., 1970.

Table 5.9-1 Definitions of municipal-waste components; reproduced from
             Recovery and Utilization of Municipal Solid Waste, U.S. En-
             vironmental Protection Agency, Washington, D.C., 1971.

newsprint · · · · · · · · · · · · ·	Newspapers. Does not include magazines, handbills, etc.
cardboard · · · · · · · · · · · ·	Corrugated boxboard and the heavier paperboard used in cartons. Light cardboard in food packages and the backing of paper pads are included with "miscellaneous mixed paper."
miscellaneous mixed paper · ·	All other paper not included above.
metallics · · · · · · · · · · · · ·	Tinned cans and aluminum cans, hardware, bottle caps, utensils, wire, and other ferrous and nonferrous metal articles.
food (garbage) waste · · · · · ·	Wastes from the handling, preparation, cooking, and serving of foods. Does not include packaging materials or papers discarded with garbage.
yard waste · · · · · · · · · · · ·	Lawn, garden, and shrubbery clippings, sod and small yard debris other than branches.
wood waste · · · · · · · · · · · ·	Branches, scrap lumber, and other wooden articles.
glass · · · · · · · · · · · · · · ·	Glass and ceramic materials.
plastic · · · · · · · · · · · · · ·	Film plastics and molded plastic articles.
miscellaneous · · · · · · · · · ·	Stones, metal oxides, articles made of natural and synthetic fibers, rubber products, and leather goods.

mate corresponds to a per capita solid-waste generation rate of approximately 1.7 t/y of solid waste.

Twenty-four percent of the total 1969 municipal waste was uncollected, 58% was disposed of in open dumps, 10% was used for sanitary landfills, 6% was incinerated, and ocean disposal and composting accounted for the remaining 2%.

The cost of handling the 190×10^6 t of municipal waste in 1969 was about $\$3.5 \times 10^9$ or an average of \$18.50 per ton. On the average, collection

Table 5.9-2 Expected ranges of municipal-waste composition; reproduced from <u>Recovery and Utilization of Municipal Solid Waste</u>, U.S. Environmental Protection Agency, Washington, D.C., 1971.

	Percent composition as received (dry weight basis)	
	anticipated range	nominal
paper ·	37 - 60	55
newsprint · · · · · · · · · · · · · · · ·	7 - 15	12
cardboard · · · · · · · · · · · · · · ·	4 - 18	11
other · · · · · · · · · · · · · · · · ·	26 - 37	32
metallics ·	7 - 10	9
ferrous · · · · · · · · · · · · · · · ·	6 - 8	7.5
nonferrous · · · · · · · · · · · · ·	1 - 2	1.5
food ·	12 - 18	14
yard ·	4 - 10	5
wood ·	1 - 4	4
glass ·	6 - 12	9
plastic ·	1 - 3	1
miscellaneous · · · · · · · · · · · · · · · ·	< 5	3

<u>moisture content</u>
   range: 20-40%
   nominal: 30%		

accounts for 80% of the cost ($\simeq$ \$15/t), disposal for the rest. Included in the economic costs of collection and disposal of municipal waste is an energy cost. An average energy use for solid-waste collection, transportation, and disposal in landfills is 0.3×10^6 Btu/t.[2] If all of the 1969 municipal waste had been disposed of by landfilling, the total energy cost would have been 7.5×10^{13} Btu or, equivalently, 3.5×10^4 bbl/d of petroleum.

[2] E. Hirst, <u>Energy Implications of Several Environmental Quality Strategies</u>, Report ORNL-NSF-EP-53, Oak Ridge National Laboratory, Oak Ridge, Tennessee, 1973.

The electricity costs of municipal-waste collection and transportation are negligible but disposal by incineration consumes, on the average, $10 \text{ kwh}_e/$ t. [2] If all of the 1969 municipal waste had been disposed of by incineration, the total electrical-energy cost would have been $2.5 \times 10^9 \text{ kwh}_e$, which is equivalent to a petroleum use rate of 1.2×10^4 bbl/d for a 33% thermal-to-electrical conversion efficiency. Thus, the energy cost for incineration alone is about one-third of that for collection, transportation and disposal in landfilling.

The heating value of solid municipal waste is approximately 5×10^3 Btu/ lb. For a thermal-to-electrical conversion efficiency of 33%, municipal waste could be used to generate electrical energy at a rate of nearly $1 \text{ Mwh}_e/$ ton. If only 10% of the 1969 solid municipal waste had been incinerated, $2.5 \times 10^{10} \text{ kwh}_e$ could have been generated and the equivalent of 4.4×10^7 bbl ($= 1.2 \times 10^5$ bbl/d) of petroleum could have been saved.

The recycling of valuable materials in municipal solid waste is an alternative to disposal. A recycling system eliminates processes such as mining, crushing, grinding, milling, separation, transportation, and oxide reduction that are associated with production processes using virgin materials. However, municipal-waste materials must be collected, shredded, separated, and transported to refiners for reprocessing. The energy required to produce many materials from recycled scrap is substantially less than the energy required to make the same products from virgin materials. For example, steel can be produced from scrap for 25% of the energy required to produce steel from virgin ore. Production of aluminum from scrap consumes only 5% as much energy as production from virgin ores.[3] The figure for paper is approximately 60 to 70%.[4] These energy estimates refer only to material reprocessing and do not include energy consumption for collection, shredding, separation, and transportation of municipal solid wastes. Because of the economic potential of recycling paper, several schemes for the large-scale recovery of cellulose fiber from municipal solid waste are being developed.

The 1970 production statistics for steel, aluminum, and paper, as well as the energy required for their production using existing methods and 100% recycled scrap, are shown in Table 5.9-3.

Another alternative to municipal-waste landfilling, incineration, or recycling is the conversion of solid wastes to fuels by pyrolysis. Workers at the Garrett Research and Development Company, a subsidiary of the Occidental Petroleum Corporation, have developed a pyrolysis process which is part of a complete system designed for utilization and disposal of municipal wastes. In the Garrett process, municipal waste is first shredded and dried, inorganic materials are separated and recycled, and the remaining organic materials are then reshredded. The finely-ground organic materials are

[3]J. C. Bravard et al, Energy Expenditures Associated with the Production and Recycle of Metals, Report ORNL-NSF-EP-24, Oak Ridge National Laboratory, Oak Ridge, Tennessee, 1972.
[4]R. G. Hunt and W. E. Franklin, "Environmental Effects of Recycling Paper," presented at the 73rd National Meeting of the American Institute of Chemical Engineers, Minneapolis, Minnesota, 1972.

Table 5.9-3 The 1970 production data and the estimated energy consumption for processing steel, aluminum, and paper; reproduced from Ref. [2].

Material	Total 1970 production, 10^6 t	Percentage of 1970 production from recycled scrap	Energy consumption for production processes using	
			existing methods,[a] 10^6 Btu/t	100% recycled scrap,[b] 10^6 Btu/t
steel	132.0	26	23	8
aluminum	4.0	4	218	9
paper	52.5	18	28	21

a. Energy consumption for production using existing methods does not include energy consumption for transportation and does not refer to energy consumption for production entirely from virgin materials, which would be characterized by higher values than those given.

b. Energy consumption for production using 100% recycled scrap includes 50 kwh_e/t for solid-waste separation, 50 kwh_e/t for miscellaneous purposes, and 10^6 Btu/ton for transportation.

sent to the pyrolysis reactor where they are heated at atmospheric pressure to about 500°C in an oxygen-free atmosphere.

The yield per ton of municipal waste of the Garrett process is approximately 135 pounds of ferrous metals, 30 pounds of nonferrous metals, 130 pounds of glass, 1 barrel of oil, 160 pounds of char, and varying amounts of low-Btu (400-500 Btu/SCF) gas. The low-Btu gas is used to provide the oxygen-free atmosphere in the pyrolysis reactor and, together with a portion of the char, is used to supply heat for the pyrolysis process. The pyrolytic oil has a high oxygen content (33% by weight), a nitrogen content of less than 1%, and contains less than 0.3% sulfur by weight. The heating value of the pyrolytic oil is about 1.05×10^4 Btu/lb or 4.78×10^6 Btu/bbl, which corresponds to more than 75% of the energy content of No. 6 fuel oil. The

pyrolytic oil is suitable for use as a fuel for electrical-power generation.

The typical properties of No. 6 fuel oil and the pyrolytic oil produced by the

Garrett process are compared in Table 5.9-4.

Table 5.9-4 Typical properties of No. 6 fuel oil and the Garrett pryolytic
oil produced from municipal wastes; based on data released
by the Garrett Research and Development Company (1973).

Property	No. 6 fuel oil	Garrett pyrolytic oil
elemental analysis, weight percent:		
carbon	85.7	57.5
hydrogen	10.5	7.6
nitrogen		0.9
oxygen	2.0	33.4
sulfur	0.7-3.5	<0.3
energy value, Btu/lb	18,200	10,500
specific gravity	0.98	1.30
density, lb/gallon	8.18	10.85
energy content, Btu/gallon	148,840	113,910
pumping temperature, $^{\circ}$F	115	160
atomization temperature, $^{\circ}$F	220	240

Workers at Garrett have estimated the capital costs of a full-scale,

2,000 t/d plant, for processing municipal waste collected from a city with a

population of 5×10^5 to be approximately $\$12 \times 10^6$. According to Garrett

engineers, in a municipally-financed plant operating 24 h/d, it would cost,

on the average, \$5/t of municipal waste to produce pyrolytic oil and other

recoverable products worth \$6, which does not include the credit for solid-

waste disposal of \$3.70/t. This plant would thus produce a return of nearly

$3.4 \times 10^6/y$ on the 12×10^6 investment, not allowing for down-time and repairs.

A summary of the materials and the estimated economic values, that are claimed to be recoverable from municipal solid waste by the Garrett pyrolysis process, is given in Table 5.9-5.

Table 5.9-5 Potential values of materials recoverable from municipal solid wastes by the Garrett pyrolysis process; based on data released by the Garrett Research and Development Company (1973).

Raw material	Composition, weight %	Commodity value, $/ton	Estimated recovery, %	Potential value, $/ton of municipal waste
water	25			
dirt and debris	2-4			
inorganic products				
magnetic metals	6-8	20-40	95	1.15- 3.00
nonmagnetic metals	1-2	100-200	95	0.95- 3.80
glass	6-10	12-20	80	0.60- 1.60
subtotal				2.70- 8.40
organic products	50-60			
pyrolytic oil		12-15	40	2.40- 3.60
pyrolytic char		4-40[a]	30	0.60- 7.20
pyrolytic gas		4-5	20	0.40- 0.60
subtotal				3.40-11.40
total				6.10-19.80

[a] This material has potential value as activated carbon.

There are non-pyrolytic processes for conversion of organic wastes to synthetic fuels. The Bureau of Mines has developed a chemical reduction process that can be applied to virtually all organic wastes. The principal reaction in the Bureau of Mines process is the abstraction of oxygen from cellulose, which is the primary component of organic wastes. In this process, organic waste is heated (240°C to 380°C) in a reactor under pressure (100 to 250 at-

mospheres) in the presence of carbon monoxide, steam, and an alkaline

catalyst such as sodium or potassium carbonate. Theoretically, nearly all

of the carbon in organic wastes is converted to oil which would yield, on the

average, 2 barrels of oil per ton of dry organic waste. In practice, the con-

version efficiency is about 85% and some of the oil is used to provide heat

and carbon monoxide for the reaction, which reduces the net yield to approx-

imately 1.25 bbl/t. The synthetic oil produced by the Bureau of Mines pro-

cess is a heavy paraffinic oil with a sulfur content of less than 0.3% and an

average heating value of 1.5×10^4 Btu/lb or 5.4×10^6 Btu/bbl, which cor-

responds to more than 85% of the energy content of No. 6 fuel oil.

The third technological process for conversion of organic wastes to

synthetic fuels is bioconversion. This process, which is less well developed

than either the Garrett or Bureau of Mines processes, is often called an-

aerobic digestion or fermentation. In this procedure, organic wastes are

mixed with water and anaerobically fermented at approximately atmospheric

pressure and at temperatures from 15°C to 50°C. Enzymes already in the

organic waste and those generated by the fermentation process decompose

the cellulose and carbohydrates to simple sugars. These sugars are then

metabolized to acids, alcohols, hydrogen, and carbon dioxide before con-

version to methane by bacteria. The complete fermentation process takes

approximately one week. The end products of the fermentation process are

methane, carbon dioxide, trace amounts of hydrogen sulfide and nitrogen gas,

and a high-protein residue, which may be converted to animal feed. The
heating value of the synthetic gas produced by this process ranges from 500 to
700 Btu/SCF. This gas may be upgraded by removing the carbon dioxide,
hydrogen sulfide, and nitrogen. The resulting methane yield is approximately
1×10^4 SCF/t of dry organic waste and has a heating value of about 1×10^3
Btu/SCF.

The organic-waste feedstock for the Garrett pyrolysis process differs
from that of the Bureau of Mines and bioconversion processes. The organic
waste used in the Garrett process is derived completely from municipal
solid waste. The Bureau of Mines and bioconversion processes are designed to use an organic-waste feedstock composed of animal wastes, logging
and wood manufacturing residues, municipal organic wastes, agricultural
crop and food wastes, industrial wastes, and municipal sewage solids. The
sources and quantities of organic solid waste produced in the U.S. in 1971, as
well as the net conversion potential to oil and methane by the Bureau of Mines
and bioconversion processes, are shown in Table 5.9-6.

A comparison of chemical reduction, pyrolysis, and bioconversion
processes for the conversion of organic solid wastes to synthetic fuels is
given in Table 5.9-7.

Additional studies of waste-utilization may be found in the current liter-

Table 5.9-6 Dry, ash-free organic solid wastes produced in the U.S. in 1971
and the net conversion potential to oil and methane; reproduced
from L. L. Anderson, Energy Potential from Organic Wastes:
A Review of the Quantities and Sources, Bureau of Mines Information Circular 8549, Washington, D. C., 1972.

Source	Wastes generated, 10^6 t	Readily collectable, 10^6 t
manure	200	26.0
urban refuse	129	71.0
logging and wood manufacturing residues	55	5.0
agricultural crops and food wastes	390	22.6
industrial wastes	44	5.2
municipal sewage solids	12	1.5
miscellaneous	50	5.0
total	880	136.3
net oil potential (10^6 bbl) for the Bureau of Mines process:	1,098	170
net methane potential (10^9 SCF) for the bioconversion process:	8.8	1.36

ature.[5, 6, 7] Generally speaking, these processes will be economically via-

ble only if revenues are ultimately derived from a number of sources, including

dumping fees, fuel value, and metal recovery.[1-7]

The utilization of one of the oil-shale recovery techniques has recently

been proposed for processing used tires.[8] The processing of 8×10^6 tires

per year is expected to yield 15×10^6 gallons of oil, 73×10^6 lb of carbon

black, and 2×10^6 lb of steel.[8]

[5]J. G. Abert, H. Alter, and J. B. Bernheisel, "The Economics of Resource
Recovery from Municipal Solid Waste," Science 183, 1052-1058 (1974).

[6]W. C. Kasper, "Solid Waste and Its Potential as a Utility Fuel," O. E. R.
Report No. 18, State of New York Public Service Commission, Albany,
New York 12208, October 1973.

[7]Chemical and Engineering News, 51, 13, June 10, 1973; ibid., 52, 16,
July 15, 1974.

[8]Chemical and Engineering News, 52, 5, June 10, 1974.

Table 5.9-7 Comparison of three processes for the conversion of organic solid wastes to synthetic fuels; reproduced from Solar Energy as a National Energy Resource, NSF/NASA Solar Energy Panel, University of Maryland, College Park, Maryland, 1972.

Process requirements	Chemical reduction	Pyrolysis	Bioconversion
form of feed	aqueous slurry (15% solids)	dried waste	aqueous slurry (3-20% solids)
temperature	320 - 350°C	500 - 900°C	20 - 50°C
pressure	130-340 atmospheres	1 atmosphere	1 atmosphere
agitation	vigorous agitation	none	slight
other requirements	uses carbon mon-oxide and an alkaline catalyst	none	none
form of product	oil	oil, char, and gas[a]	gas
yield (percent of original material)	23%	40% oil; 20% char	20-26%
heating value	15,000 Btu/lb	12,000 Btu/lb oil, 9,000 Btu/lb char	23,800 Btu/lb[b]
percent of original heat content recovered in the product[c]	65%	82% (60% if the char is not included)	less than 77%

[a] All of the gas and one-third of the char are used to supply heat.

[b] This heating value corresponds to upgraded synthetic gas.

[c] Here it is assumed that the heat content of dry organic waste is 8,000 Btu/lb.

5.10 Recycling of Waste Oil

More than 1×10^9 gallons of lubricating oils were sold during 1971 for use in cars and trucks. These oils contain large amounts of chemical additives to improve their efficacy as lubricating agents for heavy-duty applications. About one-quarter of this lubricating oil is lost or evaporated and decomposed during use. The remaining three-quarters are discarded (into streams, sewers, or on the ground). Some years ago, this waste oil was reprocessed for use in low-cost lubricants or fuel oil but re-refining has now been largely abandoned because of the difficulty and cost of treating oils with large concentrations of additives.

The U.S. Bureau of Mines has been supporting research to develop more efficient methods of treatment for these discarded lubricating oils.[1] The total potential for recovery amounts to more than 4.9×10^4 bbl/d under current operating conditions. In addition, total re-refining will remove an important pollution source from the environment.

5.11 Measures of Energy-Utilization Efficiencies

Customarily-used efficiency measures are often inadequate for a proper evaluation of relative costs among different types of energy sources. Generally speaking, a useful measure for comparison is the source-energy cost

---

[1] Bureau of Mines Energy Program, 1972, U.S. Department of the Interior, Bureau of Mines Information Circular I.C. 8612, Washington, D.C., 1972.

for accomplishing a specified job. We shall illustrate this statement by a somewhat more detailed discussion of efficiency measures for a refrigerator.

The most widely used performance characteristic for the description of efficiencies achieved in refrigerator operation is the coefficient of performance (C.P.). The dimensionless C.P. is usually defined as the ratio of unwanted thermal energy removed to the electrical energy needed to accomplish energy removal. For representative conventional refrigerators, the C.P. may be 2.1. However, the electrical energy used to drive the refrigerator is generally produced from a fossil fuel, the combustion energy of which was converted to electrical energy with an efficiency of only about 33%. Thus, a modified coefficient of performance (M.C.P), defined as the ratio of thermal energy removed to fuel-combustion energy required for removal of this thermal energy, has a value of 2.1 ÷ 3 = 0.7 since the fossil-fuel combustion energy required for conversion was three times larger than the electrical energy actually needed to drive the refrigerator. If the original fuel cost was C in $/$10^6$ Btu, then we may define an economic measure of the coefficient of performance (E.C.P.) by the following relation:

$$\text{E.C.P.} = \frac{1}{C} \times \frac{\text{thermal energy removed by the refrigerator in } 10^6 \text{ Btu}}{\substack{\text{original fuel-combustion energy needed to} \\ \text{supply electricity for driving the refriger-} \\ \text{ator when it removes } 10^6 \text{ Btu}}}$$

$$= \frac{\text{thermal energy removed by the refrigerator in } 10^6 \text{ Btu.}}{\text{cost in \$ of needed original fuel-combustion energy}}$$

A conventional refrigerator with a C.P. of 2.1 at a source-fuel cost C of $3/$10^6$ Btu has an E.C.P. of $(2.1/3) \div 3 = 0.23 \times 10^6$ Btu/$ if electricity was generated with a 33% conversion efficiency from the fuel.

If the <u>electrical-energy cost</u> is $25/10^6$ Btu, then a refrigerator using solar energy becomes competitive with a conventional design having a C.P. of 2.1 when the sum of the amortized capital and operating costs of the solar unit amount to $12/10^6$ Btu of useful thermal energy removed. In some regions of the country, costs of $25/10^6$ Btu of electrical energy, or still higher costs, were encountered by early 1975. As the result of this price escalation, solar-powered refrigerators may become economically-attractive alternatives in the near future.

CHAPTER 6

GEOPHYSICAL IMPLICATIONS OF ENERGY CONSUMPTION

A responsible society using energy to the extent that we do must answer quantitatively all questions relating to the environmental impact of energy use on highly localized regions (with characteristic lengths of a few miles), on small-scale meteorological regions (the mesoscale, corresponding to regions with characteristic lengths of tens to hundreds of miles), on regions of intermediate scale (the synoptic scale, corresponding to regions with characteristic lengths of one to a few thousand miles), and on the global, worldwide scale. Questions of environmental impact relate not only to air and water quality but also to modifications in temperature, rainfall, snowfall and associated river flows, changes in wind speeds and direction, intermediate and large-scale climatic changes and, finally, possible global effects on the earth mean temperature, melting or reformation of glaciers, global floods or new ice ages, etc.[1]

Some idea of the societal costs of naturally-occurring severe storms may be gained from the data compiled in Tables 6-1 and 6-2. It has been estimated* that failure to evacuate a heavily populated region after hurricane

---

[1]H. E. Landsberg, "Man-Made Climatic Changes," Science 170, 1265-1274 (1970).

* R. H. Simpson, National Hurricane Center, statements made after occurrence of hurricane Celia in 1970.

281

Table 6-1   A 1970 estimate of physical damage associated with severe, localized weather phenomena in the U.S.

Weather phenomenon	Approximate number of deaths per year	Property damage, 10^6/y
hail storms	150	175
tornadoes	120	120
hurricanes	80	80
lightning	?	115

Table 6-2   A 1970 estimate of property damage by winds in the U.S.; private communication from E. Aubert (1970).

Wind speed, mph	Potential loss of property valued at $9,000 in $
30	0.10
45	1.00
60	10
85	100
120	1,000
165	~ 9,000 (complete loss)

warning could produce upward of 25,000 casualties in the Gulf-Atlantic coastal regions of the United States.

It is apparent that answers to the questions posed in the introductory paragraph require a deep and quantitative understanding of global-, synoptic-, and meso-scale meteorology, with proper allowance for the three-dimensional nature of the problem and the highly non-uniform surface-boundary conditions associated with the existence of oceans, mountains, rivers, cities, etc. Unfortunately, the complete problem is not encompassed even by our most sophisticated computer programs. The evolution and development of less-than-global-scale phenomena, such as tornadoes, thunderstorms, and hurricanes are even more difficult to predict accurately than average, longer-term global weather phenomena.

In the absence of all-inclusive computer codes, which allow quantitative modelling of the interdependent physical phenomena defining our environment, it has become customary to examine component programs in the hope that a later synthesis will yield the comprehensive understanding that we require. For example, we may study the nature of an urban heat island and of its associated circulation and weather impact.[2] Or we may note that the global concentration of CO_2 has been increasing regularly with time[3] during the last 50 years and then infer from a global heat-exchange calculation that the increasing concentration of CO_2 in the atmosphere is probably responsible for an increase in the average world-wide temperatures.[4] The use of fossil fuels for energy production has increased not only the atmospheric CO_2-concentrations and local mean temperatures, but has also contributed to a significant local rise in particle concentrations. Analysis[5] of this problem for an idealized, one-dimensional model, suggests that the rise in particle

[2] D. B. Olfe and R. L. Lee, "Linearized Calculations of Urban Heat Island Convection Effects," J. Atmospheric Sciences 28, 1374-1388 (1971).

[3] Man's Impact on the Global Environment: Assessment and Recommendations for Action, Report of the Study of Critical Environmental Problems, The M.I.T. Press, Cambridge, Mass., 1970.

[4] G. N. Plass, "Carbon Dioxide and Climate," Scientific American 201, 41-47, July 1959.

[5] R. Reck, J. Atmospheric Sciences, in press (1974). For a less complete earlier analysis, see S. I. Rasool and S. H. Schneider, "Atmospheric Carbon Dioxide and Aerosols: Effects of Large Increases on Climate," Science 173, 138-141 (1971).

concentrations will either cause a decrease or an increase of surface temperature, depending on the opacity of the particle clouds formed (which, in turn,
depends on the number density and optical properties of the particles). The
interplay between particle formation and changed water and carbon dioxide
concentrations may be non-linear insofar as surface-temperature predictions
are concerned. Problems of this type are not understood for the real, three-
dimensional world. It is generally believed that the location and persistence
of ice fields and snow are the most important variables affecting the heat balance of the earth.[6]

The development of quantitative programs for environmental-impact pre-
diction is a complicated and important subject that falls beyond the scope of
this discussion. Here we shall ultimately content ourselves with comments
on known environmental changes and, following Häfele,[7] with comparisons
of man-made heat and water loads relative to natural heat and water loads.

It is difficult to draw a meaningful boundary on the scope of topics that
must be appropriately included under the heading of environmental impact of
man's activities. Certainly major catastrophic global effects of the type
associated with large storms, floods, and periods of global glaciation must

---

[6]M. I. Budyko, "The Effect of Solar Radiation Variations on the Climate of the
     Earth," Tellus 21, 612-619 (1969); W. D. Sellers, "A Global Climatic Model
     Based on the Energy Balance of the Earth-Atmosphere System," J. Appl.
     Meteorology 8, 392-400 (1969).

[7]W. Häfele, "Energy Systems," in Proceedings of IIASA Planning Conference
     on Energy Systems, pp. 9-78, International Institute for Applied Systems
     Analysis, Schloss Laxenburg, 2361 Laxenburg, Austria, July 17-20, 1973.

be considered. The impact of pollution and externalized environmental costs (an example of which will be discussed in Chapter 7 in connection with the past environmental cost of coal use) are by now classical topics relating to the impact of energy use. However, there may be more elusive topics that properly belong here, such as the impact of local weather modification on the safety of aircraft use. This last topic is almost entirely beyond our scope of analysis. In fact, quantitative study of the occurrence of aircraft accidents may be interpreted to imply that the incidence of accidents is a random variable; this conclusion is not only inconsistent with the view that significant hazards may be associated with inclement weather but also contradicts (correctly) such popular ideas as a disproportionately high rate of development of multiple-crash occurrences. We shall consider this particular subject in some detail in Section 6.1 before returning to considerations of atmospheric circulation and the magnitudes of man-made energy sources.

The development of supersonic transport planes (SST) has recently been impeded, in part, because of the suggestion that NO_x associated with engine exhausts will be responsible for ozone depletion in the stratosphere and will thus lead to excessive ultraviolet radiation at the surface of the earth. It has been estimated that 500 American SSTs will reduce the worldwide ozone shield by 20% and will also produce local reductions up to 50% in zones of high traffic.[8] This problem is currently under active investigation.[8, 9]

---

[8]H. S. Johnston, "Photochemistry in the Stratosphere - with Applications to Supersonic Transports," Acta Astronautica 1, 135-156 (1974).

[9]A. J. Grobecker, "Research Program for Assessment of Stratospheric Pollution," Acta Astronautica 1, 179-224 (1974).

An optimal sollution appears to be the redesign of the SST engine to eliminate or reduce NO_x production.

6.1 An Analysis of the Incidence of U.S. Aircraft Accidents

The rate of occurrence of U.S. air-carrier accidents during the period 1964-1969 and 1971 is reasonably well described by a Poisson distribution.

Information concerning U.S. air-carrier accidents may be found in Refs. [1] to [3]. We have used these data to construct curves showing the incidence of 1, 2, 3, etc. accidents per month as a function of the number of months when these occurrences were observed. The results are reasonably well described by the Poisson distribution. The Poisson distribution was used in the form

$$P_k = \frac{a^k \exp(-a)}{k!} , \qquad (6.1-1)$$

where k = 1, 2, 3, etc. represents the number of accidents per month and P_k is the number of months when the accident rate k per month was observed. We designate a(t) as a time-dependent Poisson parameter, evaluated separately for each calendar year, which decreases as the total number of accidents occurring per year decreases. However, the statistical data base is too

---

[1] "A Study of U.S. Air Carrier Accidents 1964-1969," Report No. NTSB-AAS-72-5, National Transportation Safety Board, Washington, D.C.

[2] "Annual Review of Aircraft Data, U.S. Air Carrier Operations Calendar Year 1969," Report No. NTSB-ARC-71-1, National Transportation Safety Board, Washington, D.C.

[3] "A Preliminary Analysis of Aircraft Accident Data, U.S. Civil Aviation 1971," Report No. NTSB-APA-72-1, National Transportation Safety Board, Washington, D.C.

restricted to allow accurate determination of a(t) and we, therefore, determine a single value of a for the period 1964-1969 and 1971. The results
derived from Eq. (6.1-1) are plotted in Fig. 6.1-1, together with the obser-
vational data listed in Refs. [1] to [3].*

We may speculate on the meaning of these findings as follows: The limited information available on the causes of air-carrier accidents are random
functions of time, for a sufficiently long-time interval. It is not clear that
a statistically-significant correlation exists with what may be another random
function of time, namely, the occurrence of bad weather (both naturally-occurring and man-made bad weather). The conclusion that air-carrier accident
rates follow a Poisson distribution is no more surprising than the well-known
results that this function provides an acceptable description for the rate at
which horses administered fatal kicks in the Prussian army, the rate at which
automobiles pass a highway marker in a fixed-time interval, or the incidence
of wars[4] of different magnitudes (defined by the logarithm to the base ten
of the number of fatalities).

6.2   Atmospheric Circulation[1]

The atmospheric circulation is conveniently divided into three categories

---

*   "Best estimates" for a(t) show the following approximate results for the
    separate years 1964-1969 and 1971; 6.6, 7.0, 6.2, 6.0, 6.0, 5.4, and 4.3.

[4] L. F. Richardson, "Statistics of Deadly Quarrels," reprinted in Vol. II of
    World of Mathematics, p. 1254 et. seq., James Newman, ed., Simon and
    Schuster, New York, 1956.

---

[1] For a qualitative introduction to this topic, see, for example, H. C. Willett
    and F. Sanders, Descriptive Meteorology, Academic Press, New York, 1959.

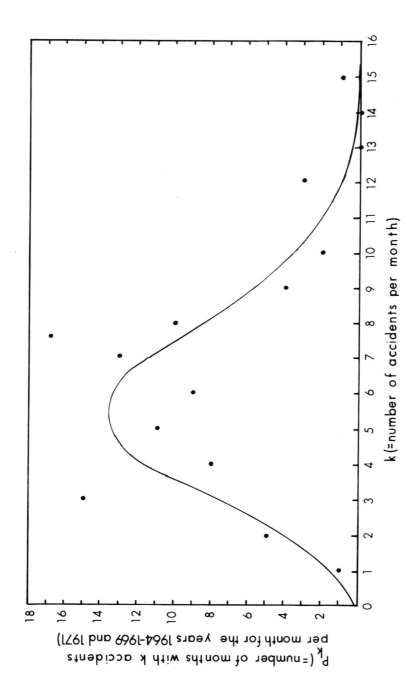

Fig. 6.1-1 The number of months P_k with k accidents per month as a function of k for the years 1964-1969 and 1971. The curve is calculated from Eq. (6.1-1) for a = 5.9.

of successively smaller scale. Thus we distinguish between primary or
planetary or general circulation produced by solar heating, which is greatly
modified by the rotation of the earth; large-scale horizontal or cellular circulation
corresponding to the secondary circulation, which dominates the weather map;
and the small-scale or localized horizontal and vertical cells which make up
the tertiary circulation that contains such local weather phenomena as land
and sea breezes, thundershowers, and tornadoes. We shall comment briefly
on the physical origin of these meteorological phenomena.

A.   The General Circulation

The general circulation is best understood by considering first a
stationary, non-rotating earth (see Fig. 6.2-1). The sun warms the equatorial
regions disproportionately, thus inducing thermal circulation between the
equatorial and polar regions (see Fig. 6.2-2). This thermal circulation is
characterized by a latitudinal (i.e., perpendicular to the latitudinal circles)
or meridional (i.e., in the direction of the meridians) flow of air in the upper
troposphere to compensate for lower pressures in the cooled polar regions.
But it follows from the principle of mass conservation that the meridional flow
in the upper troposphere must be balanced by compensating flow from the poles
toward the equator in the boundary-layer regions above the surface of the earth.
The meridional circulation in the upper troposphere transfers heat from the
equatorial region to the polar regions. The boundary-layer flow is responsible for frictional energy losses near the surface of the earth. Actually,
even if the earth did not rotate, steady circulation would not be created be-

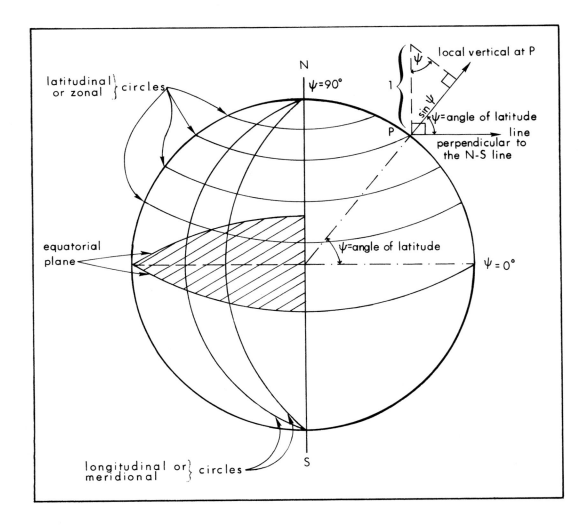

Fig. 6.2-1 Schematic diagram of the earth showing the latitudinal (or zonal)
circles, longitudinal (or meridional) circles, N-S direction,
equatorial plane, definition of the angle of latitude, and the local
vertical for an observer at P. If the frequency of angular rotation
of the earth around the N-S direction is ω, then the component of
the frequency of angular rotation around the local vertical at P is
$\omega \sin \psi$.

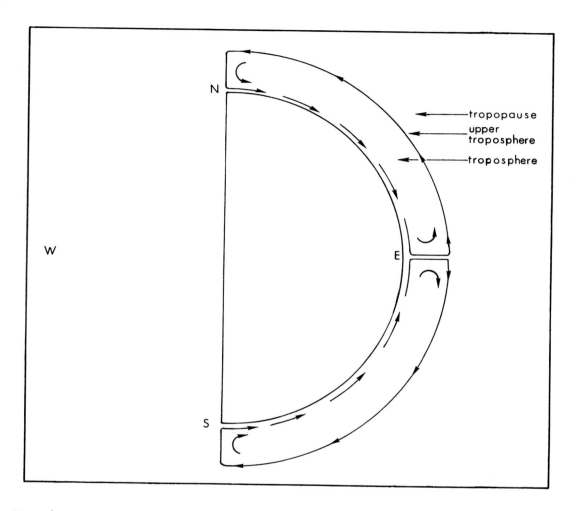

Fig. 6.2-2 Schematic diagram of the semi-earth showing the large-scale thermal circulation induced by preferential solar heating near the equator. The meridional circulation has maximum velocities near 37°N and 37°S. The pressure in the upper troposphere is higher near the equator than in the polar regions.

cause of the changing seasons. The air, which moves upward in the equatorial region, is heated by radiant-energy transfer as it rises to replace air which has moved poleward aloft. This air is later cooled by emission of radiant energy as it sinks near the polar regions.

The general-circulation model for the non-rotating earth described by Fig. 6.2-2 and in the preceding paragraph is strongly disturbed because of rotation of the earth and because of the presence of irregular land and sea masses on the surface.

B.   Induction of Strong Longitudinal or Zonal or East-West Circulation by Rotation of the Earth

Rotation of the earth (once in 23 hours, 56 minutes, 4.1 seconds) produces winds that are parallel to the isobars (rather than perpendicular to the isobars, as is the case with thermal circulation on the non-rotating earth). We call the resulting wind system the geostrophic winds. These zonal (longitudinal) winds are stronger than the meridional (latitudinal) circulation. As the result, the primary wind system in the upper troposphere becomes a system of westerlies and easterlies. It is impossible to maintain a stable circulation with only westerly or easterly winds because the mean frictional drag associated with westerlies and easterlies over the entire surface of the earth must vanish at the steady state. The preceding statement follows from the fact that the only net driving force for the winds is the thermal energy input from the sun, which is responsible for the latitudinal circulation. The stable general circulation system that develops on the earth, i.e., the balanced geostrophic wind system, is shown schematically in Fig. 6.2-3.

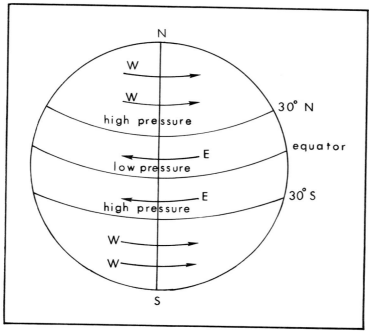

Fig. 6.2-3 Schematic diagram showing the balanced geostrophic wind
system: westerlies north and south of 30° latitude, sub-
tropical and tropical easterlies in the equatorial belt extending to 30°N and to 30°S. A net non-geostrophic circulation across isobars is created by preferential solar
heating in the equatorial region: this flow is characterized
by winds towards the equator in the frictional surface layers
of the easterlies and strong flow toward the poles in the tro-
pospheric layers. A more detailed look at the global circulation shows the existence also of weak polar easterlies.

C.   Wind Velocities in the Atmosphere

The geostrophic wind systems described in Fig. 6.2-3 may be shown to

be consistent with force balances affecting air masses. The principal forces

acting on volume elements of air will now be described briefly.

When pressure gradients are established, a pressure-gradient force

($\mathfrak{F}_{pg}$ per unit mass) accelerates the air, where

$$\mathfrak{F}_{pg} = a_{pg} = -(1/\rho)(\partial p/\partial n), \qquad (6.2-1)$$

a_{pg} = air acceleration, ρ = air density, $\partial p/\partial n$ = pressure gradient normal to the isobars; a negative sign appears in Eq. (6.2-1) because acceleration of air occurs in the direction of decreasing pressure.

The <u>gravitational force</u> per unit mass, $\mathfrak{F}_g$, produces an acceleration g equal to the gravitational acceleration and is given by the relation

$$\mathfrak{F}_g = g = -(1/\rho)(\partial p/\partial z), \qquad (6.2-2)$$

where z is the distance above the surface of the earth. If $\mathfrak{F}_g$ is the only force present, hydrostatic equilibrium is established in accord with the following change of pressure with altitude between different level surfaces:

$$dp = -\rho g dz \quad \text{or} \quad p_o - p = \rho g(z - z_o) \qquad (6.2-3)$$

for constant g, where the subscript <u>o</u> refers to surface or other reference conditions.

The frictional force per unit mass, $\mathfrak{F}_f$, is determined by velocity gradients ($\partial v/\partial n$) and the viscosity coefficient (μ) and produces the acceleration a_f. The applicable force law is

$$\mathfrak{F}_f = a_f = (1/\rho) \, \partial(\mu \, \partial v/\partial n)/\partial n \simeq (\mu/\rho)(\partial^2 v/\partial n^2). \qquad (6.2-4)$$

The frictional forces become large in regions where large velocity gradients occur (i.e., in boundary layers close to surfaces).

The effect of rotation of the earth on air motion is conveniently described by the fictitious Coriolis force. The definition of the Coriolis force is given in Fig. 6.2-4. The distance through which the volume element of air is deflected because of the rotation of the earth is AA´ = (vdt)(ωsinψ dt) and must be equal to $(1/2)a_C(dt)^2$ if a_C is the corresponding acceleration. Thus

$$\mathfrak{F}_{hdf} \equiv a_C = 2v\omega\sin\psi \qquad (6.2-4)$$

and the horizontal-deflection force ($\mathfrak{F}_{hdf}$), which acts on a unit mass of air, is seen to be $\mathfrak{F}_{hdf} = 2v\omega\sin\psi$. It should be noted that this force must always be applied in a direction perpendicular to the wind velocity and to the right side of the wind velocity in the Northern hemisphere.

At high altitudes, the principal winds are the geostrophic winds and are determined by a balance between $\mathfrak{F}_{pg}$ and $\mathfrak{F}_{hdf}$. The pressure-gradient force

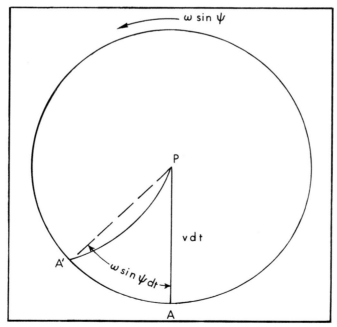

Fig. 6.2-4 An elementary volume of air, which would move from P to A in time dt with velocity v on a non-rotating earth, actually moves from P to A´ because of rotation through the angle ωsinψ dt. This rotation is accounted for by a fictitious Coriolis force.

must be directed toward lower pressures and is always perpendicular to the isobars. Per unit mass, it has been shown [see Eq. (6.2-1)] to be given by $(-1/\rho)\partial p/\partial n$. Hence the balance between the horizontal-deflection and pressure-gradient forces corresponds to the relation

$$\mathfrak{F}_{hdf} + \mathfrak{F}_{pg} = 0 \quad \text{or} \quad -2v_g \omega \sin\psi = -(1/\rho)(\partial p/\partial n), \qquad (6.2-5)$$

where we have written v_g for the geostrophic wind, which is determined by the balance between these forces. The meaning of Eq. (6.2-5) is illustrated by the pressure-balance diagram sketched in Fig. 6.2-5 for the Northern hemisphere.

The geostrophic wind velocity determined from Eq. (6.2-5) is a good approximation to the actual winds above the levels where frictional forces are important. It is perhaps worth emphasizing that the solar-energy input affects this dominant wind system through its influence on the establishment of the magnitudes and locations of the isobars.

D. Energy Requirements for Disturbing the General Circulation

The preceding discussion suggests that the supplementary energy requirements for disturbing the zonal (latitudinal or East-West) components of the general circulation above the surface of the earth must be comparable with the solar-energy flux absorbed by the atmosphere. As we shall see, this solar-energy bound is so large that the possibility of man-made interference with the average zonal component of the general circulation appears to be very remote indeed.

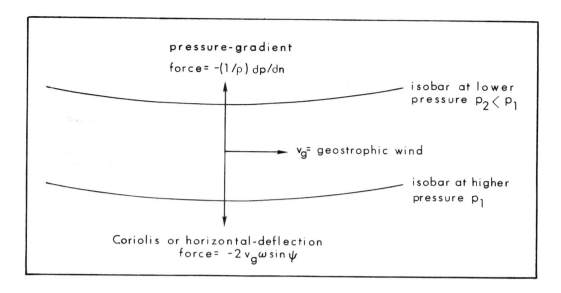

Fig. 6.2-5 Diagram showing the creation of the geostrophic wind system by
the balance between the pressure-gradient and Coriolis or horizontal-deflection forces.

The meridional (longitudinal or North-South) component of the general

circulation has been seen to be the direct result of solar heating on the

stationary earth. Hence we may expect a significant disturbance in this wind

system also when man-made energy additions approach an appreciable fraction

of the solar-energy input. A similar statement applies to the secondary circu-

lation. However, changes in the tertiary circulation may arise for much

smaller total energy additions, with the scale of the disturbance measured

essentially by the size of the region over which man-made influences are com-

parable with natural effects or are capable of inducing suitable feed-back

mechanisms to produce significant disturbances.

That feed-back is generally required to disturb natural balances on a sig-

nificant scale is apparent if we note, for example, that the total energy dissipation during the life of a mature hurricane has been estimated to be as large as 2×10^{26} to 6×10^{27} ergs, or about 0.3 to 10 times the annual U.S. energy consumption in 1970.[*] Clearly, a phenomenon of this type cannot be created by local, man-made heat sources such as giant thermal plumes from nuclear-reactor farms, unless these act as a trigger in releasing a sequence of supplementary natural thermal phenomena which ultimately produce hurricane-like winds as the result of cooperative effects. Unfortunately, understanding cooperative feed-back phenomena in nature requires a level of physical insight and a sophistication in analysis which is currently beyond our comprehension. For this reason, we must generally content ourselves with qualitative statements such as "this local, man-made heat source corresponds only to a small fraction of a known natural heat source and, therefore, we do not expect it to induce an important change in the balance of natural phenomena." Unexpressed in this type of statement is the tacit appendix "provided the man-made heat source does not serve as a trigger for a sequence of natural phenomena, which we do not understand, but which may escalate into a large-scale disaster".

6.3 Comparison of Man-Made and Naturally-Occurring Power Densities

A schematic diagram, showing the flow of energy to and from the earth, has been given in Fig. 2.17-1; similar representations have been published by others.[1]

---

[*] Energy dissipation rates in hurricanes are listed as 2×10^{25} to 6×10^{26} ergs/day with about 98% in thermal energy and 2% in rotational energy. We have taken a hurricane life of 10 days.

[1] M. King Hubbert, "The Energy Sources of the Earth," Scientific American **224**, 61-70, September 1971.

The numerical values given in Fig. 2.17-1 refer to averages over the entire sur-

face of the earth. Since the radius of a sphere with the same volume as the

earth is[2] $6.37\ 12213 \times 10^6$ meters $\simeq 3.95889 \times 10^3$ miles, the averaged

solar-energy input over the entire surface of the earth becomes S = 1.73 ×

10^{15} w/$4\pi \times (6.371 \times 10^6)^2 \text{m}^2 \simeq 340$ w/m^2.* The quantity S is referred to as

the solar constant.

The data listed in Fig. 2.17-1 may be used to estimate power densities

associated with natural phenomena. A compilation of these power densities

is given in Table 6.3-1.

Table 6.3-1 Power densities associated with natural phenomena, in w/m^2,
compiled from various sources and averaged over the entire
surface of the earth.

solar energy input into the outer atmosphere	340
solar radiation reflected directly from the atmosphere of the earth	102
absorbed solar radiation which is converted to heat energy on the earth	159
power density associated with evaporation and precipitation	79
power density associated with waves, convection, and currents	0.73
power density used for photosynthesis	0.079

[2]Handbook of Chemistry and Physics, p. F-144, 51st Edition, The Chemical
Rubber Co., Cleveland, Ohio, 1970.

*See Section 2.17 for a comparison of this estimate with the average flux density
incident on the illuminated side of the earth and an evaluation of the fraction
actually received at the surface of the earth.

Since we are concerned with the possible environmental impacts of energy use on the surface of the earth, we summarize in Table 6.3-2 other applicable data for our planet.

Following Häfele,[3] we list in Table 6.3-3, some examples of man-made power densities associated with energy use, as well as the data input required for estimation of the listed power densities; the designations w and kw refer to total equivalent power use (i.e., w_t and kw_t). Similar data[4] for selected cities are listed in Table 6.3-4.

Comparison of the data listed in Tables 6.3-1, 6.3-3, and 6.3-4 shows that we may expect concentrated man-made sources with energy densities in the vicinities of nuclear-reactor farms nearly sixty times larger than the normal solar energy-density input, that highly industrial regions like the Ruhr Valley of West Germany will provide energy output about 30% as large as the average global solar input by the year 2000, and that continuation of past energy-use trends will provide many heat-source regions (elsewhere in Western Europe, North America, Japan, the U.S.S.R., and industrial centers in other parts of the world) with atmospheric loadings that will similarly exceed the normal average load carried by our planet. These estimates give us reasons for concern although, as has been noted previously, our detailed knowledge of environmental implications is inadequate for quantification of impact-assessment. An optimist might argue that the projected world-wide energy input in the year 2000 on the land

---

[3]Ref. [7] in the Introduction to Chapter 6.

[4]Inadvertent Climate Modification, The M.I.T. Press, p. 58, Cambridge, Mass., 1971.

Table 6.3-2 A compilation of data referring to the earth; (a), from Ref. [2]; (b) from M. R. Gustavson, _Dimensions of World Energy_, Report M71-71, The Mitre Corporation, McLean, Virginia, 1971.

equatorial radius[a]	6.37839×10^6 m = 3.9633×10^3 mi
polar radius[a]	6.35691×10^6 m = 3.94999×10^3 mi
$1°$ latitude at the equator[a]	69.41 mi
$1°$ latitude at the poles[a]	68.70 mi
mean density[a]	5.522 g/cm^3 = 344.7 lb/ft^3
total mass[a]	5.983×10^{24} kg = 6.595×10^{21} t
mean surface density of continents[a]	2.67 g/cm^3 = 166.7 lb/ft^3
mean linear velocity in orbit[a]	29.77 km/sec = 18.50 mi/sec
mean rotational speed at the equator[a]	0.465 km/sec = 0.289 mi/sec
land area[a]	1.48847×10^8 km^2 = 5.7470×10^7 mi^2
ocean area[a]	3.61254×10^8 km^2 = 1.3948×10^8 mi^2
highest mountain (Mount Everest)[a]	8.840×10^3 m = 2.9003×10^4 ft
greatest sea depth[a]	1.0430×10^4 m = 3.4219×10^4 ft
mean distance to the moon[a]	3.84393×10^5 km = 2.38854×10^5 mi
mean distance to the sun[a]	1.495×10^8 km = 9.290×10^7 mi
approximate thermal gradient in the crust[a]	$30°$C/km = $48°$C/mi
geothermal heat to 10 km depth[b]	4×10^{19} Btu
heat capacity of the oceans per $°$C [b]	5.4×10^{21} Btu/$°$C
energy used per year for evaporation[b]	9.8×10^{20} Btu/y
energy required to evaporate the average water-vapor content of the atmosphere[b]	3×10^{19} Btu
heat capacity per $°$C of the atmosphere[b]	5×10^{18} Btu/$°$C

Table 6.3-3 Some examples of man-made power densities associated with energy use.

Physical system	Data input	Power density, w/m^2
1970, World land area	average per capita continuous power consumption for 4.0×10^9 people: 2.0kw/p	$\dfrac{(2,000w/p) \times (4.0 \times 10^9 p)}{1.488 \times 10^{14}\ m^2} = 0.054 w/m^2$
1970, U.S.	12 kw/p, 2×10^8 p, $9.4 \times 10^{12}\ m^2$	0.26
1970, West Germany	4 kw/p, 6×10^7 p, $2.5 \times 10^{11}\ m^2$	0.96
1970, Ruhr area of West Germany	18 kw/p, 6×10^6 p, $6.5 \times 10^9\ m^2$	16.60
2000, World land area	10 kw/p, 7×10^9 p, $1.488 \times 10^{14}\ m^2$	0.47
2050, World land area	20 kw/p, 1×10^{10} p, $1.488 \times 10^{14}\ m^2$	1.34
2000, U.S.	18 kw/p, 3×10^8 p, $9.4 \times 10^{12}\ m^2$	0.57
2000, West Germany	20 kw/p, 6×10^7 p, $2.5 \times 10^{11}\ m^2$	4.80
2000, Ruhr area of West Germany	100 kw/p, 1×10^7 p, $10^{10}\ m^2$	1×10^2
large nuclear-reactor farm	$3 \times 10^4\ Mw_e \simeq 7 \times 10^4\ Mw_t$, $3.5 \times 10^6\ m^2$	2×10^4

Table 6.3-4 Power densities in selected metropolitan areas for 1965-1968; reproduced with modifications from Ref. [4].

Metropolitan area, km^2	Population, 10^6	Man-made power density, w/m^2	Per capita power consumption, kw/p	Average solar input into the metropolitan area, w/m^2
West Berlin: 234[a]	2.3	19.7	2.0	57
Moscow: 878	6.42	122.8	16.8[b]	42
Sheffield (1952): 48[a]	0.5	16.7	1.6	46
Hamburg: 747	1.83	12.2	5.0	55
Cincinnati: 200[a]	0.54	25.1	9.3	99
Los Angeles: 3,500[a]	7.0	20.6	10.3	108
Manhattan (New York City): 59	1.7	605.1	21.0	93
Fairbanks, Alaska: 37	0.03	17.7	21.8	18
region including 21 metropolitan areas between Boston and Washington: 87,000	33	4.2	11.2	~90

a. Built-up area only.

b. Related to industrial production.

areas will reach an average density of less than 0. 14% of the solar input and of

less than 0. 6% of the mean energy density associated with evaporation and preci-

pitation and that there is no indication that this type of incremental loading

cannot be handled comfortably by our planet.   On the other hand, a pessimist

might argue that the compounding of strong localized energy sources will exert

a major influence on global meteorology that may well produce disastrous local,

mesoscale, and even synoptic-scale changes.   The truth is that we simply do

not know what will happen, that we should be concerned about what we are doing,

and that we must spend the required effort for quantitative impact-assessment

well before the year 2000.

6.4   Normal Water Flows and Water Consumption

Häfele[1] has expanded the semi-quantitative discussion of environmental

loading by man to include examination of the earth-water cycle and the potential

of embedding energy in the hydrosphere.   The earth-water cycle is reproduced

in Fig. 6.4-1 from Lvovich.[2]   The steady-state ocean volume of $1.37 \times 10^9 \text{km}^3$

is seen to be consistent with the heat-capacity estimate of $5.4 \times 10^{21} \text{Btu}/^{\circ}\text{C} =$

$1.37 \times 10^{24} \text{ cal}/^{\circ}\text{C}$ given in Table 6.3-2.   If the year 2000 world-wide energy

consumption of $2.1 \times 10^{18} \text{Btu}$ were uniformly used to heat the world's oceans,

the corresponding temperature rise would be only $3.9 \times 10^{-4} \, ^{\circ}\text{C}$ and would prob-

ably be negligible insofar as environmental impact is concerned.

---

[1] Ref. [3] in Section 6.3.

[2] M. I. Lvovich, "World Water Balance," Publications de l'Association
    Internationale d'Hydrologie Scientifique 93, 401-415 (1970).

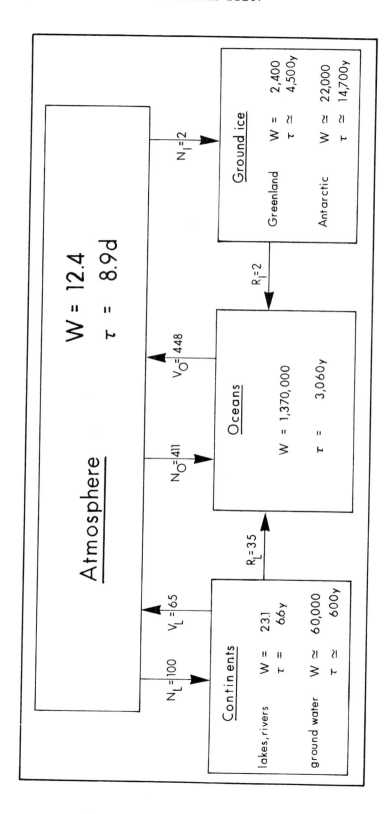

Fig. 6.4-1 Water cycle of the earth; based on the data of Lvovich. [2] Water content: W in 10^3km^3; transports: to (N) and from (V) the earth, in $10^3 \text{km}^3/\text{y}$; residence time: $\tau = W/F$ with F equal to the sum of the outgoing volume-flow rates; total for the earth: $V_E = N_E = 513 \times 10^3 \text{km}^3/\text{y} \rightleftharpoons$ 101 cm/y; run-off to the oceans: R in $10^3 \text{km}^3/\text{y}$.

Water consumption data for 1965 and estimates for the year 2000 have also been compiled by Lvovich.[3] These results are summarized in Table 6.4-1. We note a 1965 global consumption (for evaporation and waste) corresponding to 8.1% of normal run-off whereas the projected year 2000 consumption estimate of 12,700 km^3/y corresponds to 36.3% of the normal global run-off. These numerical values suggest that we are rapidly approaching saturation for use of normally-available global water resources. Needless to say, in heavily-industrialized regions, we are already using upward of one-third of the normally-available water run-off. The principal consumptive uses (see Table 6.4-1 for details) for water are irrigation, industrial use including cooling of energy sources, and removal of waste heat in manufacturing. Of these, irrigation is expected to increase relatively slowly (see Table 6.4-1), whereas waste-water production associated with power-plant cooling and industrial use is growing most rapidly.

Table 6.4-1 Estimated water consumption in km^3/y for the year 1965 and projected water consumption to the year 2000; based on the data of Lvovich.[3]

Application	The year 1965 use for			The year 2000 use for		
	evaporation	waste	total	evaporation	waste	total
irrigation	1,700	600	2,300	3,850	400	4,250
industrial use	40	160	200	600	2,400	3,000
power-plant cooling	15	235	250	250	4,250	4,500
other urban uses	42	56	98	190	760	950
totals	1,797	1,051	2,848	4,890	7,810	12,700

[3] M. I. Lvovich, "Water Resources of the Future," unpublished (1969); reprinted in Ref. [1].

6.5 Supplementary Water and Energy Requirements for Large-Scale Irrigation Development

Häfele[1] has emphasized the requirement for significant supplementary water and energy use in case of development of large-scale irrigation in arid regions for agricultural and other purposes. His reference data[1] are based on practical experience in Egypt, where it was found that a supplementary water input of about 200 cm/y is required to convert arid to cultivated land.

Of the 1.49×10^8 km^2 of land area, it has been suggested that as much as 0.3×10^8 km^2 is located in favorable climates where irrigation could convert the arid land to cultivated land. For a required water input of 200 cm/y, the corresponding supplementary global water requirement for irrigation becomes 6×10^4 km^3/y. If this water is supplied by evaporation of ocean water, the required supplementary thermal energy per year is seen to be 128Q/y ($\simeq$ 61 times the estimated year 2000 world-wide consumption) for a heat of evaporation of 540 cal/g = 2.13 Btu/g. Thus, large-scale global irrigation with water supplied by distillation of salt water appears to imply a prohibitively-high energy cost. The use of more economical desalination procedures requires[1] 50 kwh/m^3 = 43 cal/g of H_2O and reduces the energy requirement for supplying 200 cm/y for 0.3×10^8 km^2 to 10.2 Q/y or 4.86 times the estimated year 2000 world-wide energy consumption.

It should be noted that the total run-off water of 3.5×10^4 km^3/y corresponds to an equivalent average global rainfall of $(3.5 \times 10^4$ km^3/y$) \times (10^5$ cm/km$)$

[1]Ref. [3] in Section 6.3.

$\div$ (1.49 $\times$ 10^8 km^2) = 23.5 cm/y. The total heat of evaporation of this run-off

water corresponds to 1.9 $\times$ 10^{22} cal/y = 7.5 $\times$ 10^{19} Btu/y while the total con-

densation of water to the lands and oceans releases about (513/35) = 14.7 times

more energy or 11 $\times$ 10^{20} Btu/y (which is seen to be in rough accord with the

appropriate entry of 9.8 $\times$ 10^{20} Btu/y listed in Table 6.3-2).

6.6   Use of Run-Off Water and of the Atmosphere for Power-Plant Cooling

If all of the run-off water were used to cool electrical generating stations

and if an average temperature rise as high as 5°C for the run-off water were

allowed, then we could absorb 1.75 $\times$ 10^{20} cal/y. About one-third of this energy

could be made available as electricity, i.e., about 7.7 $\times$ 10^{6}Mw$_e$ would corres-

pond to the ultimate, continuously-usable, installed capacity.

On the other hand, if all of the run-off water were evaporated, the ulti-

mate installed generating capacity would be increased by a factor of 540/5 = 108

and would correspond to 8.3$\times$ 10^8 Mw$_e$. We expect that the year 2000 installed

world-wide generating capacity will reach about 4 $\times$ 10^6 Mw$_e$ and that it is,

therefore, apparent that evaporative cooling will be required if water is to be

the principal heat-transfer medium.

According to Table 6.3-2, the heat capacity of the atmosphere is 5 $\times$ 10^{18}

Btu/$^\circ$C = 5Q/$^\circ$C. Hence, if the year 2000 energy-utilization rate were all used

for electricity generation with a 33% conversion efficiency, then an atmospheric

temperature rise of 0.67 $\times$ 2.1Q/(5Q/$^\circ$C) = 0.28°C would occur if only atmo-

spheric cooling is employed; the subsequent use of the electrical energy will, of course, be responsible for further heat addition in some form. It is not clear that a temperature rise of the estimated magnitude is tolerable.

6.7 Epilogue

The dimensions of approaching world-wide energy use are so large that the problem of significant global impact appears to be very real indeed. Probably nothing short of a crash effect-assessment study will provide us with an indication of possible saturation in environmental capability before disastrous consequences become apparent.

Admittedly incomplete computer studies of global-climatic changes have suggested that a 1.6% decrease in solar radiation or, equivalently, a 5 to 10% increase in the average planetary albedo will produce a major period of glaciation.[1]

A record of temperature variations kept along the Eastern seaboard for 230 years shows both warming (during the late 18th century and from 1900 to 1945) and cooling (during much of the 19th century and since 1945) trends, with typical yearly fluctuations in temperature that are far larger than the long-term changes.[1] Similar short- and long-term variations have been observed in precipitation rates.[1]

Man-made additions to the atmosphere of some chemical pollutants already exceed normally-present constituents and have produced long-term concentration changes. For example, the monitoring station at Mauna Loa in Hawaii shows an average increase in atmospheric CO_2-concentration from 312 ppm in 1958

[1] H. E. Landsberg, "Man-Made Climatic Changes," Science 170, 1265-1274 (1970).

to 321 ppm in 1970.[2] The anticipated rise in CO_2-concentration, in view of known

fossil-fuel combustion, was actually considerably higher and would have led to an

increase in CO_2-concentration to 326 ppm by 1970 if not for unknown sinks that

removed more CO_2 than was anticipated.[2] The rate of exchange of CO_2 between

the atmosphere and the oceans has been extensively studied by H. E.

Suess.[3-6] Suess' investigations suggest an average residence time in the

atmosphere of about 10 years, which defines the rate at which CO_2 produced

by fossil-fuel combustion is absorbed in the oceans. Over geologic times,

the atmospheric CO_2-concentration has presumably been regulated by the

tendency to establish equilibrium between silicates, carbonates, silica, and

CO_2.[7]

In conclusion, we note that energy loading is only one of many influences

exerted by man on his environment. As another example, the relation between

[2] Man's Impact on the Global Environment, p. 48, The M.I.T. Press, Cambridge, Mass., 1970.

[3] H. E. Suess, "Natural Radiocarbon and the Rate of Exchange of Carbon Dioxide Between the Atmosphere and the Sea," Proceedings of the Conference on Nuclear Processes in Geologic Settings, pp. 52-56, National Academy of Sciences-National Research Council Publication, Washington, D. C., 1953.

[4] R. Revelle and H. E. Suess, "Carbon Dioxide Exchange Between Atmosphere and Ocean and the Question of an Increase of Atmospheric CO_2 during the Past Decades," Tellus 9, 18-27 (1957).

[5] H. E. Suess, "Transfer of Carbon 14 and Tritium from the Atmosphere to the Ocean," J. Geophys. Res. 75, 2363-2364 (1970).

[6] J. Houtermans, H. E. Suess and W. Munk, "Effects of Industrial Fuel Combustion on the Carbon-14 Level of Atmospheric CO_2," in Radioactive Dating and Methods of Low-Level Counting, pp. 57-68, International Atomic Energy Agency, Vienna, Austria, 1967.

[7] H. C. Urey, The Planets, Yale University Press, New Haven, Connecticut, 1952.

man's mobilization of selected materials within the ecosystem and the naturally-occurring flows of these materials is shown in Table 6.7-1. The long-term environmental influence of these materials, as well as of sulfur-compound and CO_2 introduction into the atmosphere, is only now beginning to be assessed.[8]

That numerically small changes in climatic variables (e.g., in the solar constant) may be responsible for significant environmental changes has recently been emphasized by Bryson,[9] who notes that human activity may be interfering significantly with some of the dominant control variables (e.g., CO_2- and particle concentrations). Climatic changes occur very rapidly once a critical triggering mechanism has been released. The time-determining steps for change are associated with the times required for melting and reformation of glaciers and characteristic times for change in the active layers near the surface of the earth. According to Bryson,[9] ice ages may be initiated or terminated in a century or two.

[8] John P. Holdren and Paul R. Ehrlich, "Human Population and the Global Environment," American Scientist 62, 282-292 (1974).

[9] R. A. Bryson, "A Perspective on Climatic Change," Science 184, 753-760 (1974).

Table 6.7-1 Man's mobilization of selected materials compared with movement of these same materials in river flows; based on data from H.J.M. Bowen, Trace Elements in Biochemistry, Academic Press, London, 1966 and the Minerals Yearbook, U.S. Department of the Interior, U.S. Government Printing Office, Washington, D.C., 1974.

Material	Normal river flows of material,[a] 10^3 mt/y	World mining and production rate in 1972, 10^3 mt/y
metallic ores and concentrates		
iron	23,000	756,000
manganese	420	21,000
molybdenum	12	80
nickel	350	640
titanium	300	3,600
metals		
aluminum	8,400	11,000
copper	350	6,600
gold	2	1
lead	175	3,400
magnesium	144,000	230
mercury	3	10
silver	5	9
tin	1	240
zinc	350	5,100
nonmetals		
nitrogen	8,000	35,000
sulfur	130,000	25,800

[a] A river water-flow rate of 35 $\times 10^3$ km^3/y is assumed (see Fig. 6.4-1).

CHAPTER 7

THE PAST SOCIETAL COSTS OF COAL USE
IN ELECTRICITY GENERATION

Nearly all books on ecology contain at least one chapter on the environmental costs of coal use. Discussions on the disastrous effects of coal mining and coal burning range from subsidence to acid drainage to pneumoconiosis to atmospheric pollution. Quantification of social costs requires a more difficult analysis. We shall follow M. Granger Morgan and his colleagues in their evaluation of the societal costs of coal use. Before describing this analysis in Section 7.2, we present a brief commentary of a more conventional variety on the environmental costs of coal mining.

7.1 Environmental Costs of Coal Mining

The following qualitative description of environmental damage refers to factors that are customarily associated with coal mining without, however, emphasizing properly the dominant past costs associated with SO_2, NO_x, and particulate production.

A. Subsidence[1]

About 56% of the bituminous coal used in the United States during 1970 was obtained from underground mining. There were about 8×10^6 acres of under-

---

[1]See, for example, G. Garvey, _Energy, Ecology, Economy_, W. W. Norton and Co., New York, 1971.

mined land, of which 77% was produced by coal mining. Most of this land was located in the Appalachian region of the Eastern United States. About 0.158×10^6 acres of urban land showed significant subsidence in mid-1970. By the year 2000, an additional 3 to 5×10^6 acres are expected to show noticeable subsidence. By mid-1970, about 395×10^6 had been expended on building repairs in subsidence areas. It has been estimated that in Wilkes-Barre, Pennsylvania, every dollar spent on subsidence control saved $8 in post-subsidence damage.[1]

B.   Acid Drainage[1]

Deep mining dislocates the relative positions of rock strata and thereby disturbs the water table. Mine drainage pollutes rivers and impounded waters with sulfuric acid. It has been estimated by workers at the U.S. Department of the Interior that 75% of the observed acid drainage is associated with deep mining and 25% with strip mining. According to a study performed at the Thompson-Ramo-Wooldridge Corporation,[1] 500×10^9 gallons of mine drainage, containing 4×10^6 tons of H_2SO_4, have polluted nearly 11,000 stream miles and 1.5×10^4 acres of impounded water. Most (about 80%) of the strip-mine banks are devoid of vegetation because of excess acidity (pH = 3 to 5), which is lethal to plants for a pH less than about 4. Mine-acid drainage exceeds environmental absorption capacities by a substantial margin.

The acid drainage may be neutralized with an alkali such as lime. The total weight of sulfuric acid produced corresponds roughly to 10% of the weight of coal mined.   The estimated costs for effective neutralization of

acid drainage in the Appalachian region vary from about $0.05/(ton of coal

produced) to as high as $2/t.   Spent mines can be sealed at costs ranging

from a few thousand to perhaps twenty thousand dollars per seal, with the

effectiveness of the seals highly variable.   To reduce mine run-off by up

to 75%, drainage channels may be diverted at costs ranging from $300 to

$3,000 per acre. [1]

Control may also be achieved by covering refuse piles with soil, estab-

lishing a vegetative cover, and providing adequate drainage to minimize

erosion. [2]

C.   Mine Fires[1]

Fires occur sporadically in virgin, active, and abandoned mines.   The

mine fires are costly to control and are responsible for air pollution.   The

1960 cost to the State of Pennsylvania alone for mine-fire control was $60 \times 10^6.

D.   Soil Erosion[1]

Strip mining is accompanied by the production of mountains of refuse

that line the excavated areas or have been allowed to fall into stream beds.

In Appalachia, about 1% of the land has been strip mined.   Subsequent soil

erosion produced fouled waterways.   The soil erosion remains after the

refuse has been cleared.   This problem is the more severe the larger the

---

[2]Z. V. Kosowski, "Control of Mine Drainage from Coal Mine Mineral Wastes,
    Phase II: Pollution Abatement and Monitoring," Office of Research and
    Monitoring, U.S. Environmental Protection Agency, Washington, D.C.,
    20460, May 1973.

overburden protecting the coal layer. Hence, it tends to be aggravated in regions where strip mining of marginal deposits occurs. Only about 60% of strip-mined soil regains natural vegetation. Proper soil reconstruction generally requires leaching of acid and replanting. About 1 acre of land is adversely affected for every acre that is strip mined. Furthermore, strip mining affects, through subsequent erosion, undisturbed forests near the mined areas. The fallen debris and waste impede the water flows in the river beds. It has been estimated[1] that water flows have been reduced by an average of 60% and that only about 25% of the silt load created is carried to the major river systems. The creation of spoil banks accelerates erosion, perhaps as much as tenfold.

E.   Land-Reclamation Costs

Reclamation costs for strip-mined lands vary greatly, from a few hundred dollars to as much as $1,500 per acre, depending on the nature of the land and on the planned extent of reconstruction. The quantitative aspects of this problem will be discussed more completely in the following Section 7.2. The following estimate has been made[1] for the total cumulative damage in Appalachia to 1970: 2.8×10^9; of this total, 1.15×10^9 was allocated for waste reclamation and soil conservation, 1.00×10^9 for subsidence, 0.50×10^9 for acid drainage, and 0.15×10^9 for fire control.

Entirely omitted from the preceding discussion are environmental costs associated with coal use. As we shall see, these societal charges are substantially larger than those accounted for in the specified production costs.

The problem of rehabilitation of Western coal lands after strip mining is well formulated and carefully discussed in a recent publication.[3]

7.2   An Estimate for the Societal Cost of Coal Use[1]

The methodology developed by Morgan et al[1] for estimating the societal cost of coal production and use will serve as a prototype of how assessments of this type should be made. Although some of the detailed cost studies may well be subject to revision, the overview provided by this type of analysis should ultimately become a universal requirement for societal-cost evaluations connected with all types of technological applications.

A.   Summary of Results

Referring specifically to the application of coal for electricity generation, the following summary statements indicate the principal conclusions reached by Morgan et al.[1]

The 1970 direct cost of coal use for producing electrical energy was 7 to 8 mills/kwh$_e$ (1 mill = 1×10^{-3} = 0.1 cent). The social cost of this coal application, which was born by society at large, was $\geq 11.5 \pm 2$ mills/kwh$_e$.

---

[3]Rehabilitation Potential of Western Coal Lands, Environmental Studies Board, National Academy of Sciences/National Academy of Engineering, Ballinger Publishing Co., Cambridge, Mass., 1974.

---

[1]M. G. Morgan, B. R. Barkovich, and A. K. Meier, "The Social Costs of Producing Electric Power from Coal: A First-Order Calculation," Proceedings of the IEEE 61, 1431-1442 (1973).

If an optimal control strategy were implemented, the direct cost of coal use for producing electrical energy would rise by $\geq 3 \pm 1$ mills/kwh$_e$ because of the supplementary costs associated with installation of control systems, while the social cost would decrease from $\geq 11.5 \pm 2$ mills/kwh$_e$ to $\geq 4.5 \pm 1.5$ mills/kwh$_e$.

The possible global impact of CO_2 production and of thermal pollution has not been included in arriving at the specified numbers (see Sections 6.3 and 6.7 for brief discussions of these topics).

B.   Optimization Methodology for Production, Use, and Societal Costs

Let ℓ_i represent the level of control of an undesirable effect i (e.g., subsidence, acid drainage, pneumoconiosis, sulfur dioxide concentration in the atmosphere associated with coal use, particle concentration near a boiler using coal, etc). We may then divide the total cost C_i, associated with the undesirable effect i, into a societal-cost component $C_s(\ell_i)$ and a control-cost component $C_c(\ell_i)$. The costs $C_s(\ell_i)$ are paid, respectively, by society at large and by the coal-producer or coal-user to achieve the control level ℓ_i for the ith undesirable effect, with $C_c(\ell_i)$ referring to either or both production control and use control. Thus

$$C_i = C_s(\ell_i) + C_c(\ell_i);$$

also

$$C \equiv \sum_{i=1}^{m} C_i = \sum_{i=1}^{m} [C_s(\ell_i) + C_c(\ell_i)] \qquad (7.2-1)$$

represents the total cost of coal use, including both societal and control components. The summation over i, from i = 1 to m, includes all items

for which a societal cost can be assigned and for which it is, therefore,

worthwhile to ask if a more economical method of use cannot be found by

instituting suitable controls, including, for example, partial or complete

removal of sulfur compounds before or after burning, partial or complete

soil restitution, partial or complete filtering of particles from the mines

to eliminate pneumoconiosis, etc. Schematically, the costs must vary

with institution of controls as is shown in Fig. 7.2-1 and we, therefore,

expect to find an optimized control strategy at a particular control level

ℓ_i^* for each deleterious effect i. Here we assume that the undesirable

influences may be treated independently, i.e., we neglect the possible

occurrence of synergistic coupling between deleterious effects (even

though it is clear that this type of interplay will, in fact, occur since,

for example, the combined health hazards of high particle and SO_2 con-

centrations may be greater than those associated with the sum of these

phenomena occurring alone).

The analysis of Morgan et al[1] refers to a 1,000-Mw_e station with a 70%

plant use factor and annual fixed charges of 14%.

We shall now describe briefly how the summary results given in Section

7.2A were obtained.

C.   Cost of Land Use in Strip Mining

The costs for reconstructing a Western softwood forest are shown in

Fig. 7.2-2, with the percentage recovery of maximum timber volume per

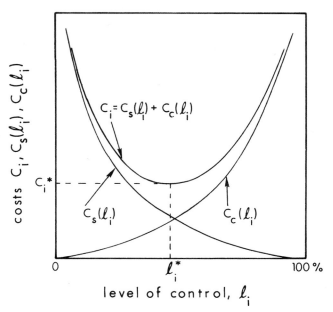

Fig. 7.2-1 Schematic diagram showing total, societal, and control costs as functions of control level for the ith undesirable effect; l_i^* is the optimized value of l_i corresponding to cost minimization at C_i^*.

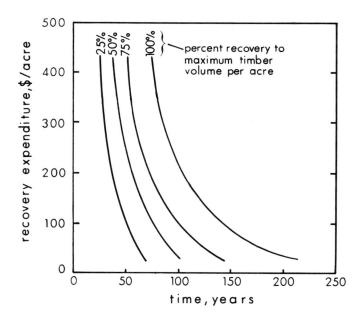

Fig. 7.2-2 Lumbering costs for a Western forest; reproduced from Ref. [1].

acre as a variable parameter. Immediate reconstruction of land by replanting
fully-grown trees is prohibitively expensive. The full recovery cost in
200 years amounts to about $40/acre, but does not include an assessment
for the aesthetic cost paid over such a long period of time by people who
have had to be satisfied with much less than a completely-matured forest.

A first-order estimate may be made for the aesthetic cost by charging
land-rental fees, consistent with applicable standards for land use in the
particular area where reforesting is in progress. Even at the minimum
federal value for land of $10/acre, the incremental cost for full reforesting
is seen to be large, amounting to $2,500/acre for a 250-year period without
allowance for partial recovery, or to some appropriate fraction of this amount
if a suitable formula can be found for prorating the value of partial recovery.

Experience in the Rhineland of Germany with recovery of strip-mined
brown-coal or lignite fields has shown total recovery costs of $3,000 to
$4,500 per acre to obtain agricultural land in about five years. The U.S.
costs are likely to be comparable and may be broken down as follows: $500
to $3,000 per acre for grading, $300 per acre for planting or $60 to $100 per
acre for hydroseeding, and $800 to $1,000 per acre for mulching.

One might, of course, consider alternative land reconstruction. For
example, it would generally be far cheaper and much quicker to convert
a strip-mined forest to agricultural use. Before a decision of this type can
be made, the relative societal advantages and disadvantages of converting
forested land to agricultural land must be examined.

If we choose a mean recovery cost vs. time curve (see Fig. 7.2-3) and then add fixed annual land-rental fees, we may derive a cost-control curve (see Fig. 7.2-4) for each annual rental fee. At $10/acre for rental, the societal cost for land recovery is seen to be at least 2.5×10^3 (see Fig. 7.2-4). For this rental value, the incremental cost for generating electricity associated with land reconstruction, for a coal field that yields 1.8×10^6 tons/mi^2 if each ton of coal can be converted to 2.2×10^3 kwh$_e$ of electrical energy, becomes

$$\frac{(\$2.5 \times 10^3/\text{acre}) \times (640 \text{ acre/mi}^2)}{(1.8 \times 10^6 \text{ ton of coal/mi}^2) \times (2.2 \times 10^3 \text{kwh}_e/\text{ton of coal})}$$

$$= \$4 \times 10^{-4}/\text{kwh}_e = 0.4 \text{ mill/kwh}_e.$$

The corresponding estimate at $40/acre-y rental fee is easily seen to be about 0.9 mill/kwh$_e$.

The preceding analysis is clearly incomplete. In particular, the elusive aesthetic costs of temporary land degradation have not been evaluated. Nevertheless, the methodology used is interesting and deserves amplification. Different techniques to arrive at societal-cost estimates were employed[1] for other deleterious effects, as will be indicated briefly in the following subsections.

D. Control of Acid-Mine Drainage[1]

The 1969 U.S. Department of the Interior estimate of the capital investment required to control 95% of all acid-mine drainage was $6.6 \times$

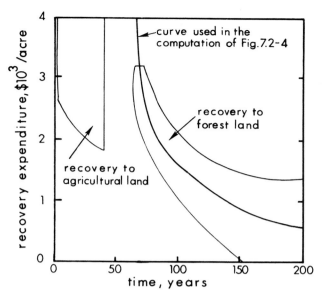

Fig. 7.2-3   Mean recovery expenditure for reforesting or conversion to agricultural land use. The recovery to agricultural land includes a lower limit line and a cut-off (vertical line) at about 40 years. Reproduced from Ref. [1].

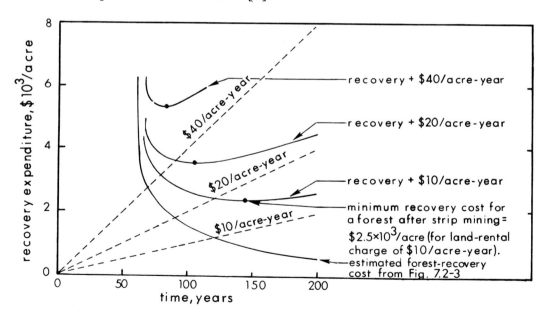

Fig.   7.2-4   Total land recovery expenditure as a function of time using the average recovery-cost curve for reforesting from Fig. 7.2-3 and various annual land-rental charges; reproduced from Ref. [1].

10^9 over a period of twenty years. Using this estimate and noting that a total of 73×10^9 tons of coal had been mined to 1970, the incremental cost for electrical-energy production associated with acid-mine drainage becomes

$$\frac{\$6.6 \times 10^9}{(73 \times 10^9 \text{ ton of coal}) \times (2.2 \times 10^3 \text{kwh}_e/\text{ton of coal})}$$

$$\simeq \$4 \times 10^{-5}/\text{kwh}_e = 0.04 \text{ mill/kwh}_e.$$

The preceding cost refers to reconstruction only and does not allow for the past long-term damages and losses associated with acid-mine drainage, nor is a proper cost included for partial losses during the twenty-year reconstruction period.

E.   Subsidence[1]

Only a portion of the subsidence cost has been paid by the government and, therefore, represents a societal cost. The remaining fraction of the cost for subsidence control was paid by the coal producers and was then included in the direct cost of coal. The societal portion amounted to $0.05/ ton of coal in 1968 or

$$\frac{\$0.05}{(\text{ton of coal}) \times (2.2 \times 10^3 \text{kwh}_e/\text{ton of coal})}$$

$$\simeq \$2 \times 10^{-5}/\text{kwh}_e = 0.02 \text{ mill/kwh}_e.$$

F.   Removal of Refuse Banks

Although the total accumulated bituminous refuse as of 1970 was 2.8 $\times 10^9$ tons (corresponding to a 75-ft deep layer covering 23,000 acres), its removal cost is easily seen to represent a negligible addition to the cost of electrical-energy production.

G.   Pneumoconiosis

In 1970, there were between 38,000 and 125,000 coal miners with black-lung disease, the effect varying from severe to slight for these populations. In order to avoid the disease, the total dust concentration must be maintained below 2 mg/m^3, whereas the average level reached near automated mining equipment was 8 mg/m^3. The Federal Coal Mine Safety Act of 1969 established 2 mg/m^3 as the maximum allowable level after January 1, 1973. It has incidentally been estimated that implementation of this act has led to a 15 to 30% decrease in underground mining productivity.

An Appalachian Commission report by Lucille Langlois[2] has placed the total cost for pneumoconiosis victims at 5×10^7/y or at $1,000/y for every affected miner if the average number of affected miners is taken to be 50,000. The corresponding incremental societal cost for electrical-energy production from coal use in 1968 is seen to be

$$\frac{(\$5 \times 10^7/y) \times 0.53 \ (= \text{fraction of coal used for electricity production})}{(1.43 \times 10^{12} kwh_e/y) \times 0.46 (= \text{fraction of total electricity production associated with coal burning})}$$

$$\simeq \$4.0 \times 10^{-5}/kwh_e = 0.04 \ mill/kwh_e.$$

---

[2] L. Langlois, The Cost and Prevention of Coal Workers Pneumoconiosis, Appalachian Regional Commission Monograph, 1971.

The computed <u>control</u> cost for complete elimination of the disease has been pegged at 0.024 mill/kwh$_e$.

Morgan et al[1] use a somewhat different analysis that leads to a value of 0.08 mill/kwh$_e$ for the societal cost of pneumoconiosis. This estimate raises the average compensation for each afflicted miner to \$2,000/y and may still be too low.

H.   Fatal Accidents

In 1968, when total electrical-energy production corresponded to 1.43 $\times 10^{12}$ kwh$_e$, there were 311 fatal accidents in coal mining. Assuming a value of \$220,000 for each fatal accident, we find an incremental societal cost of

$$\frac{(\$220,000 \times 311/\text{y}) \times 0.53 \ (= \text{fraction of coal used for electricity production})}{(1.43 \times 10^{12} \text{ kwh}_e/\text{y}) \times 0.46 \ (= \text{fraction of total electricity production associated with coal burning})}$$

$$\simeq 0.05 \text{ mill/kwh}_e.$$

I.   Non-Fatal Accidents

During 1968, there were 9,495 non-fatal injuries. At an estimated cost of \$22,000 per non-fatal injury, the incremental societal cost becomes

$$\frac{(\$22,000 \times 9,495/\text{y}) \times 0.53 \ (= \text{fraction of coal used for electricity production})}{(1.43 \times 10^{12} \text{kwh}_e/\text{y}) \times 0.46 \ (= \text{fraction of total electricity production associated with coal burning})} \simeq 0.17 \text{ mill/kwh}_e.$$

J.   Total Health-Related Costs

The sum of the societal health-related costs is seen to be 0.30 mill/kwh$_e$ if we use the larger value of 0.08 mill/kwh$_e$ for the cost of pneumoconiosis. Here we are not making a proper distinction between the relative health hazards associated with underground and surface mining.

K.   SO$_x$ Pollution

We now turn to a brief consideration of environmental charges associated with coal use if the coal is not properly purified. Investigators at the Council on Environmental Quality[3] estimated in 1971 that the total annual cost in 1968 associated with oxides of sulfur pollution was 8.3×10^9. This estimate may be converted into an incremental societal cost for coal use as follows:

$$\frac{(\$8.3 \times 10^9/y) \times 0.51\;(= \text{fraction of SO}_x \text{ production by electric-power generation}) \times 0.92\;(= \text{fraction of total SO}_x \text{ production by electric-power generation derived from coal})}{(1.43 \times 10^{12}\,\text{kwh}_e/y) \times 0.46\;(= \text{fraction of total electricity production associated with coal burning})}$$

$$\simeq 6 \text{ mills/kwh}_e.$$

Acceptable sulfur-control techniques for high-sulfur-coal use remain to be worked out. Examples of proposed techniques for SO$_x$ removal are fluidized combustion of coal, wet scrubbing in the presence of limestone, catalytic oxidation with MgO scrubbing, adsorption of SO$_x$ on alkaline alumina or CuO or

----

[3]The President's 1971 Environmental Program, compiled by the Council on Environmental Quality, U.S. Government Printing Office, Washington, D.C., 1971.

charcoal, reduction of SO_x with CO or NH_3 and recovery of S_x, and steam
scrubbing.

L. NO_x Pollution

The "pindex" method[*] for evaluation of total air pollution provides relative ratings for SO_x and NO_x damages based on air-quality standards.   In
1968, the estimated average weight ratio of SO_x-to-NO_x production in coal-
fired boilers to make steam for electrical-generating plants was 5.2 to 1.[4]
For equal weights, the SO_2-to-NO_x damage ratio is 1 to 1.3 so that the cost
for NO_x pollution may be estimated to be 1.5 mills/kwh$_e$ in 1968.

M.   Particle Pollution

The generation of electric power by the use of coal-fired boilers in steam-
electric plants released over 5×10^6 t/y of particulate matter during 1970.
Only about 30% of the total number of particles present is removed if 99.7%
(by weight) of the particulate matter is abstracted in such devices as Cottrel
precipitators, because these systems are ineffective for the control of particles
with diameters smaller than about 5μ.

Investigators at the Council on Environmental Quality[3] estimated in 1971
that the total annual cost in 1968 associated with particulate air pollutants was
$\$5.9 \times 10^9$.   This estimate may be converted into an incremental societal

----

[*] The pindex method is described in Appendix 7-A.

[4] The 1970 National Power Survey, U.S. Federal Power Commission, U.S.
   Government Printing Office, Washington, D.C., 1971.

cost for coal use as follows:

$$(\$5.9 \times 10^9/y) \times 0.20 \; (= \text{fraction of partic-} \times 0.99 \; (= \text{fraction of total partic-}$$

ulate production   ulate production by
by electric-power   electric-power gener-
generation)   ation derived from coal)

$$\overline{(1.43 \times 10^{12}\text{kwh}_e/y) \times 0.46 \; (= \text{fraction of total electricity production associ-}}$$
ated with coal burning)

$$\simeq 1.8 \text{ mills/kwh}_e.$$

In 1968, the estimated average weight ratio of SO_x-to-particulate production in coal-steam electrical-generating plants was 2.8 to 1.[4] The pindex
method gives a SO_2-to-particulate damage cost ratio of 1 to 1.77. Hence,
the earlier estimate of 6 mills/kwh$_e$ for SO_x pollution corresponds to a particulate damage cost of 3.8 mills/kwh$_e$.

Estimates[1] for the complete control of particle production have yielded
a control cost of only 0.1 mill/kwh$_e$.

N. Heavy Metals

It has been estimated [5] that 23% of the mercury found in urban atmos-
pheres comes from coal. Conventional precipitators remove less than 4% of
the mercury present. A damage estimate has not been given for this pollutant.
Similarly, damage estimates are not available for other metal contaminants
such as radium and thorium.

O. Radiation Damage

Coal-fired boilers produce ash (containing radium and thorium) which,

_____

[5]O. I. Joensuu, "Fossil Fuels as a Source of Mercury Pollution," Science 172,
1027-1028 (1971).

in turn, is responsible for local radiation exposures about 400 times larger
than those allowed in nuclear reactors of the pressurized-water variety and
180 times less than that permitted for boiling-water reactors, assuming a 9%
ash content of coal, 97.5% ash removal, and equivalent stack-discharge
heights. [6]

P.   Thermal Pollution

The long-term problems associated with thermal pollution have been
discussed in Chapter 6. Here we note that Morgan et al[1] have estimated
local thermal control costs at 0.4 to 1.0 mill/kwh$_e$.

Q.   Summary of the Social-Cost Evaluation for Coal Use

The data derived in the preceding subsections, along with the data pre-
sented by Morgan et al,[1] have been used in the compilation presented in
Table 7.2-1, which is consistent with the assessment summary given in
Section 7.2A.

[6] J. E. Martin, E. D. Harward and D. T. Oakley, "Radiation Doses from
Fossil-Fuel and Nuclear Power Plants" in Power Generation and Environ-
mental Change, D. A. Berkowitz and A. M. Squires, eds., The M.I.T.
Press, Cambridge, Mass., 1971.

Table 7.2-1 Summary of social-cost assessment for coal production and use; based, in part, on data presented in Ref. [1].

Damage type or reconstruction	Social-cost estimate in mills/kwh$_e$ for		Cost for controls in an optimized system, mills/kwh$_e$
	current operation	optimized control	
land reconstruction	>1	0.4 to 0.9	0.1 to 0.4
acid drainage	--	--	0.04
subsidence	0.02	--	--
health hazards	≥0.30	0.30	≤0.30
SO$_x$ pollution	6	2.3	1.8
NO$_x$ pollution	0.17 to 2.2	0.16 to 0.26	0.07 to 0.1
particle pollution	1.8 to 3.8	--	0.1
heavy metals	?	?	?
thermal pollution	>1.5	0.4 to 1.5	0.4 to 1.0
radiation	?	?	?
lower bound for the total cost of using strip-mined coal	10.5	3.3	2.5
lower bound for the total cost of using deep-mined coal	9.8	3.2	2.7
Morgan et al,[1] best estimate	≥ 11.5 ± 2	≥4.5 ± 1.5	≥3 ± 1

7-A   Appendix - The Pindex Method for Relative Damage Assessment

The pindex method[1] is a scheme, based on air-quality standards, for estimating total air pollution. This method accounts for photochemical reactions between pollutants and particle-sulfur-oxides synergism. When applying the pindex method, the level (weight per unit volume) of each pollutant is divided by the corresponding pollutant tolerance factor, based on air-quality standards, to yield a dimensionless pollutant indicator. Then the six (sulfur oxides, nitrogen oxides, particulate matter, carbon monoxide, hydrocarbons, oxidants) pollutant indicators, as well as the term accounting for synergistic effects (which is set equal to the ratio of the weight per unit volume to the tolerance factor of the limiting reactant), are added to determine a dimensionless index of overall pollution.

The pindex method of weighting air-polluting emissions according to their toxicity may be used to develop relative damage costs of various pollutants.[2] The damage cost associated with the emission of a given pollutant is proportional to the toxicity, defined as the reciprocal of the tolerance factor for pollutants which do not react photochemically. The derivation of the toxicity for pollutants which react photochemically involves additional considerations which account for the production of other pollutants in the photochemical process.

---

[1] L. R. Babcock, "A Combined Pollution Index for Measurement of Total Air Pollution," Journal of the Air Pollution Control Association 20, 653-659 (1970).

[2] A. M. Schneider, "An Effluent Fee Schedule for Air Pollutants Based on Pindex," Journal of the Air Pollution Control Association 23, 486-489 (1973).

The relative damage costs for common pollutants calculated by the
pindex method and based on the 1971 federal air-quality standards are shown
in Table 7-A-1. The validity of these relative damage costs depends on the
assumption that air-quality standards are indicative of the relative damage
potential of various pollutants.

Table 7-A-1 Relative pollutant damage costs; based on the data of Ref. [2].

Pollutant	Relative damage cost based on equal emitted weights
SO_2	1.000
CO	0.034
NO_2	1.070
NO	1.640
NO_x (50% NO, 50% NO_2 by volume)	1.295
N (in compounds)	3.510
hydrocarbons	$0.564/n$ [a]
particulate matter	1.770

a. n is the weight of hydrocarbons emitted per
    unit weight of nitrogen oxides.

CHAPTER 8

A COMMENTARY ON U.S. ENERGY POLICY
AND RESOURCE DEVELOPMENT

The grand design of policy, politics, and economics which impacts on energy

use is sometimes referred to as energy policy. In making energy policy, we

must be aware of energy demands, of the economic and environmental impact

of energy use, of energy resources and availability, of the cost of energy supplies,

of capital requirements for the development of new energy supplies, of the so-

cial impact of energy use, of the political impact of energy use on trade partners,

of foreign competition for energy resources, of the relation between world sup-

plies of food and energy sources, of the technological impact of energy consump-

tion, of the effect of technological innovations on energy reserves, etc., etc.

In short, in order to make energy policy intelligently, we must understand every-

thing. Some wise people believe that it would be better not to make energy policy

at all because we can, in fact, never know everything and a policy made on the

basis of inadequate input may actually be worse than no policy at all. In the ab-

sence of a policy, in the absence of direction by an inadequately informed super-

planner, there is some possibility that adjustments and corrections will lead to

a viable de facto system. Modifications leading to an acceptable operational

procedure may not occur at all, or may be more difficult to accomplish, under

the guidance of a less than omnipotent intelligence.

Having noted the pitfalls of inadequate energy policy, we shall nevertheless attempt to arrive at overall guidelines for long-term energy planning. This more modest objective is, to some extent, amenable to analysis as we shall now proceed to show.

8.1 A Moderately Optimistic Energy-Growth Scenario

Our previous discussion of the economic value of energy use (see Chapter 4) suggests that, without reconstruction of our social system, the following four factors may be considered to be of dominant importance in the making of energy policy:

1. The U.S. <u>per capita</u> GNP per unit of energy consumed, assuming reasonable savings associated with improved efficiencies in manufacturing and improved economies in energy use.

2. The estimated population growth for the U.S.

3. The unit energy costs and the capital-cost requirements for the conversion of potential energy resources to accessible energy reserves for programmed applications.

4. The U.S. foreign-trade complexion, with special consideration for the guaranteed availability of foreign supplies, our ability to pay for energy imports (e.g., by the export of foodstuff or of such high-technology items as computers and advanced aircraft).

A.   The Personal GNP in Dollars per Barrel of Petroleum Consumed,
      Assuming Significant Future Energy Savings

The U.S. values of per capita energy consumption [in $(bbl/py)_e$], of

GNP (in \$/py), and of their ratio have been plotted in Fig. 4.1-4 for the one-

hundred year period 1870 to 1970.   We have repeatedly emphasized that signif-

icant opportunities exist for energy savings, not only in the transportation sector

but for all manufacturing, service functions, etc. (see, especially, Chapter 5).

During the 1973-74 oil shortage, curtailments of energy use by 10 to 15% were

implemented without extensive dislocation of the economic sector and without

undue discomfort to the population at large.   Such changes as lowering highway

speed limits may actually constitute desirable social accommodations in their

own right.   With careful planning for energy conservation, it is therefore reason-

able to expect that we shall be able to effect simultaneously increasing per capita

income for the population at large and decreasing energy consumption per dollar

of GNP.   Our goals for energy savings for the proposed scenario, in (bbl/\$ of

$GNP)_e$, are summarized in Table 8.1-1.   The 1970 entry in Table 8.1-1 is the

reciprocal of the applicable value plotted in the top part of Fig. 4.1-4 but ad-

justed for a GNP price-inflation factor of 1.35 between 1958 and 1970.

B.   Slow Population Growth in the U.S.

The U.S. Bureau of the Census has provided the past U.S. population

estimates summarized in Table 8.1-2.

The fertility rate is defined as the average number of births during the en-

tire lifetime of 1,000 females in the U.S. population.   Some past estimates of

Table 8.1-1 Goals for energy consumption per unit of GNP, in $(bbl/\$ \text{ of } GNP)_e$, in an expanding economy with optimal energy conservation. The entries refer to constant 1970 dollars.

Year	Energy consumption per unit of GNP, $(bbl/\$ \text{ of } GNP)_e$	Percentage reduction relative to 1970
1970	1.20×10^{-2}	-----
1980	1.15×10^{-2}	4.2
1985	1.00×10^{-2}	17
1995	0.95×10^{-2}	21

Table 8.1-2 U.S. population estimates from the U.S. Bureau of the Census based on data from the Pocket Data Book: USA 1973, p. 37, U.S. Government Printing Office, Washington, D.C., 1973.

Year	U.S. population, $10^6 p$
1940	131.7
1950	151.3
1960	179.3
1970	203.2
1972	209.0

fertility rates are summarized in Table 8.1-3. The replacement level fertility rate, which corresponded to constant population for 1973 mortality rates, was 2,110.

Estimates of future population growth are made by the U.S. Bureau of the Census. Projections refer to various fertility rates. Actual or "reasonable" values of population growth cannot be predicted. In the optimistic scenario

which we are developing, we shall not only accept the very large energy savings
indicated in Table 8.1-1 but we shall also use relatively low population growth
rates. Corresponding to the median U.S. Census projection, we shall assume
a 1985 U.S. population of 231×10^6 p and a 1995 U.S. population of 246×10^6 p.

Table 8.1-3   Past U.S. fertility rates; based on data from the Pocket Data
Book: USA 1973, p. 70, U.S. Government Printing Office,
Washington, D.C., 1973.

Year	Fertility rate
1945	2,490
1950	3,090
1960	3,650
1970	2,470
1972	2,040

C.   A Moderate Projection of Personal-Income Growth

Personal income (in $/py) for the one-hundred year period from 1870 to
1970 has been plotted in Fig. 4.1-4. In our moderately optimistic scenario,
we shall assume an income growth of 3%/y in the post-1970 period accompany-
ing the contemplated drastic energy economies (compare Section 8.1A). This
assumption will allow a considerable increase in the average standard of living,
hopefully benefitting especially the lowest U.S. income levels. The resulting
personal GNP values are summarized in Table 8.1-4, where the 1970 entry
corresponds to 1.35 times the value shown in Fig. 4.1-4 in order to correct
for the 1958 to 1970 price-inflation factor of 1.35.

Table 8.1-4   Estimated future personal GNP values corresponding to a compounded 3% annual growth rate after 1970. All entries refer to 1970 dollars.

Year	GNP, $/py
1970	4,800
1985	7,480
1995	10,050

8.2   The Year 1985 Energy Needs and Supplies[*]

Using the data summarized in Section 8.1, we may now determine the total required energy supply in the year 1985 from the following relation:

total energy requirements for the U.S. in 1985

$=$ 1985 personal GNP in $/py

$\times$ U.S. population in 1985

$\times$ 1985 estimate of energy consumption per unit of GNP in $(bbl/\$)_e$.

In this manner, we obtain a 1985 energy requirement of 1.73×10^{10} $(bbl/y)_e$ or of 47.3×10^{6} $(bbl/d)_e$.

We now turn to the questions of energy-supply sources, energy self-sufficiency by 1985, and possible projected energy-trade deficits if energy self-sufficiency is unattainable.

The total year 1973 U.S. energy production amounted to 30.5×10^{6} $(bbl/d)_e$. We have reached a point in time where maximum stimulation of currently-

---

[*]One of us (SSP) has been a participant in a NASA/TRW/University of Texas workshop (Monterey, Calif., August 26 to 30, 1974), where methodologies related to those described in the text were considered by a panel headed by A. Goldburg.

utilized energy sources, other than those which will be especially singled out

in the subsequent discussion, will at best maintain the year 1973 supply of

30.5×10^6 (bbl/d)$_e$. Here we include recovery of petroleum at higher costs

from marginal wells,[*] substantially more costly supplies to supplement our

dwindling natural-gas reserves produced by gas stimulation and other tech-

niques, capacity operation of existing coal mines and of installed nuclear re-

actors, etc. Comparison of the identified year 1985 needs for our particular

scenario (considerable augmentation of energy efficiency, relatively slow popu-

lation growth, moderate but continued improvement in the standard of living

as measured by real personal yearly income) with this hopefully constant U. S.

energy-supply source shows that we must obtain by 1985 additional energy sup-

plies of 16.8×10^6 (bbl/d)$_e$.

We list in Table 8.2-1 our estimate of possible supplementary energy

supplies that would be obtainable by 1985 under a crash U.S. energy-resource

development plan. Also listed in Table 8.2-1 are reasonably assured new

supplies of energy in view of technological developments and administrative

steps that had already been taken by the beginning of 1974. Reference to Table

8.2-1 shows that, even for the modest projected growth schedule we have as-

sumed, energy self-sufficiency by 1985 is unattainable unless about 50% of the

supplementary supplies associated with the identified crash programs in Table

---

[*]Among the techniques used in <u>secondary recovery</u> of petroleum is the injection of gas or water under pressure into oil bearing rocks, which increases recovery above the <u>primary</u> yields of 15 to 35% to perhaps as
much as 45%; examples of as yet largely experimental <u>tertiary recovery</u>
procedures are injection of surfactant (detergent) material into rocks
or air injection followed by partial combustion in fuel-rich mixtures. By
the use of these procedures, considerable additional amounts of oil should
be recoverable from existing oil wells.

Table 8.2-1 A compendium of supplementary domestic energy supplies [rounded off to the nearest 0.5×10^6 (bbl/d)$_e$] that may be obtainable by 1985. Supplies identified by an asterisk may not become available without changes in applicable legal regulations, relaxation of environmental standards, or gross dislocations of industrial activities.

Supplementary energy source	Reasonably assured supplies, $(10^6$ bbl/d)$_e$	Supplies that may be achievable through a crash program, $(10^6$ bbl/d)$_e$
Alaska North Slope	2	4
West Coast of Alaska	-	1*
Santa Barbara Channel in California	1	1
Atlantic Coast and Gulf Coast off Florida	-	2*
shale oil (conventional mining)	0.5	1
coal (including use for gasification and liquefaction)	3	4*
nuclear reactors	4	5*
solar heating and cooling	-	0.5
hydroelectric development	0.5	0.5
geothermal (including natural steam and dry rock sources)	-	0.5
energy recovery from waste	-	1
in situ recovery of fossil fuels	-	0.5*
tidal and wind energy, energy farms, breeder and fusion reactors, photovoltaic power conversion, solar-sea power plants	-	-
total	11	21

8.2-1 can be implemented. In the absence of this activity, our projected

energy deficiency in 1985 will correspond to a trade deficit (in 1970 dollars) of 5.8×10^7/d if the imported energy sources cost \$10/bbl. This trade deficit of \$21 $\times$ 10^9/y is actually quite close to the trade deficit for fossil fuels encountered in 1974. We conclude that a crash energy-development program is required even if energy-values, measured in terms of bbl/\$ of GNP, are decreased by 17% below applicable 1970 values, the population grows by little more than 10% between 1970 and 1985, and we settle for a moderate GNP growth rate of 3% between 1970 and 1985. It should be noted that this average 3% growth rate may include a significant decline in personal GNP for the period 1973 to 1975 since the personal GNP growth rate exceeded 3% between 1970 and 1973.

Reference to the last column in Table 8.2-1 shows that there are a number of alternatives in crash-program selection to achieve energy self-sufficiency by 1985. Our estimate of 47.3 $\times 10^6$ (bbl/d)$_e$ by 1985 is significantly below the low-growth projection (compare Fig. 1.5-10) made by the National Petroleum Council,[1] which corresponds to a year 1985 energy use of 52.7 $\times 10^6$ (bbl/d)$_e$. A recent Ford Foundation project[2] has led to the following year 1985 energy-use projections: 43.8 $\times 10^6$ (bbl/d)$_e$ for "zero energy growth", 45.2 $\times$ 10^6 (bbl/d)$_e$ for a "technical-fix scenario ", and 54.1 $\times 10^6$ (bbl/d)$_e$ for an "historical-growth scenario".

8.3 The Year 1995 Energy Needs and Supplies

Subject to the assumptions and procedures outlined in Section 8.2, we estimate the year 1995 energy requirements as 64.3 $\times 10^6$ (bbl/d)$_e$. A conceivable

[1] U.S. Energy Outlook, National Petroleum Council, Washington, D.C., 1972.

[2] Exploring Energy Choices, Ford Foundation Energy Policy Project, Washington, D.C., 1974.

development schedule for energy supplies, supplementary to the assumed con-

stant 30.5×10^6 $(bbl/d)_e$ produced in the U.S. during 1973, is summarized in

Table 8.3-1.   These data suggest that, with implementation of energy economies,

moderate population growth, and a compound growth in GNP of 3%/y, energy

self-sufficiency is an achievable U.S. goal by 1995.

8.4   Energy Policy

In the preceding discussion, we have developed in some detail the implica-

tions of a _representative_ scenario.   The making of energy policy requires the

evaluation of very many scenarios and policy decisions and implementation

schedules that produce the desired scenario.

What is the desired or desirable scenario?   An increase in GNP/py, with

zero population growth?   A decrease of population to, say, the 1940 values, to-

gether with a reduction in per capita energy use to 1970 world means?   We are

no longer able to make analytical judgments.   We have, in fact, left the arena

of energy policy _per se_ and are now addressing the larger problem of energy

policy that is consistent with the goals of a better society.   The definition of

these goals, however, falls beyond the scope of this cursory excursion into

policy.

In the preceding sections, we have made sweeping and perhaps indefensible

assumptions.   How will we maintain the 1973 energy-supply levels constant?

What are the detailed specifications for technological implementation that will

allow us to achieve this objective?   Exactly what types of nuclear reactors will

be used to supply 4×10^6 $(bbl/d)_e$ by 1985 and 9×10^6 $(bbl/d)_e$ by 1995?   Under

Table 8.3-1 A compendium of supplementary domestic energy supplies
[rounded off to the nearest 0.5×10^6 (bbl/d)$_e$] that may be
obtainable by 1995. Supplies identified by an asterisk may
not become available without changes in applicable legal regulations, relaxation of environmental standards, or gross
dislocations of industrial activities.

Supplementary energy source	1995 supply goals, $(10^6 \text{ bbl/d})_e$
Alaska North Slope	5
West Coast of Alaska	3*
Santa Barbara Channel in California	1
Atlantic Coast and Gulf Coast off Florida	4*
shale oil (conventional mining)	1.5
shale oil (in situ mining)	1.5
coal (conventional and in situ mining)	5
nuclear reactors	9
solar heating and cooling	1
hydroelectric development	1
geothermal (natural steam reservoirs)	0.5
geothermal (dry rock sources)	1
energy recovery from waste	3
tidal and wind energy, energy farms, breeder and fusion reactors, photovoltaic power conversion, solar-sea power plants	1
more efficient energy conversion using MHD systems	1
total	38.5

what environmental constraints will this growth in nuclear-reactor development

be allowed to occur? By what means and at what environmental cost shall we

be able to develop a 3×10^6 (bbl/d)$_e$ oil shale industry in the U.S. by 1995?

Each of the preceding questions, and many others in addition, must be answered

in detail before the present excursion into energy policy attains the significance

of a meaningful evaluation.

In our scenarios of energy-supply development, we have not commented on

the capital investments required to achieve the specified goals. Is our private

capitalistic system capable of supplying the needed funds? If not, what are al-

ternative development procedures? We are now again addressing a difficult

special topic for which quantitative assessment is required by a competent

group of economic planners. Here we content ourselves with the observation

that the National Petroleum Council projections[1] implied growths of energy

supplies larger than those assumed in this discussion and yet the authors of

that evaluation did not foresee basic problems in financing the enormous required

capital investments. In view of recent rapid price escalations, the earlier opti-

mistic conclusion may, however, require amendment. The capital supply prob-

lem requires continuous reassessment and updating in the same manner as the

technological innovations.

---

[1]
   Ref. [1] in Section 8.2.

8.5 A Schedule for Energy-Resource Development[1]

The development of a priority schedule for energy-resource utilization depends on the meaningful construction of U.S. energy policy. The particular question of capitalization for specific areas of activity, in view of competition for available funds, cannot be addressed until we know exactly where we are going. The following primary assessments must be made: What is the cost for development of each resource when proper allowance is made for environmental reconstruction? What is the magnitude and schedule on which new energy supplies become available? How competitive is the ultimate product with alternative sources of supplies, including foreign imports?

Although the type of evaluation specified in the preceding paragraph has not been made, we present nevertheless a master schedule for implementation of large-scale energy-production facilities, prototype or pilot-plant development, and supporting research. This priority list has been constructed in order to achieve two objectives, with first priority assigned to minimization of the economic impact of embargoes on foreign fossil-fuel shipments to the United States and second priority assigned to the early construction of facilities for abundant energy production in the United States without the use of fossil fuels.

Given the present economic stresses, we must develop a mixed strategy

---

[1]S.S. Penner, "A Condensed Schedule for Energy-Resource Development, " Annals of Nuclear Science and Engineering 1, 339-341 (1974).

for early production of energy resources within the United States and friendly countries, while developing complete long-term solutions to our needs for cheap and abundant energy. The nature of the current crisis dictates immediate emphasis on offshore and mainland oil and gas exploration (F-1 in Table 8.5-1), on increased coal production (F-2 in Table 8.5-1), on oil recovery from the Athabasca (Alberta, Canada) tar sands (F-4 in Table 8.5-1), on construction of nuclear-fission reactors (N-1 and N-2 in Table 8.5-1), on expansion of hydroelectric facilities (H-1 in Table 8.5-1), on exploitation of hydrothermal facilities (H-2 in Table 8.5-1), on the development of electrical-power-generating plants using selected tidal basins (H-3 in Table 8.5-1), and perhaps application of magnetohydrodynamic power conversion (F-10 in Table 8.5-1). These are technologies which we should apply soon in order to relieve shortages during the next decade.

By the year 2100, our current problems with energy generation should be totally resolved. The problem may be resolved by full development of one or more total long-term solutions: controlled nuclear-fusion reactors, geothermal power generation using the outer earth mantle as a heat source, the solar-sea generator, land-based solar-generating stations, all combined with a hydrogen-fuel technology. This is the fossil-fuel-free energy resource schedule to which we must change. Knowing where we are and where we are going, we arrive at the kind of energy-development map displayed in Table 8.5-1.

Table 8.5-1 is an estimate for technological-priority schedules relating to full-scale implementation, pilot-plant or prototype development, and research priorities.   Entries are listed in order of presumed decreasing relative impor-

tance for selected time periods.   Disappearance of priority entries in later

time schedules indicates expectation of completion of research, development,

or essential large-scale implementation.   The time scheduling has been designed

to place maximum sustainable stress on all of the technological components of

the energy-resource enterprise.   Failure to meet specified time schedules

should imply establishment of relatively lower priority in subsequent time inter-

vals or abolition of the technology involved as an important component of energy-

resource planning.   Research priorities, which disappear before large-scale

implementation, are considered to have relatively low chances for making im-

portant contributions to the total energy-resource evolution.   Table 8.5-1 (which

surely has many defensible variations at the present time) should, of course,

be revised and updated at five-year intervals by groups of active workers who

are involved in all aspects of energy-resource planning.

Some political-priority schedules required for implementation are sum-

marized in Table 8.5-2.   Research-direction priorities are listed in Table

8.5-3.

In the following Volumes II and III of this series of publications, we shall

be concerned with discussions of new energy technologies that must be assessed

before Table 8.5-1 can be redrawn in a defensible manner.   At the end of this

excursion, we shall return to the troublesome problem of the making of energy

policy.

Table 8.5-1 Technological-priority schedules, listed in relative order of promise for early, large-scale application; reproduced from Ref. [1].

Time period	Full-scale technological implementation*	Pilot-plant or prototype development	Research priorities
1974 ↘ 1978	F-1, F-2, F-3, F-4, N-1, N-2, H-1, H-2, H-3, F-10	N-3, F-7, F-6, F-8, N-4, S-1, S-2, S-3, H-5, H-4, B-2, S-4	N-5, F-5, F-9, F-11, F-12, B-7, B-6, B-5, B-1, B-3, B-4, B-8
1979 ↘ 1983	F-1, F-2, F-3, F-4, F-5, F-7, F-10, N-1, N-2, S-1, S-2, B-2, H-3, H-4	N-3, F-5, F-6, F-8, N-4, F-9, S-3, H-5, S-4, B-7, B-6	N-5, F-11, F-12, B-5, B-1, B-3, B-4, B-8
1984 ↘ 1988	F-2, F4, F-5, F-6, F-7, F-8, F-10, N-2, N-3, N-4, F-9, S-3, H-5, S-4	B-7, B-6, F-11, F-12, B-5	N-5, B-1, B-3, B-4, B-8
1989 ↘ 1998	F-2, F-5, F-6, F-7, F-8, F-9, F-10, N-2, N-3, N-4, S-3, H-5, S-4, F-11, F-12	N-5	N-5, B-1, B-3, B-4, B-8
1998 ↘ 2020	F-2, F-5, F-6, F-7, F-8, F-9, F-10, N-3, N-4, S-3, H-5, S-4, F-11, F-12, B-7	N-5	N-5, B-1, B-8
2020 ↘ 2050	N-5, F-5, F-6, F-8, F-9, N-3, N-4, S-3, H-5, S-4	N-5	N-5
2050 ↘ 2100	N-5, F-5, F-6, S-3, H-5, S-4		
2100 ↘	N-5, H-5, S-3, S-4		

*This term is meant to imply large-scale new construction; conversely, absence of an entry implies that new construction is to be discouraged for environmental or other conservation reasons. Thus, we are recommending a ten-year time limit for mainland and offshore exploration, a 35-year time limit for construction of new coal-mining facilities and of new coal-gasification and coal-liquefaction units, a 65-year exploitation program for shale oil, etc.

Definition of Symbols in Table 8.5-1

A. Fossil-fuel technology
    F-1. Offshore and mainland oil and gas exploration
    F-2. Increased coal production by conventional methods
    F-3. Construction of Alaskan pipeline(s)
    F-4. Construction of plants to recover more oil from Canadian tar sands by conventional methods (it should be noted that this entry does not refer to a U.S. resource development)
    F-5. Development of in situ technology for oil recovery from tar sands, oil shale, and coal

F-6. Recovery of oil from oil shale by conventional, above-ground retorting
F-7. Construction of coal-gasification units
F-8. Construction of coal-liquefaction units
F-9. Deep ocean oil and gas exploration
F-10. Magnetohydrodynamic power conversion
F-11. Large-scale generation of H_2 using electrolysis or sequential chemical reaction schemes
F-12. Implementation of a hydrogen economy with large-scale distribution and utilization of H_2

B. Hydroelectric, geothermal, tidal, and wind technology
H-1. Expansion of hydroelectric power-generation facilities
H-2. Construction of hydrothermal power-generation stations
H-3. Development of generating capacity using selected tidal basins
H-4. Wind-driven power generators
H-5. Geothermal developments using the hot earth mantle

C. Nuclear-reactor development
N-1. Construction of light-water nuclear reactors
N-2. Construction of high-temperature gas-cooled nuclear reactors
N-3. Construction of liquid-metal-fast-breeder reactors
N-4. Construction of gas-cooled breeder reactors
N-5. Construction of fusion reactors

D. Solar-energy development
S-1. Implementation of solar water heaters
S-2. Implementation of solar space heaters
S-3. Power generation using solar-sea stations
S-4. Development of land-based solar-generating plants

E. Basic studies
B-1. Photovoltaic power conversion
B-2. Fuel cell development
B-3. Thermoelectric power generation
B-4. Thermionic power conversion
B-5. Application development of H_2 technology
B-6. H_2-distribution networks
B-7. Superconducting power lines
B-8. Extraterrestrial solar-energy collectors with transmission to ground-based receivers

Table 8.5-2 Political-priority schedules, listed in relative order of
importance, to facilitate large-scale development of U.S.
energy resources.

1. Abolish unrealistic and artificial price constraints. Allow

    prices to rise to levels at which they are controlled by

    competitive market factors.

2. Reduce political and environmental obstacles to research

    objectives by defining reasonable, maximum-allowable time

    schedules for review of priority programs.

3. In view of likely substantial price increases for energy

    supplies, some type of subsidy for low-income wage earners

    may be required.

Table 8.5-3 Research-direction priority schedules.

1. Place authority for funding of research grants and contracts

    under the direction of highly-competent senior investigators.

    Avoid the use of junior contract administrators without

    extensive research and development experience.

2. Direct research funding schedules along mission-application

    lines, with relative support levels reflecting relative

    implementation priorities.

3. Coordinate and supervise research accomplishments by

    advisory panels composed primarily of active workers in

    the field.

PROBLEMS

Problems marked with a dagger (†) deal with the environmental impact of energy production, transportation, or use.

Problems marked with a single asterisk (*) should be deleted in courses addressed to a lower-division class.

Problems marked with a double asterisk (**) require reading and literature search of original source material.

Problems for Chapter 1

1. Using the data in Table 1.2-2, perform the following conversions of
    energy equivalents:
    (a) 10 cords of wood to bbl of petroleum;
    (b) fusion energy of the deuterium from 1 km^3 of seawater to tons of
         TNT equivalent;
    (c) 10^6 tons of TNT (which is equivalent to a 1-metagon nuclear bomb)
         to bbl of petroleum;
    (d) 10^3 hph to bbl of petroleum.

2. Using the data in Table 1.2-2, make the following estimates of equivalent
    per capita energy consumption:
    (a) the world in the year 1970 in gallons of petroleum/p-d and in SCF
         of natural gas/p-d;
    (b) the world in the year 2000 in gallons of petroleum/p-d and in SCF
         of natural gas/p-d;
    (c) the world in the year 2050 in gallons of petroleum/p-d and in SCF
         of natural gas/p-d.

3. Replot Fig. 1.5-1 on the assumption that the growth rate of total demand
    will be curtailed to 3% per year between 1970 and 1990, while the growth
    rates for petroleum, coal, natural gas, and hydroelectric power are each
    limited to 2% per year. Discuss the implications for the resulting growth
    rate in nuclear-energy use.

4. If Saudi Arabia were to become the fifty-first state in the Union, how would
    the estimated U.S. years supply of petroleum and natural-gas reserves
    change after 1973? Use the implied U.S. use rate corresponding to the
    entries in the third line of Table 1.5-6.

5. How long would the estimated U.S. oil reserves (see Table 1.5-6) last if

the people in the U.S. were to reduce their per capita oil consumption to that of the Italians in 1970? Use the data given in Fig. 1.5-11 to answer this question.

6. Discuss the effect of total prohibition of natural-gas movement across state lines on the people of California. Use the data in Fig. 1.6-1.

7. Using only the information given in Section 1.6, how would you regulate the flow and use of natural gas in the U.S.?

8.[†] Oil spills from pipeline shipments of crude oil average about 0.023 lb/bbl of oil shipped. If the crude oil from Prudhoe Bay in Alaska weighs, on the average, 300 lb/bbl, how many barrels of oil are likely to be spilled in Alaska during 1977 when the projected delivery schedule is 0.6×10^6 bbl/d?

9.[†] In 1970, 1.89×10^6 horsepower were developed to pump crude oil through pipelines in the U.S. Approximately 16.5% of the 1970 horsepower requirements were supplied by diesel fuel. During 1970, the average specific fuel consumption of the pumping stations was 0.38 lb of fuel per horsepower-hour and the average diesel fuel density was 7.1 lb/gallon.

 (a) If a 10% downtime is assumed, how much diesel fuel was required for pumping in 1970?

 (b) If 142 lb of SO_2 were emitted per 10^3 gallons of fuel consumed, how many tons of SO_2 were emitted from crude-oil pumping stations in 1970?

 (c) If 80 lb of NO_x were emitted per 10^3 gallons of fuel consumed, how many tons of sulfur and nitrogen pollutants were emitted from crude-oil pumping stations in 1970?

10.[†] During 1970, 17.8×10^{12} SCF of natural gas were transmitted to distribution centers in the U.S. If the combustion of natural gas produces 7.3×10^3 lb of NO_x per 10^3 SCF of natural gas burned and 4.1% of the transmitted natural gas was burned to supply the energy required for natural-gas transmission, how much NO_x production was associated with the transmission of natural gas in 1970?

11.[†] During the period from 1965 to 1969, the energy consumption of crude-oil refineries averaged 7.04×10^5 Btu/bbl of crude oil processed of which 97% was supplied by fuel oil. If fuel oil with the maximum sulfur content meeting the federal emission regulations of 0.8 lb of SO_2 emitted per 10^6 Btu of oil burned were consumed at the average fuel use rate, how many pounds of SO_2 per 10^3 bbl of processed crude would be emitted from a typical refinery?

12.[†] A typical value for nitrogen-oxide emissions from refineries is about 130 lb/10^3 bbl of crude processed. The refining capacity of the U.S. was about 13×10^6 bbl/d in 1973. If all U.S. refineries had been operated at 100% of capacity during 1973, how many tons of nitrogen-oxide emissions would have been released into the atmosphere from the refineries?

13.[†] Hydrocarbon emissions originating from storage tanks, loading and transfer facilities, and accidental spills and leaks in petroleum range from 0.1 to 0.6 weight percent of the crude oil processed.

   (a) If crude oil weighs, on the average, 300 lb/bbl and a nominal value of 0.35 weight percent for the emission factor is assumed, how many pounds of hydrocarbon emissions per 10^3 bbl of crude oil processed would be released from a typical refinery?

   (b) How many tons of hydrocarbons would have been emitted from refineries in the U.S. if all of the 13×10^6 bbl/d refinery capacity in 1973 was fully utilized?

14.[*] What is your interpretation of the physical significance of the expression for total electricity demand given in Eq. (1.7-7)? How would you expect this relation to be modified for a highly industrial region like Chicago?

15.** What is known about the chemical compositions of kerogen and bitumen?

16.** Elaborate the chemical constitutions of anthracite and bituminous coals.

Problems for Chapter 2

1. Discuss the physical meaning of the large deviations of the dQ_d/dt data from the smoothed dotted curve shown in Fig. 2.1-3.

2. The dependence of the rate of oil discovery on cumulative exploratory footage drilled is shown in Fig. 2.2-1. Explain the large initial discovery rates and peak in this curve. To what do you ascribe the fact that the rate of discovery did not decrease significantly between 6×10^8 and 15×10^8 ft of cumulative exploratory drilling?

3. Using the arguments presented in Section 2.18, calculate the available hydrothermal energy in units of Mwy for a 50-year exhaustion schedule at a 25% conversion efficiency if 5% of the hydrothermal energy available to a depth of 3 km and 0.5% of the hydrothermal energy between 3 and 10 km depths could be utilized.

4. Indicate your best estimate for the time scales in years when you would expect exhaustion of the following domestic non-renewable energy resources if consumption remained constant at the year 1970 U.S. total energy use rate:
    - (a) petroleum;
    - (b) natural gas;
    - (c) coal;
    - (d) oil from oil shale;
    - (e) U_3O_8 at a cost of not more than \$10/lb if it is used only in conventional light-water reactors;
    - (f) U_3O_8 at a cost of not more than \$10/lb if it is used only in breeder reactors.

    Specify the data and references used in making your time estimates.

5.   Using world resource estimates, list the following renewable and/or partially renewable resources in order of decreasing total magnitude: hydroelectric energy, solar heat energy, wind energy, tidal energy, hydrothermal energy, and dry geothermal energy.

6.[†]   A typical oil well requires 0.25 acre of land. If the average oil well produces 6,200 bbl of oil per year, what is the land commitment necessary to produce 12×10^6 bbl/d of crude oil?

7.[†]   The 1969 work injury rate for the exploration, drilling, and production of crude oil and natural gas was 9.7 disabling injuries for each million man-hours worked. In 1969, 450,000 employees in the oil and natural gas industries worked 9.39×10^8 man-hours and the production of energy from oil and natural gas amounted to 4.12×10^{16} Btu. If the same productivity and injury rates persist, approximately how many disabling injuries would be expected to occur if 5×10^{16} Btu of energy were produced from oil and natural gas?

8.[†]   In federal areas off the Louisiana coast, approximately 1×10^6 bbl/d of crude oil are produced. Forty-three percent of the 1.76×10^7 gallons of waste water produced per day is discharged into the surrounding water.

   (a) If the current regulations permit only an average discharge of 50 parts per million of oil in the waste water, how many barrels of oil may be discharged into the surrounding water per year?

   (b) What percent of the oil production may be discharged with the waste water?

9.[*]   Show analytically that the time dependence of the rate of change of remaining reserves (dQ_r/dt) has been indicated correctly in Fig. 2.1-2.

10.[*]   Prepare a production rate-time curve for crude oil in the U.S. on the assumption that unexpected new discoveries will raise $Q_{d,\infty}$ to 800×10^9 bbl (see Figs. 2.2-2 and 2.2-3 for related curves).

11.* Assume that the U.S. energy consumption will grow at the rate of 3% per year from 1970 to the year 2000 and will remain constant thereafter. Define the relative amounts of coal, liquid petroleum, and natural gas that must be used to account for 80% of the total energy needed in the U.S. in such a way that each of these fuels will be exhausted at the same time. What is the fossil-fuel exhaustion date with this scenario? Specify the precise resource input data which you are using in the analysis.

12.* If 20% of the U.S. energy is to be supplied by nuclear reactors for the scenario specified in Problem 11, what efficiency in conversion is required when 857×10^3 tons of U_3O_8 (compare Table 2.15-1) are used and the exhaustion date of this low-cost U_3O_8 is to coincide with that of the fossil fuels defined in Problem 11?

13.* Describe a shale-oil production program of sufficient magnitude to supply 10% of the U.S. energy needs after the year 1990 according to the scenario of Problem 11.

14.* Assume that the capital investment costs for solar energy are $\$10^3/kw_e$. What are the required capital investments if solar energy is to supply 5% of the U.S. energy needs by the year 2000, 10% by 2020, 20% by 2050, 50% by 2070, and 90% by the year 2100? Use the energy-consumption schedule specified in Problem 11.

15.* At 40% conversion efficiency to electricity, how many km^3 of seawater will be needed to supply the deuterium required in the year 2100 for the generation of the electrical energy equivalent of the year 2100 total energy consumption in the U.S. according to the scenario of Problem 11? How many tons of lithium would have to be processed per year if all of the electricity were generated in 2100 by using $_3^6Li$ according to Eq. (2.16-4) with a 40% conversion efficiency to electricity?

16.*   Assume that the scenario for energy requirements given in Problem 11 applies in the year 2000 and that all of the energy is extracted from the winds. If the average station output power is 500 Mw_e, how many wind-generator stations will be required? Use the assumption that the required electrical energy equals the total energy needs. If Los Angeles County uses 8% of the total U.S. electrical energy, how many wind-generator stations will be located along the shoreline? If the average coastal length required per power station is 1 mile, how many miles of shoreline would be required for the year 2100 wind-generator stations supplying Los Angeles?

17.**   Refering to the published literature, describe the time dependence of the volume of natural gas discovered, on the average, per bbl of oil discovered. What type of regional variation occurs in this ratio? How reliable are the published data? Do you believe that this ratio depends on the price of natural gas?

18.**   Prepare a map of the type shown in Fig. 2.8-5 for per capita energy consumption during 1970.

Problems for Chapter 3

1.   If aluminum had been replaced entirely by an equivalent weight of steel in 1968, how much of the total U.S. energy consumption would have been saved? Use the data in Table 3.2-1.

2.   If carbonated beverages had been replaced in 1968 by an equivalent number of gallons of distilled beverages, what would have been the total incremental energy use in the U.S., expressed in bbl of petroleum per year? Specify the source of the data used to answer this question.

3.   Assume an average soft-drink consumption of 1 gallon per week per person in a city with a population of 2×10^6 people. What would be the energy savings expressed in bbl of petroleum per year if the city were to convert from 50% throwaway and 50% glass containers with 15 returnable refills

to 100% glass containers with 15 returnable refills? Use the data given in Table 3.2-4c.

4. Using the data given in Table 3.3-2, calculate the transportation cost in Btu per passenger-mile for 100% occupancy of the following aircraft: 747 jet, 707 jet, SST (U.S.). Compare these results with the entries listed in Table 3.3-6.

5. Compare the energy cost in Btu per passenger-mile for a cross-country train with a 20% occupancy with that of a fully-loaded 747 jet; compare a fully-loaded four-passenger automobile with a fast train having an occupancy of 15%. Do these data suggest that energy savings can be effected only if public transportation systems become generally accepted and high occupancy occurs?

6. Discuss the energy impact of time savings associated with the use of relatively faster transportation systems for passenger movement. Comment on the sociological and health impacts of more walking or bicycling in inner-city transportation.

7. At 6 mph, the average fuel consumption of oil tankers is 0.0612 lb per hour per ton of cargo. The average weight of crude oil is 300 lb/bbl and the average energy content is 5.8×10^6 Btu/bbl.

    (a) For a 6 mph average transport speed, what is the average fuel consumption per barrel transported per mile?

    (b) If diesel fuel has an average heating valve of 19,800 Btu/lb, what is the transport energy requirement per barrel transported per mile for a 6 mph average transport speed?

    (c) What is the approximate fuel energy requirement per million Btu-mile of oil transported at an average speed of 6 mph?

8. Consider the energy-application diagram shown in Fig. 3.4-1 and discuss the likely impact of a governmental master plan to allocate energy use to the consuming sectors by decree.

9.   Calculate the estimated percentage of rejected energy in 1960, 1970, and
      1980 from the plots of Fig. 3.4-3.   Calculate the estimated percentage
      allocation of energy use in 1985 for the principal user categories from
      the data shown in Fig. 3.4-4; calculate the energy allocation for the
      forms in which energy is applied in 1970 from the plots of Fig. 3.4-5;
      calculate the estimated 1985 percentage distribution among energy sources
      from Fig. 3.4-6.

10.[†] During 1971, 3,185 tank barges with a cumulative cargo capacity of
      6.33×10^6 tons were operating in the U.S.   The total petroleum products
      shipped by tank barges in 1971 amounted to 2.115×10^8 tons.   If the aver-
      age oil loss per barge per year was 0.1% of the barge capacity and the
      average weight of the petroleum products shipped was 300 lb/bbl, what
      was the average weight of spillage per barrel of petroleum products
      shipped?

11.[†] Consider a fish with a characteristic length of 5 ft, weighing 100 lb, and
      swimming at a maximum speed of 20 mph.
         (a) What is the estimated specific horsepower for this creature in hp/t?
         (b) What is the estimated lower limit of the specific horsepower for
              swimming at a maximum speed of 20 mph?

12.[**] Describe the chemical and physical properties of gasoline, distillate fuel
      oil, residual fuel oil, natural-gas liquids, lubricants, kerosene, and jet
      fuel.

Problems for Chapter 4

1.   Evaluate the ratio for the U.S. of per capita income per year (in $/py)
      to per capita energy consumption per year in units of (gallons of petroleum/
      $py)_e$ for 1875, 1890, 1920, and 1970.   What would this ratio be in the year
      2000 if per capita income grew at the rate of 4% per year from 1970 to 2000

while energy use increased at the rate of 3% per year during this same time period? Use the data of Fig. 4.1-4.

2. Revise Table 4.2-4 by using the following prices: in 1975, \$11.50/bbl of petroleum and \$1.50/10^3 SCF of natural gas; in 1985, \$14.50/bbl of petroleum and \$2.25/10^3 SCF of natural gas. Discuss the anticipated U.S. trade deficits in energy fuels for 1975 and 1985. What is your proposal for coping with this foreign-trade problem over the near term, assuming that is not possible to develop new energy sources on a sufficient scale and sufficiently rapidly to increase domestic supplies above those implicit in the NPC projection for Case I?

3. On the basis of the information presented in Chapter 4, how would you project Fig. 4.4-1 to the year 1985?

4. Assume that the data in Table 4.4-1 remain valid in the year 2000 (in 1972 dollars).

    (a) What will be the average increase in electricity cost associated with the following source distribution for U_3O_8: 30% at \$8/lb, 30% at \$10/lb, 10% at \$15/lb, 5% at \$30/lb, and 25% at \$50/lb?

    (b) If 30% of the total electricity is produced in nuclear reactors in the year 2000, what will be the average impact on electricity costs of the specified escalation in the price of U_3O_8?

5.* Compare the power-plant cost estimates presented in Sections 4.5 and 4.6. Plot in Fig. 4.6-2 the appropriate line for natural-gas costs of \$1.00/10^6 Btu. Increase all other costs by 30% above the values shown in Fig. 4.6-2. What will be the production cost for electricity in mills/kwh_e for the higher fuel and other costs in a 1,000-Mw_e power plant burning natural gas?

Problems for Chapter 5

1. What would have been the impact in 1968 on U.S. energy consumption in units of bbl of petroleum equivalent per year if the following reductions in consumption had been achieved: 15% for space heating, 20% for water heating, 25% for cooking, 30% for all other applications listed in Table 5.1-1?

2. Are energy-utilization systems with optimal fuel-energy conversion efficiencies necessarily the most economical to use? Why are we not ready to replace the internal combustion engine by fuel cells? How would you insure the preferential sale of cooling units with efficiencies in excess of 10 Btu/wh$_e$?

3. Consider a city of 2×10^6 people using 1% of the total U.S. energy when total U.S. consumption corresponds to 35×10^6 bbl/d of petroleum equivalent. In this city, 30% of the space and water heaters, electric ranges, and clothes dryers use electrical energy. This sector of the economy consumes 18% of the total energy used in the city.

    (a) Assume that the data of Table 5.3-2 apply. What energy savings in units of $(bbl/y)_e$ could be realized by making the use of electricity illegal for the specified applications?

    (b) What percentage of the operating costs would be saved if the data of Table 5.3-3 apply?

4. If gasoline consumption was decreased by 50% and all other energy costs for automobile manufacturing and services were reduced by 30% through the introduction of smaller cars, what would be the reduction in total U.S. energy consumption? Use the data given in Section 5.6 for this calculation.

5. Estimate the maximum energy savings that could be obtained by replacing automobiles with bicycles. State the assumptions on which your estimate is based.

6.[†]   In 1969, the production of municipal solid waste in the U.S. was 250×10^6 tons. The average heating value of municipal waste as received is 4,200 Btu/lb. If this waste had been utilized for power generation in a power plant operating with a 100% plant factor and a heat rate of 10,000 Btu/kwh$_e$, what would have been the resulting electrical-power output?

7.[†]   In 1969, the production of industrial solid wastes and agricultural wastes was 110×10^6 tons and $2,280 \times 10^6$ tons, respectively. If the average heating value of industrial wastes was 5,200 Btu/lb and the average heating value for agricultural wastes was 7,600 Btu/lb, what was the total available thermal energy from agricultural and industrial wastes in 1969?

8.[†]   The electrical-power generating capacity of the U.S. was 313,000 Mw$_e$ in 1969.

   (a) If all of the solid wastes produced in the U.S. in 1969 had been used to generate electrical power in a power plant operating with a 100% plant factor and a heat rate of 10,000 Btu/kwh$_e$, what percentage of the installed generating capacity could have been fueled by solid wastes? Use the waste-production data given in Problems 6 and 7 for this calculation.

   (b) If the energy content of fuel oil is 5.8×10^6 Btu/bbl, how much fuel oil could have been conserved during 1969 by utilizing solid wastes for electrical-power production?

9.[**] Develop a scheme for slowing the electricity use rate in the U.S. according to the methodology described in Section 5.8.

10.[**] Discuss the problems and promise of municipal-waste utilization for your city. Use realistic estimates for current waste collection and disposal costs. Develop a methodology for recovering energy and raw materials from waste.

Problems for Chapter 6

1. Describe a physical process by which a man-made energy load smaller than the solar-energy input could conceivably produce disastrous environmental effects.

2. What types of monitoring would you perform in order to assure that man-made energy use does not produce disastrous environmental impacts?

3. It is often stated erroneously that solar-energy utilization does not affect the global heat balance.

   (a) Why is this idea erroneous?

   (b) Is the opposite view correct that, at equal utilization efficiency, solar-energy use provides essentially the same thermal loading as any other energy source?

4.*,** Update Tables 6-1 and 6-2 to 1974.

5.*,** Describe the development of the geostrophic wind system analytically. How could this wind system be disturbed by man-made energy additions?

6.*,** Prepare the required entries for Table 6.3-3 for your city, county, and state in the years 1970, 2000, and 2050.

7.*,** Discuss and evaluate the short-term environmental impact of the data of Table 6.7-1. Speculate on the long-term environmental impact of the same data. Which entry in Table 6.7-1 has potentially the most damaging environmental impact? Briefly describe the environmental consequences associated with the specified entry.

Problems for Chapter 7

1. List in order of decreasing importance the following factors associated with past coal use for electricity production that produced the greatest

environmental damage expressed in terms of societal costs in units of mills/kwh$_e$: pneumoconiosis, sulfur pollution, acid drainage, subsidence, NO_x pollution, particle pollution, and health hazards to miners other than pneumoconiosis. Discuss the consistency of this ordering with the usual environmental arguments against coal utilization.

2.[†] During 1970, 2.942×10^8 tons of coal were mined in the Appalachian region from seams with an average thickness of 4.9 ft. The average bituminous coal density is 82.6 lb/ft^3 and 7.15 gallons of acid drainage were produced on the average per year per ft^2 of exposed mine roof.

    (a) How many gallons of acid drainage were produced, on the average, per ton of coal mined?

    (b) What was the total acid drainage produced during 1970 in the region?

3.[†] Assume that a 1,000-Mw$_e$ power plant converts coal to electricity with an overall efficiency of 33% and operates with a 70% plant factor.

    (a) If the coal has a sulfur content of 0.2% which is totally converted to SO_2, how many tons of SO_2 are produced per year by the power plant without sulfur-removal from the flue gases?

    (b) If 1 lb of CO is produced per ton of coal burned, how many tons of CO are produced per year by the power plant?

    (c) If the power plant produces 3.85 lb of SO_2 per ton of coal burned and the conversion efficiency of sulfur in coal to SO_2 is 100%, what is the percentage by weight of sulfur in the coal?

4.[†] On the average, coal mining produces injuries and pneumoconiosis amounting to an equivalent loss of 4.8807 days/6.71×10^9 Btu of coal mined. How many work days are lost by miners who supply the coal feed for one year of operation of a 1,000-Mw$_e$ plant operating with a heat rate of 10,000 Btu/kwh$_e$ and a 70% plant factor?

5.[†] Assume that a 1,000-Mw_e power plant converts coal to electricity with a
heat rate of 10,000 Btu/kwh_e and operates with an 80% plant factor.

    (a) If 5.694 acres of land are required per 6.71×10^{11} Btu of coal
mined and the land-rental charges are \$100/acre-year, what
is the annual rental value of the land required to supply the coal
for the power plant?

    (b) If 750 acres of land per 400 tons of coal mined per hour are re-
quired by the average mine, how many acres of land must be
allocated to the 1,000-Mw_e power plant? Assume that the average
mine is operated 6,000 hours per year and the average heating
value of the coal mined is 25×10^6 Btu/ton.

6.[†] Discuss the effect of changes in the air-quality standards on the estimates
of the societal and direct costs of coal use for electricity production.

Problems for Chapter 8

1. What are the 1985 U.S. energy requirements for the following scenario:
energy use per \$ of personal GNP, population, and gross national product
all grow at a 5% annual rate after 1970? What is your prescription for obtaining the needed energy supplies in 1985?

2. What are the 1995 energy requirements in the U.S. for the following
scenario: energy use per \$ of personal GNP is reduced by 50% below ap-
plicable 1970 values, the gross national product increases at a 1% annual
rate from 1970, and the total U.S. population declines to 180×10^6 p?
What is your prescription for obtaining the energy supplies needed in 1995?

3.[**] Describe your preferred evolution for the U.S. to 1995 and estimate the
corresponding year 1995 energy requirements. How do you propose to accomplish your preferred developments for the U.S. to 1995?

4.^{*, **} Replace Table 8.5-1 by a defensible energy-development map of your
own. Give reasons why the prescriptions of Tables 8.5-2 and 8.5-3
may be considered to be either irrelevant or unworkable.

INDEX